WITHDRAWN

Thinking Politics

Thinking Politics

Intellectuals and Democracy in Chile, 1973-1988

JEFFREY M. PURYEAR

The Johns Hopkins University Press · Baltimore and London

The Johns Hopkins University Press
2715 North Charles Street
Baltimore, Maryland 21218-4319
The Johns Hopkins Press Ltd., London

Library of Congress Cataloging-in-Publication Data

Puryear, Jeffrey.
  Thinking politics : intellectuals and democracy in Chile,
1973–1988 / Jeffrey M. Puryear.
    p. cm.
  Includes bibliographical references and index.
  ISBN 0-8018-4839-3 (acid-free paper). — ISBN 0-8018-4841-5 (pbk. :
acid-free paper)
  1. Chile—Politics and government—1973–1988. 2. Intellectuals—Chile.
3. Democracy—Chile. 4. Authoritarianism—Chile.
I. Title.
JL2681.P87 1994
320'.893'09'048—dc20   93-47402

A catalog record for this book is available from the British Library.

To Miri, Mile, and Manchi

Contents

Preface

This study is about how intellectuals helped engineer a successful transition to democracy in Chile. The victory by an opposition coalition over General Augusto Pinochet on 5 October 1988 in a nationwide plebiscite on his continued rule marked a crucial turning point in Chile's long struggle against one of Latin America's most repressive military dictatorships. Indeed, the presidential and parliamentary elections that followed a year later were almost anticlimactic. The fundamental issue—whether Pinochet would stay in power, postponing free elections until 1997, or give up power through open presidential and parliamentary elections in 1989—had been settled in the plebiscite.

Until then, Pinochet had seemed nearly invincible. Since taking power in a bloody 1973 coup, he had established a powerful military regime that radically transformed Chile's social and economic institutions. He had weathered a spectacular banking failure in 1982 and had managed to rekindle steady economic growth. He had controlled, with an artful combination of guile and repression, the widespread protests the economic crisis had generated in 1983. He had maintained the near-unanimous support of business and the armed forces, counting supporters across the entire society. And Pinochet's political opposition, despite several years of high hopes and hard work, had made little progress in igniting a broad movement against him.

Many doubted that Pinochet would even permit the free and fair vote on his continuing in office until 1997, when it was called for in the Constitution he and his supporters had imposed on the country through a questionable plebiscite in 1980. And even if he did, few thought that the fractious collection of center and left parties that opposed Pinochet would be able to devise an alternative—and a campaign—attractive enough to unseat him. But he did, they did, and he lost.

Transitions to democracy have occurred frequently in Latin America, particularly since 1980. Since that year, fifteen military regimes have yielded power to elected civilian governments, and today Cuba is the lone remaining Latin American dictatorship. Although differing greatly in sequence and pace, none of these transitions has been truly revolutionary. Instead, each has evolved deliberately, more or less in accord with a timetable determined in advance. And all have involved a decision, for highly varied reasons, by military leaders to give up power.

Chile's transition was no exception. Although the military junta did not turn power over to politicians immediately after the 1973 coup, as many had expected, it did establish a committee to study constitutional reforms. By 1980, an entirely new Constitution came into force that mandated a return to democracy. But the process was long—Pinochet would remain president until 1989 and might even stay until 1997. And the democracy envisioned was riddled with authoritarian elements, including a set of senators appointed for life and permanent military tutelage over political affairs.

What is distinctive about Chile's transition to democracy is the extraordinary role played by intellectuals. Elsewhere, some combination of military officers, party leaders, and economic elites has usually taken the lead in orchestrating democratic transitions. Intellectuals, although sometimes inspiring or quickening change with their critiques, have seldom participated directly and extensively. Instead, they have tended to restrict themselves (despite the occasional conspicuous exception) to traditional academic functions. And more broadly across history, as Lewis Coser has pointed out: "Knowledge may bring power, but, even so, men of knowledge have only rarely been men of power" (*Men of Ideas: A Sociologist's View* [New York: Free Press, 1965], 135).

But something different happened in Chile. Most observers who regularly visited Chile during the dictatorship were struck by the visibility and vigor of a large group of private research centers, staffed by talented, foreign-trained intellectuals. Most of those intellectuals were social scientists who engaged almost exclusively in academic activities—research, publication, and debate. Many of them were simply trying to continue working as academics after being forced out of university or government positions. Yet they also seemed to be at the center of opposition politics. Their political impact was not clear at the time but turned out to be extraordinary. In Chile, intellectuals tested the limits of traditional roles and showed us something new about how intellectuals might contribute to democratic transition.

Chile's case is exceptional for another reason. Until 1973 Chile had no recent history of authoritarian government or political instability. It boasted one of the longest-lived democracies in the world, with a strong and competitive party system, an independent legislature, and a military that had seldom intervened in politics. Yet the military regime that followed the 1973 coup became one of the harshest and most enduring to emerge in Latin America during the 1960s and 1970s. More than other military regimes, it sought fundamental economic, political, and social change. Thus by 1988 Chile was not only one of the few countries in South America that had not reverted to democratic government, it had also undergone the most radical economic transformation of any Latin American country since Cuba's shift to communism in the 1960s.

I was sent to Chile by the Ford Foundation in December 1973, shortly after the military takeover of power. Since then I have followed events there from foundation positions in New York, and as director of the foundation's regional office in Lima, Peru. I have been both observer and supporter, analyzing conditions in Chile and funding intellectuals and others through foundation grants. My work has enabled me to visit Chile regularly over nearly two decades and to develop extensive relationships with many of the intellectuals and politicians who played important roles in the transition to democracy. I have thus had an uncommon vantage point from which to observe events spanning the post-coup repression of 1973 and the inauguration of President Patricio Aylwin in 1990.

This book draws on those experiences. It is based as well on comprehensive interviews, ranging from thirty minutes to two hours, with nearly seventy intellectuals and political leaders who participated in the transition. After consulting with a wide variety of local intellectuals and political leaders, I chose the interviewees for their direct knowledge of various aspects of the transition process. I carried out all the interviews myself, in Spanish, between December 1990 and September 1992. Interviewees were allowed to speak off the record if they wished; virtually none of them did. I taped each interview, and the tapes were subsequently transcribed directly onto computer diskettes by experienced transcribers in Santiago. I compared each transcription with the original tape for accuracy. My analysis draws also on a broad array of academic and journalistic sources, many of which are available only in Spanish, and a few of which are as yet unpublished. All translations are my own.

I have written this book for several reasons. First, I wanted to record clearly and accurately the contributions that an extraordinary group of intellectuals made to Chilean politics at a time of extreme political crisis. Second, I wanted to abstract from those events to see whether Chile's experience might tell us something more generally about transitions to democracy, and the potential of intellectuals to assist them. Third, I was interested more broadly in the impact intellectuals can have on development in third-world countries, and thereby the arguments for providing them with foreign assistance. And finally, I wanted to present my analysis and conclusions in a style that would be attractive and accessible to both academics and practitioners.

One word about emphasis: My objective has been to connect the activities of intellectuals to the broader set of events that were central to Chile's shift from authoritarian to democratic rule. That has meant referring when appropriate to the contributions of other actors, but without the detail and depth given to the contributions of intellectuals. My emphasis is deliberate. I wanted to document the role played by intellectuals, a group that has otherwise received little attention in discussions of democratic transition. I do not, however, mean to suggest that other groups played minor roles. Many actors, including opposition political leaders, the church, human rights activists, and several foreign governments, contributed importantly to Chile's transition to democracy. Unfortunately, analyzing their contributions in greater detail would have limited my ability to address properly the extraordinary role played by intellectuals and would have gone substantially beyond the comparative advantage that I brought to this study.

This book, therefore, is an exercise in the sociology of knowledge, not in historiography. I have not tried to write a definitive history of Chile's transition to democracy. My concern throughout is with the impact of a particular group rather than with the impacts of all relevant groups. I have sought to identify one pattern among many and to ask whether that pattern has meaning for other historical settings. I hope that effort will enrich the more definitive account that will eventually emerge from the efforts of a variety of scholars.

Acknowledgments

Hundreds of people enriched this book by contributing their time and insights. Two of those—Abraham Lowenthal and Guillermo O'Donnell—were especially helpful during the planning stages, when I was struggling with basic questions of direction and method. Their encouragement and criticism made a major difference in the questions I asked. Another, José Joaquín Brunner, unselfishly offered ideas, criticism, and inspiration throughout each stage of the study. Among the many others who offered valuable comments, criticism, or suggestions, I particularly want to thank Alan Angell, Genaro Arriagada, Peter Bell, Sergio Bitar, Angel Flisfisch, Alejandro Foxley, Edmundo Fuenzalida, Manuel Antonio Garretón, Oscar Godoy, Peter Hakim, Albert Hirschman, Carlos Huneeus, Terry Karl, Marta Lagos, Norbert Lechner, Dan Levy, María Teresa Lladser, Javier Martínez, Patricio Meller, Chris Mitchell, Oscar Muñoz, Joe Ramos, Michael Shifter, Gary Sick, Al Stepan, Eugenio Tironi, Ignacio Walker, and Lawrence Weschler. Also, I want to thank the approximately seventy Chilean intellectuals and political leaders who consented to lengthy taped interviews and provided extraordinary insight regarding the complex factors that explain Chile's transition to democracy.

Thanks also go to the Ford Foundation, not only for providing the bulk of the funds necessary to carry out the study but also for first sending me to Chile in 1973, and then regularly sending me back over nearly two decades. Without the rare continuity that experience has given to my involvement in Chilean affairs, this book simply could not have been written. I thank, as well, the Center for Latin American and Caribbean Studies at New York University, which provided me with an office, infrastructure, and professional collegiality for my work in New York. Similarly, I want to thank the entire staff at the Corporation for Latin American Economic Research (CIEPLAN), who provided those same resources for me during my work in Chile. Violeta Cuevas and Rosa Jaime transcribed, accurately and rapidly, more than 100 hours of taped interviews. Solange Phillips regularly made hard-to-find documents appear overnight. The Latin American Institute for Doctrine and Social Studies (ILADES) and the Latin American Faculty of the Social Sciences (FLACSO) kindly provided me access to their valuable collections of documents and books. Bobbe Hughey of the Johns Hopkins University Press significantly improved the manuscript with her green pencil, teaching me more than I expected to learn about my own writing.

Acronyms of Principal Chilean
Private Research Institutions

AHC   Academy of Christian Humanism

CED   Center for Development Studies

CEP   Center for Public Studies

CERC   Center for the Study of Chilean Reality

CIDE   Center for Educational Research and Development

CIEPLAN   Corporation for Latin American Economic Research

CISEC   Center for Socioeconomic Research

CLACSO   Latin American Council of Social Sciences

CLEPI   Latin American Center for Research on Political Economy

CPU   Corporation for University Promotion

FLACSO   Latin American Faculty of the Social Sciences

GEA   Agro-Regional Studies Group

GIA   Agrarian Research Group

ICHEH   Chilean Institute for Humanistic Studies

IDEP   Institute of Political Studies

ILADES   Latin American Institute for Doctrine and Social Studies

ILET   Institute of Latin American Transnational Studies

PET   Program on Labor Economics

PIIE   Interdisciplinary Program of Educational Research

PROSPEL   Latin American Foreign Policy Monitoring Program

SUR   Sur Professional Consultants

VECTOR   Center for Economic and Social Studies

Thinking Politics

Introduction

*In periods marked by relatively stable social structures and routinized poli-
tics, the affairs of state prove recalcitrant to intellectuals' attempts to gain
political ascendance. But revolutionary periods may afford them the chance
to gain state power.*

— LEWIS COSER, *Men of Ideas*

In March 1990 Ricardo Lagos, a Duke University Ph.D. in economics who taught for nearly twenty years at the University of Chile, became
Chile's minister of education. Alejandro Foxley, a Ph.D. in economics
from the University of Wisconsin and founder of one of Latin America's
most prestigious research institutes, was named finance minister. Edgardo Boeninger, a former rector of the University of Chile, became minister of the general presidential staff—and the president's chief political
strategist. Enrique Correa, a former professor of philosophy at the State
Technical University, was named to head another key ministry. René
Cortázar, a Ph.D. from the Massachusetts Institute of Technology and
prolific researcher, was named minister of labor. Carlos Ominami, a former member of the radical Revolutionary Left Movement (MIR), who
had completed doctoral studies at the University of Paris, was chosen to
be minister of economic affairs. Berkeley-trained sociologist Germán
Correa became minister of transportation. Francisco Cumplido, a lawyer
who headed up a research program on the sociology of law at the Latin
American Faculty of the Social Sciences (FLACSO) during the 1970s,
became minister of justice. José Antonio Viera-Gallo, a former professor
of political theory at Chile's Catholic University and director of a private
research center, was elected president of the Chamber of Deputies.
Throughout the new, democratically elected government, large numbers
of intellectuals, many of them foreign trained and with considerable research and teaching experience, were assuming key positions.

The occasion was the inauguration of Christian Democratic leader
Patricio Aylwin as Chile's first freely elected president in two decades.
Backed by a diverse, seventeen-party coalition, he had decisively defeated

two conservative candidates in a presidential election three months earlier, and his fellow coalition members won an absolute majority in both houses of Congress. His election was made possible when voters rejected the continuation in office of General Augusto Pinochet in a plebiscite held in October 1988. Pinochet's seventeen-year dictatorship had ended.

At a gala reception held in the Palacio de la Moneda, Chile's government palace, several thousand official guests circulated tirelessly, so consumed by smiles and excitement they barely sipped their champagne. They were joyful and solemn at the same time. It was hard to believe they had won. It was hard to imagine what democracy would be like. They would, for the first time in seventeen years, have a say in the affairs of their country.

Three years earlier, the outlook could hardly have been more desolate. After struggling since 1983 to topple the Pinochet government through disruptive public protests, the opposition was frustrated and depressed. Its social mobilization strategy had failed to bring Pinochet to the bargaining table. Instead, he and his supporters had closed ranks and countered with rising force, causing violence and casualties to mount. The discovery in late 1986 of massive arms caches smuggled into the country from Cuba by extreme-left terrorist groups and a failed attempt by those groups to assassinate Pinochet had further discredited the mobilization strategy and caused the government to declare a state of siege. The country seemed to be on the road to civil war rather than democracy.

Pinochet had emerged from those challenges almost triumphant. His regime was cohesive, supported by the political right, business, and a disciplined military establishment. The economy had recovered from a disastrous crisis in 1982 and was again showing signs of growth. Levels of social protest were dropping. He faced an opposition that was discouraged and in disarray. His government projected order and purpose, in sharp contrast to the constant disagreements among opposition parties over strategy and leadership. For many, Pinochet represented the new Chile, stable and prosperous; the opposition stood for the chaotic past.

What explains the change? How did a traditionally divided opposition facing serious government restrictions on the press and on political activity realize that, despite Pinochet's strength, relatively broad support, and resurgent economy, they had a chance to use his own political rules against him? How did they come to abandon their mobilization strategy, accept Pinochet's Constitution, form a coalition, and devise a campaign good enough to win the 1988 plebiscite? And why did so many intellectuals emerge as key figures in the new democratic regime?

This book attempts to answer those questions. It targets just one aspect of the answer: the role played by intellectuals. It examines how intellectuals influenced the transition process, and particularly how they altered the opposition's choice of transition strategies.

The rapidly expanding academic literature on democratic transitions says little about intellectuals.[1] There is, to be sure, a strong focus on the crucial roles played by elites and "elite pacts" in shifting from dictatorship to democracy, but the elites mentioned tend to be political, economic, and military. They are seldom intellectual. Similarly, the norms and values held by political elites are seen to be important determinants in the success or failure of democratic transitions, but few studies have attempted to link the activities of intellectuals to changes in elite political culture, and to specific instances of democratic transition. O'Donnell and Schmitter constitute a partial exception, emphasizing the roles played by intellectuals and artists in the "resurrection of civil society" that often precedes democratic transition. Those groups, through their "capacity to express themselves by oblique metaphors" and their "membership in a de facto world system of cultural exchange," tend to "lead the way in manifesting public opposition to authoritarian rule, often before the transition has been launched."[2] But O'Donnell and Schmitter discuss only the expressive capacity of intellectuals—their ability to transform discontent into defiance when political parties are unable to act. They do not discuss the potential impact of intellectuals on political culture more generally, on the thinking of party elites, or on transition strategy. Nor do they discuss the possibility that intellectual cadres might constitute a source of political leadership during the transition period.

The limited mention of intellectuals in the democratic transition literature may, of course, be because intellectuals have, de facto, seldom played important roles. The only region in which intellectuals are commonly assumed to have played a recent, significant role in democratic transitions is Eastern Europe. There, efforts by such dissident writers as György Konrád, Adam Michnik, and Václav Havel are generally credited with hastening the fall of the Communist regimes in Hungary, Poland, and Czechoslovakia. Typically, observers have pointed to a political underground in which "very gradually, indirectly, in convoluted and largely unpredictable ways, the pressure of individuals living in truth and dignity and associating in loose structures of 'social self-organization' . . . must eventually change the way that society is governed."[3] Some of the most visible members of that underground were intellectuals, many of them novelists and playwrights. They produced samizdat, criticized authoritarianism, reaffirmed the legitimacy of liberty and democracy, and generally expressed the dissidence welling up in their societies.

On the other hand, the case for a strong role by intellectuals in Eastern Europe's transitions to democracy, even as articulators of dissent, has not been systematically made. In his analysis of the Polish case, Goodwin dismisses much of the conventional wisdom because of its "journalistic and scholarly over-identification with the sundry . . . roles played by intellectuals in the politics of protest" and its "signal failure" to "specify evidential connections between idea and action." Similarly, Laba downplays the impact of intellectuals: "The roots of Solidarity were in the Baltic working class, and the intellectuals made a necessary but not causal or creative contribution." There is, in addition, a significant literature faulting Eastern European intellectuals for their complicity with authoritarian practices, and their failure to exploit their capacity for critical, independent thinking and dissent.[4] Thus, although existing materials suggest some impact by intellectuals on the transitions to democracy in Eastern Europe, the breadth and strength of that impact have yet to be demonstrated with any rigor.

Similarly, a review of work on democratic transition in Latin America over the past decade suggests that the impact of intellectuals has been minor at best, and usually insignificant.[5] Accounts of Brazil's efforts at democratic transition, for example, make almost no mention of intellectuals.[6] In Peru there is little evidence that participation by intellectuals in Juan Velasco Alvarado's military government had any impact on the military's decision to restore democratic rule in the late 1970s.[7] Hartlyn's analysis of Colombia concludes that the concrete actions of political leaders have been more important than prodemocracy political culture and intellectual groups in determining the evolution of democracy.[8] In Argentina, analysts do not argue that intellectuals influenced the 1983 transition to democracy despite the Raul Alfonsín government's subsequently appointing several intellectuals to key positions.[9] Overall, intellectuals are virtually a null set in the literature on Latin American transitions to democracy. Perhaps, under Latin American dictatorships intellectuals have been particularly weak, or perhaps the barriers to their participation in politics have been especially great.[10] Clearly, however, the key elites in most of those transitions have been military, political, and economic.

Nonetheless, events in Chile took a different turn. There, intellectuals played a major role in the transition to democracy, one that they probably have not played anywhere else in Latin America. Their influence on the transition process was prolonged, beginning shortly after the 1973 military coup and continuing right through the establishment of a new democratic regime some seventeen years later. They also contributed in different ways at different points in time, helping to moderate opposition political thought, rethink transition strategy, modernize politics, design a successful plebiscite campaign, and, in a few cases, lead political parties. Their contributions, however, have not been analyzed with the same care given to other actors, such as politicians and military leaders, in the transition process. Indeed, most analysts assume that Chile's transition came about almost entirely at the behest of political and military elites.[11] Yet one of the most distinctive aspects of Chile's transition was the important role played by intellectuals. In this book I seek to document that role, explain it, and assess its significance.

In doing so, I recognize the importance of the political, social, and historical context—particularly the parameters established by the military regime—in conditioning opposition decisions. Political change is a complex process, often driven by broad historical forces and seldom dependent on a single factor. In Chile's case, a transition of sorts—painfully slow and to a democracy full of authoritarian features—had already been decreed by the Pinochet government in 1980 with the establishment of a new Constitution. (Among the authoritarian features of the Constitution's democracy were a significant number of lifetime senators appointed by the Pinochet regime, and a permanent tutelary role for the military in politics.) The Constitution mandated a gradual transition to the new democracy, beginning with a plebiscite on Pinochet's continued rule in 1988 and ending, depending on how the plebiscite turned out, with full presidential and congressional elections either in 1989 or 1997. To ensure that this scenario was carried out absolutely, the Constitution made amendments almost impossible.

The 1988 plebiscite was central to Pinochet's plans, and he fully expected to win it. The plebiscite was intended to bolster the regime's legitimacy eight years after the constitutional referendum and to provide eight more years to consolidate its quasi-authoritarian approach to democracy. Opposition leaders, however, made three difficult decisions in early 1988 that enabled them to defeat Pinochet in the plebiscite. First, they agreed to participate in the plebiscite, something they had vehemently ruled out since 1980. Second, they overcame their bitter historical divisions and agreed to form a fourteen-party coalition (the Concertación de Partidos para la Democracia) that would contest the plebiscite as a single force. Third, they entrusted the organization of the plebiscite campaign to a single, multiparty committee (the Technical Committee for the No) staffed by some of the opposition's most talented social scientists.

Those decisions were crucial to the plebiscite victory in October 1988. They meant accepting Pinochet's political framework rather than holding out for reform and possibly not participating in the plebiscite at all. They meant offering voters a unified opposition, in contrast to the specter of opposition conflict and chaos the regime had used so effectively to justify its continued rule. And they meant devising a single, coherent campaign strategy rather than many different strategies tailored to the views of each opposition party. Had any of those decisions not been taken, Pinochet might have won the plebiscite, and democracy might have been put off for eight more years.

The victory over Pinochet in the plebiscite forced full and open presidential elections in 1989 instead of 1997 and convinced the regime to negotiate, prior to those elections, a package of fifty-four reforms that significantly weakened the authoritarian aspects of the 1980 Constitution. The transition to democracy would occur in 1990 rather than in 1997, and with fewer authoritarian features than the regime originally intended. In 1989, the opposition coalition emerged victorious in the presidential elections with 55.2 percent of the vote and won a majority of the contested seats in the Chamber of Deputies and the Senate. Democracy had returned to Chile.

This analysis assumes that several different paths could have been chosen under the circumstances that existed in Chile during the mid-1980s and views events as the outcome not only of broad historical processes but also of conscious decisions made by opposition political elites. It argues that intellectuals played an important and often crucial role in determining which choices opposition political elites made, a role they do not appear to have played in recent transitions to democracy elsewhere, and it documents the important role played by foreign assistance in enabling intellectuals to influence the political process.

The relationship between intellectuals and politics is at the center of this book, and I need to begin by making clear what I mean by *intellectuals*. The term is particularly complex and value charged, the subject of a long and distinguished academic debate.[12] Definitions range from the relatively broad ("those who create, distribute and apply culture") to the relatively narrow ("experts, operating within or on the margins of government, who advise, consult, serve in various official capacities, and comment tirelessly on public issues"). For Michels, intellectuals are those who are "vocationally concerned with things of the mind." Merton defines them as "individuals who devote themselves to cultivating and formulating knowledge." Some emphasize their relationship to culture, and others their relationship to power.[13] There is no magic in any of those definitions, and it is perhaps most important to choose one that is appropriate to the topic and reality at hand. I have therefore taken a practical approach, letting a definition emerge from the reality under study, and then taking note of its relevance and limits.

A look at contemporary Chile yields some immediate facts: virtually all intellectuals who played leading roles in the transition to democracy were social scientists who had carried out graduate study abroad. They started their careers as academics, although many subsequently left the academy, at least temporarily. Most have published at least one book; many have published several. The majority are economists or sociologists, reflecting the extraordinary advances made in those two disciplines in Chile over the past three decades. Most of the rest are political scientists or historians. Some originally studied law but moved on to a social science discipline. A very few are lawyers who pursued an academic career. Intellectuals from the natural sciences or the arts were much less conspicuous in the transition, although a few played largely symbolic roles in the free elections movement of 1987. For the most part, however, we are talking about social scientists with graduate training in Europe or the United States. Almost all were male.

The interviews carried out in conjunction with this book confirm that profile, adding two other dimensions. First, many interviewees stressed the grey area that marks the boundary between intellectuals and politicians in Chile. They cited a traditional interpenetration of intellectual and political elites, wherein academics may become leaders of political parties, and politicians maintain various kinds of ties with academics. One economist (himself an intellectual active in politics) observed: "Here . . . all the parties and political leaders encouraged a relation . . . and valued the contribution of the intellectual to political life."[14]

Two oft-cited examples help clarify these observations. Genaro Arriagada, a lawyer by training, vice-president of the Christian Democratic party, and perhaps the country's most able political strategist, has also written solid academic books on such topics as the government of Salvador Allende, political theory, and civil-military relations. Despite having no graduate training and never having taught, Arriagada was regularly classed as an intellectual. Conversely, Angel Flisfisch, who did graduate work in political science at the University of Michigan and is one of the country's most prolific and respected political scientists, had been a member of the Socialist party's governing board for nearly twenty years and accepted a high position in the Aylwin government. The interviewees repeatedly observed that intellectuals and politicians in Chile have a remarkably close, and often metamorphic, relationship.

Second, the interviewees divided on whether to include technocrats in the intellectual category. A slight majority tended to emphasize the broadly reflective and critical roles of intellectuals over their roles as "experts" in narrow subject areas. Thus specialists in international trade or industrial relations, for example, despite distinguished academic careers, were often excluded unless they also reflected more broadly on social issues. Most lawyers, except those who had gone on to study a social science discipline, were excluded. Indeed, one common definition of *intellectual* that emerges from the interviews is based firmly on broad-gauged social research, reflection, and criticism—functions generally carried out only by some members of the academy.

José Joaquín Brunner, perhaps Chile's most distinguished specialist in the sociology of knowledge, expresses this concept most clearly: "I am speaking basically of the intellectual as . . . the principal producer in the ideological sphere of society . . . where reason, and therefore reasoned argument, encounters the interests, passions, desires, yearnings and dreams of a society."[15] He sees the intellectual as someone who combines the world of reason and science with the world of values and aspirations, to interpret reality and to guide action. This definition, typically implicit rather than explicit among interviewees, was common. It is clearly a subset of the broader definitions cited earlier and excludes the functions we usually refer to as technocratic.

Technocrats, on the other hand, were often included to make a broader point: the professionalization of government policy-making. Here the emphasis was on the success of highly trained experts in wresting authority from politicians over specific policy areas. Chilean politicians, the argument goes, no longer have the political arena to themselves. Increasingly, they must share policy-making power with the experts.[16] Repeatedly in the interviews one encountered the idea that a well-educated, modern professional class had appeared on the scene and was struggling with traditional politicians for power throughout the political (and policy) arena. Here the definition of *intellectual* included policy professionals with recent, usually foreign, graduate training. Again, however, only social scientists, and principally economists, were mentioned.

Thus the definition of *intellectuals* that emerges from this study is restricted in several ways. It is limited de facto to social scientists who pursued graduate training abroad and began their careers as academics. It emphasizes those who produce ideologies, bringing the broad world of ideas and a critical attitude to bear on their surroundings. But it permits, somewhat ambiguously, a second dimension: the modern, well-trained expert who applies knowledge to a narrow policy area. As we will see, this distinction is important, often marking the difference between two functions that intellectuals have played in Chile's transition to democracy (and perhaps between two historical periods).

Why have social scientists apparently played a more important role in Chile's transition to democracy than have their colleagues in the arts and natural sciences? In part, probably because the fundamental issues here (political, economic, and social change) are the issues that social scientists work on. One could hardly expect natural scientists to compete successfully in areas where they are at a comparative disadvantage; the category therefore is probably self-selecting.

But another factor is almost certainly at work as well: the substantial investments made over the past thirty years to establish a modern social science in Chile. Beginning around 1960 the Chilean government and a host of foreign public and private donors invested millions of dollars to send Chilean students abroad for graduate training, first in economics and sociology and later in political science, and to establish modern, well-equipped departments in the country's principal universities. After the coup, foreign donors provided funds for nearly two decades to keep many of those well-trained social scientists on hand and working in the country in newly created private research centers, despite the repression of the military regime. Those investments eventually yielded a large political dividend at a critical moment in Chile's history. They established and maintained a cadre of modern, highly committed professionals who were able to play an important role in the country's return to democratic rule.

The Historical Context

With social thought turning so rapidly into attempted social engineering, a high incidence of failed experiments is the price that is often paid for the influence intellectuals wield.
— ALBERT HIRSCHMAN, *Essays in Trespassing*

A country of the learned and ideologues, of jurists and communicators, of legislators and intellectuals who dream of imposing, each group or party, each school or sect, its own "model country." A country of limited substance, baptized a thousand times more by words than by transforming things by hand, or by machine. A country more sacramental than productive, of gestures and rituals more than of enterprises and instruments.
— JOSE JOAQUIN BRUNNER, *Un Espejo Trizado*

Education

The spectacular collapse of Chile's longstanding democracy on 11 September 1973, was especially surprising because it occurred in one of the most highly educated and politically sophisticated countries in Latin America. By the 1960s, development literature consistently placed Chile near the top of Latin American countries, exceeded on most measures only by Argentina, Uruguay, and Costa Rica. A strong and highly centralized state had developed shortly after independence and had come to play an important role in social policy. Chile was one of the first countries in Latin America to establish a national health service and a social security system. It was among the most urbanized countries in the region and boasted one of the highest rates of political participation. It was also one of Latin America's most politically stable countries, having managed to govern itself democratically for most of its history. By almost any measure of development, Chile was among the most advanced of the third-world countries.[1]

Chile was also especially successful in obtaining development assistance from wealthier countries. Its combination of democratic politics, a strong and effective state, and openness to new ideas was particularly attractive to the United States. The growing concern for "underdeveloped" countries that emerged in the United States in the late 1950s and led in 1961 to the creation of the Agency for International Development (AID) and the Alliance for Progress, found fertile ground among Chile's political and economic elites. Chile's reformist, capitalist model offered U.S. policymakers an attractive counter to the revolutionary communism emerging in Fidel Castro's Cuba. Thus U.S. economic assistance more than tripled during the 1960s. One source estimates that Chile received 14 percent of all U.S. economic aid and 16 percent of Export-Import Bank credits to Latin America during the Kennedy administration, and 11 and 21 percent, respectively, during the Johnson administration.[2] Since Chile's population constituted less than 4 percent of the total Latin American and Caribbean population, its treatment by the United States was indeed extraordinary.

Chile's system of education had long been one of Latin America's best. The country's strong state had generated relatively high and sustained public investment in education over many years, raising enrollments and lowering illiteracy. Chile's adult literacy reached 84 percent in 1960, far ahead of most other countries in the region. Regular contacts with European and American educators brought recent pedagogical advances to Chilean classrooms. Chile's secondary school system, patterned on the French lycée, was one of Latin America's finest. At the turn of the century, approximately one-third of school-age children were enrolled in schools; by 1950, nearly two-thirds were enrolled.[3]

Schiefelbein and Farrell summarize the system's early achievements:

> Drawing upon a provision of the Constitution of 1833 that declared public education to be a state responsibility, Chile became in 1842 the first Latin American nation to establish a system of public instruction. Before the middle of the century, the first normal school had been founded, the University of Chile had been established, and the university-preparatory *liceo* had expanded its classical-humanist curriculum to include experimental science. Under an organic law passed in 1860, elementary education was made free, and additional secondary and normal schools were established. Toward the end of the 19th century, Chile became the first Latin American nation to admit women to the university and permit them to practice the liberal professions, secondary education opened its doors to women, and European professors were invited to the *Instituto Pedagógico* of the University of Chile, where they had a profound influence on the training of teachers and on the development of the educational system.[4]

Chile's system of higher education had also expanded and become cosmopolitan. By 1970 there were eight heavily subsidized public and private universities enrolling over 9 percent of the relevant age group. Although precise measures are hard to find, the quality of the system appears to have been among the highest in the region. Admission was based on a centrally administered test of academic aptitude. The proportion of full-time faculty with graduate training was growing steadily, and professors were beginning to return from study abroad. Programs and curriculum had for some years been influenced by innovations in European and North American higher education. Several universities were making deliberate efforts to promote scientific research, often with support from foreign donors.[5] Indeed, a number of foreign assistance programs had provided substantial funds, staff, and training aimed at strengthening Chile's university system and underwriting new approaches.[6]

An ambitious university reform that began in 1967 under the reformist Christian Democrats and continued under Salvador Allende's Popular Unity government significantly modernized and expanded the system. Government funding, as a percentage of gross domestic product, more than doubled during the period. Enrollments grew from 56,000 in 1967 to 77,000 in 1969. They then doubled to 147,000 in 1973 after the Allende government sharply expanded university funding. The number of full-time professors increased significantly, as did the number of those undertaking research. A concerted effort was made to strengthen the sciences. Several new forms of organization were introduced, including the departmental model and separate research centers. University governance was significantly democratized, with the election of top officials and broader representation in decision making.[7]

Thus by the 1970s, Chile was, in the words of the U.S. State Department's *Area Handbook,* "one of the most literate of Latin American countries."[8] Primary and secondary schooling were widely available and of good quality. The country's universities were among the region's strongest, playing a fundamental role in training modern elites and shaping the ideas that dominated public debate. Education, and particularly higher education, had become a potent force in Chilean society.

The Social Sciences

Chile's progress in the social sciences between 1955 and 1970 was especially impressive and came about as part of a broader effort to institutionalize scientific research within Chilean universities. Until the mid-1950s, the country's universities had an overwhelmingly professional orientation, relying almost entirely on part-time professors and incorporating little concern for, or encouragement of, research. They were, in the words of one analyst, "loose federations of professional schools whose overriding purpose was to educate the lawyers, physicians, engineers, architects, secondary school teachers, agronomists and other professionals needed by a modern and complex society in intense interaction with the rest of the world, particularly Western Europe, and, more recently, the United States."[9] Research was occasionally carried out in Chilean universities before 1955, but it was not part of their institutional goal.

That situation began to change in the early 1950s, when Juan Gómez Millas was elected rector of the University of Chile. Gómez Millas, a historian and former dean of the Faculty of Education and Philosophy, believed strongly that scientific research was important to society and should be a central part of the university's mission. His strong views on the importance of research were reflected in his 1956 address inaugurating the academic year: "Not a few people repeat the phrase popular in some circles, 'Let others do the science, we will take advantage of its results and applications,' a phrase that reveals a position among the most immoral that I know of because it represents a premature renunciation of the life of the spirit. . . . Why not renounce art as well, or the state, or religion, or any other of the higher forms of existence of the human in man?" (70–71). Gómez Millas expressed a viewpoint that was gathering force in Chile and sparked a major, systematic effort to institutionalize scientific research in Chilean universities.

Those efforts met with considerable success. The government responded immediately, creating a national fund to finance scientific research. By 1965, the University of Chile had established a research-oriented Faculty of Sciences, and the country's other major universities, particularly the Catholic University and the University of Concepción, had embarked on major efforts to incorporate scientific research through structural reforms and major infusions of new funds. A consensus was developing among Chilean academic and political elites that scientific research in general was crucial to social and economic development. That consensus was shared by major foreign donors, including the Ford and Rockefeller foundations and the U.S. government, who began to provide substantial funds to develop the research capacity of Chilean universities. The result was a sustained effort over nearly two decades to train professors abroad, establish appropriate infrastructure within universities, and promote research across a broad variety of disciplines.[10]

It is important to note the size and duration of these initiatives. The Chilean government passed a law in 1954 that channeled .5 percent of all nonmunicipal taxes, as well as all customs and export taxes, into a University Construction and Research fund and established a Science and

Technology Committee to advise on national policy (72). The University of Chile, the Catholic University, and the University of Concepción embarked on extensive debates over the role of research, leading to fundamental changes in university structure. The U.S. Agency for International Development (USAID) and the Ford and Rockefeller foundations accorded high priority to university development in the third world during the 1960s and became particularly active in Chile.[11] A policy consensus had developed, and major funding was provided. The time had come for scientific research in Chilean universities.

The Rockefeller Foundation, which began supporting the medical school at the University of Chile in 1942, provided over $1 million to Chilean universities for research and teaching in the medical and biological sciences between 1955 and 1965. In the mid-1960s, USAID provided a $3 million loan over forty years (at .75%) to finance engineering and economic studies and to train Chileans in modern planning techniques, and a $10 million loan over forty years (at 1% over the first ten years and 2.5% thereafter) to strengthen the country's educational sector. In 1965 the Ford Foundation committed $10 million over ten years to strengthen the University of Chile through a program of exchanges with California's university system. That program was particularly successful in agriculture and veterinary medicine and resulted in graduate degrees from the University of California for more than 125 Chilean professors between 1965 and 1978, and some one thousand books, articles, papers, theses, and films. The Ford Foundation also provided $800,000 for the University of Concepción's Central Institutes of Basic Science, complementing a $1 million donation from the United Nations.[12]

These efforts included not only the hard sciences but the social sciences as well, chiefly sociology and economics. The country already possessed a long tradition of social studies that encompassed history, philosophy, social criticism, and literature.[13] That tradition was not institutionalized in the country's universities, however, and had only a tenuous relationship to the advances in academic sociology under way in Europe and the United States.

Scientific sociology arrived only in the late 1950s, when former law student Eduardo Hamuy returned from graduate study in the United States. Hamuy wanted to complement the existing "speculative" sociological tradition with an empirically based science that incorporated such U.S. methodological advances as scales and polls. With the backing of Rector Gómez Millas and local funding, he established the Institute of Sociological Research at the University of Chile.[14] In 1958, the first twenty-two students ever to major in sociology at the University of Chile enrolled, and research assistants were sent for training in the United States and Western Europe.[15]

At about the same time, the Latin American Faculty of Social Sciences (FLACSO) was established in Santiago as part of a U.N. Educational, Scientific, and Cultural Organization (UNESCO) initiative to train the first generation of Latin American social scientists in the region rather than sending them to the United States or Western Europe. FLACSO's multinational character was especially significant because it brought European professors to Santiago, along with students from several Latin American countries. Its principal training program, the Latin American School of Sociology (ELAS) also benefited from two extraordinarily talented foreign directors—José Medina Echavarría of Spain and Peter Heintz of Switzerland. It had become, by the late 1960s, Latin America's premier graduate training program in sociology and was attracting outstanding students from throughout the region.[16]

In 1958, Roger Vekemans Van Cauwelaert, a charismatic Belgian Jesuit with a special talent for fund-raising, established a School of Sociology at the Catholic University of Chile. Vekemans had been sent to Chile in 1957 as part of a church effort to strengthen its programs in the face of a growing fear that Marxist (and Freemason) Salvador Allende might be elected president. The program incorporated a number of European visiting professors and sent several junior professors off for graduate study in the United States. (The Ford Foundation provided $380,000 to the program in 1964 to improve its academic infrastructure and to underwrite graduate training abroad for junior staff members.) Vekemans also established separately a private economic and social development institute—the Center for Latin American Economic and Social Development (DESAL)—that soon generated extraordinary levels of foreign funding and was to have a major influence over the next decade on many of the country's talented young social scientists.[17]

Thus in the space of two years, three serious, research-oriented teaching programs in sociology were established in Chile. Each was led by modern, foreign-trained, highly committed sociologists. Each was launched with considerable local support and legitimacy. Each benefited from regular and close ties to professional sociologists in Europe and the United States. And each received major funding from U.S. sources, principally the Ford and Rockefeller foundations, with UNESCO, the Organization of American States (OAS), and several smaller European sources also contributing. It is unlikely that the discipline of sociology was established under more auspicious conditions anywhere else in Latin America.

By 1967, the two university-based programs were enrolling some one hundred new students each year. In 1969 a third school of sociology was established at the University of Concepción. By 1970, some seven hundred students were studying sociology in Chilean universities, and the country's first Institute of Political Science had been created at the Catholic University. The social sciences were established and growing rapidly. The proportion of university graduates majoring in the social sciences rose, according to one estimate, from 8 percent in 1960 to 18 percent in 1970.[18]

The rapid development of modern sociology in Chile was complemented by developments in economics. The University of Chile already had, by the mid-1950s, a strong teaching program in economics, possibly the strongest in Latin America. The program had been influenced by staff (among them, Argentine economist Raúl Prebisch) based at the United Nations Economic Commission for Latin America (ECLA) in Santiago, who often taught part-time at the university's School of Economics. In 1955, the program was fundamentally reorganized under a new dean, Luis Escobar, and incorporated U.S. economist Joseph Grunwald as director of its research institute. In 1957, it established Latin America's first graduate training program in economics (ESCO-LATINA). Over the next eight years, the University of Chile became the region's strongest source of academic research in economics.[19]

As in the case of sociology, advances at the University of Chile were matched by advances at the Catholic University. In 1956 the Catholic University signed an agreement with the University of Chicago's Department of Economics to establish a program of modern teaching and research at the Catholic University's School of Economics and Administration. Some forty Catholic University students were sent to the University of Chicago for training in economics over the next decade. By the mid-1960s, the Catholic University had developed a solid program with a well-trained faculty, a modern curriculum, and a growing capacity for carrying out research. The relationship with Chicago was to continue for at least three decades, giving rise during the 1970s to the "Chicago Boys," whose neoconservative approach revolutionized economic policy under the military regime and later altered economic thinking more broadly across Latin America.[20]

The programs at the University of Chile and the Catholic University both received substantial funding from USAID, the Ford and Rockefeller foundations, and the OAS. The Ford Foundation, for example, provided some $2 million for strengthening Chile's economics programs between 1961 and 1971. USAID had spent $812,000 on the Catholic University program by 1964. The Rockefeller Foundation provided more than $40,000 for the Catholic University program, and in excess of $200,000 for the University of Chile program during the late 1950s.[21] A significant portion of these foreign funds underwrote graduate training in the United States for Chilean students who would later return to teach and carry out research. Other funds covered visiting foreign professors, in-country research, and local infrastructure.

As a result of these efforts, Chile became one of the region's strongest centers for teaching and research in economics. According to one estimate, Chile's trained economists grew sixfold (from 121 to 727) between 1960 and 1970. The number of those holding foreign graduate degrees grew from just a few in 1959 to forty-six by 1971.[22] A half-dozen new research and teaching institutions had been established in the two universities, including the Center of National Planning Studies (CEPLAN) and the Department of Agricultural Economics at the Catholic University, and the Center of Planning (CEPLA) at the University of Chile. And the tools of contemporary economic analysis began to be applied to public policy through a newly established national planning office. Like modern sociology, modern economics had taken root in Chile.

Chile's advances in the social sciences were complemented by a growing presence in Santiago of well-trained foreign social scientists. The country's highly educated population, long democratic traditions, and openness to ideas had made it an intellectual center for the region. Several international and regional organizations had established their headquarters in Santiago. Besides ECLA and FLACSO, the Latin American Institute for Economic and Social Planning (ILPES) and the International Labor Organization's Regional Employment Program (PREALC) were based in Santiago and interacted regularly with the local academic community. The United Nations Children's Fund (UNICEF) and UNESCO both had regional offices in Chile. At the time of the military coup, probably more social science talent was concentrated in Santiago than in any other Latin American capital.

By 1970, then, the social sciences were well established in Chile and had begun to play an important role in society. The country's teaching and research capacity in the social sciences may well have been the strongest in Latin America. The reformist policies of Eduardo Frei's government had created an unprecedented demand for "social analysts," and many of Frei's key policymakers had been drawn from the University of Chile's economics program. The critiques of social scientists were beginning to penetrate the media and the political parties. And the "revolutionary socialism" of the Allende government would soon offer social scientists even greater influence in government decision making. The supply of social scientists and the demand for their services were both increasing rapidly. It was, according to Brunner and Barrios, "the golden age of progressive intellectuals."[23]

Chilean Intellectuals

By the early 1970s, Chile's intellectual community was strong and prestigious. As a group, intellectuals tended to be well trained, sophisticated, and connected to their professional peers in Europe and the United States. Through the media, political parties, and professional associations, they had considerable access to the country's elites. Most were based in universities. A few worked at the international organizations that had offices in Santiago, or in a handful of private research institutions. And a growing number held government positions, reflecting the demand for social analysts occasioned by the reforms of the Frei and Allende governments. By reason of an uncommon combination of training and status, Chile's intellectuals had more influence in political affairs than their counterparts in any other Latin American country.

By most accounts, however, that community was dominated by a certain kind of intellectual, one who emphasized society as a whole rather than as a collection of separate parts. Most prominent intellectuals favored a comprehensive perspective, addressing broad social problems that had basic structural causes and required sweeping solutions. They resisted and even discouraged analysis that was partial, tentative, or specialized. Their goal was "to produce a general image of society, a diagnostic of the totality, and to propose alternative models for its restructuring."[24]

The contrasting notion—of intellectuals as technocrats, concerned with instrumental issues and the specific details of social change—was firmly out of favor during this period. Its unpopularity may have been, as Silva suggests, a reaction to efforts by the right-of-center Jorge Alessandri government (1958–64) to expand free-market policies and halt the expansion of the public sector. Alessandri's efforts, which many labeled a technocratic approach to government, were resisted not only by labor and leftist political parties but also by business sectors that had long benefited from Chile's statist and protectionist policies. Thus by the early 1960s technocracy "had considerable political weight and created controversy in national affairs."[25] Technocratic approaches had become, at best, suspect.

Instead, Chilean intellectuals were strongly oriented toward ideology. They sought, in Brunner's words, "recognition on that purely discursive level, distancing themselves from instrumental or specialized tasks, from the production of knowledge directed towards specific managerial or organizational objectives." Their principal concern was to interpret history in terms of society's values and to chart the way to the future. They were expected to provide a broad vision of events and scientifically derived principles for how society should be organized. Brunner and Barrios's meditation on sociologists of the period was probably valid across the social sciences: "To be a sociologist was, for several years, the equivalent of being partisan. The sociologist was called, over all, to be an intellectual in the tradition of the ideological 'great intellectual,' who has knowledge of the totality, who knows the secret keys of society, its laws of development and its levels of false and true consciousness. The specialist, by contrast, was seen as a cut-down intellectual, partial, always exposed to contamination by dominant ideologies; in short, a narrow empiricist. The intellectuals that the revolution loved were the hedgehogs, not the foxes."[26] Ideology, in its grandest sense, became the principal currency of Chilean intellectuals.

The emphasis Chilean intellectuals placed on ideology was complemented by another notion that dominated during this period: that revolution and the refounding of society were necessary for achieving real social progress. Intellectuals of leftist and "social-Christian" persuasion often argued that the capitalist model of development was proving nonviable in Latin America. As Socialist intellectual and politician José Antonio Viera-Gallo put it: "It seemed to us that the institutional forms of the *estado de compromiso* had reached their limits and that, henceforth, far from favoring the much-delayed incorporation of the popular sectors, they would contribute to their exclusion." A key figure in the Social Democratic party expressed similar views: "We had all come to agree more or less explicitly that the constitution we had was no good, that the economy required a profound revolution, that our social and political organizations were in crisis. . . . We all agreed one way or another that things had to be radically transformed."[27] Thus gradualist and reformist measures came to be seen as palliatives that reinforced the status quo. Society needed to be fundamentally restructured; only radical change would do.

With time, the emphasis on profound social crisis and radical change structured thinking and debate in terms of competition between essentially different models of society. Latin America in general, and Chile in particular, were seen to be facing a historical choice between socialism and fascism. The Cuban Revolution provided a sharp contrast to the shortcomings of Chile's gradualist approach to development. Increasingly, debate was over comprehensive models of development and the "historical necessity" of revolutionary change.[28] Even the centrist Christian Democrats proposed a "revolution in liberty."

Moulian describes vividly the prevailing view of many on the left: "We fed on a religious vision of politics, that led us to see Marxism as 'total knowledge'; . . . hypnotized by what we believed were laws of revolutionary development: the rigid distinction between reform and revolution, distrust of gradual and step-by-step reforms, the demand to destroy the bourgeois state, the impossibility of capitalist development in a peripheral country, the need for the middle classes to be subordinated to the workers in all moments of the transition to socialism."[29] More and more, political actors were forced to choose from among competing, nonnegotiable models, intensifying debate and political polarization. The pressure to choose sides placed people at odds; it emphasized their differences rather than their similarities. Those not opting for revolution, particularly on the right, felt increasingly threatened by the direction and drift of democratic politics.

The role of intellectuals in that debate, more often than not, was to sharpen the differences between political alternatives. They underscored the contradictions and drew the lines, often reducing complex problems to a single simple idea. They were seldom moderate or conciliatory. An intellectual who later moved into politics, Alejandro Foxley, describes how intellectuals interacted with the political world during this period: "The intellectual became, often, a reaffirmer of ideologies and a sharpener of ideological conflicts between distinct political forces. The intellectual was, almost always, a factor of rigidity, dogmatism and sometimes even arrogance and exclusion." He continues: "Moderation was always interpreted in Chile as a sign of weakness. Anyone who was moderate was presumed to have some kind of complex."[30] Intellectuals were not particularly concerned with bridging differences and seeking common ground. Increasingly, they came to favor absolutist viewpoints that stressed the differences among groups over pluralist viewpoints that acknowledged their similarities. Their role was to divide rather than to unite.

Yet another central thread in intellectual thinking was a tendency to view politics in predominantly instrumental terms. Politics, as Brunner observes, was seen as a means of implementing ideologies and not "a limited subsystem that regulates party competition and permits the selection of groups that will periodically and alternatively exercise power." The intelligentsia saw politics as "a vehicle for globalizing proposals to transform society" and thus "loaded it with promises and saturated it with expectations, since it seemed like the source of society's whole impulse to change." Society was not something that produced itself gradually and from below, but rather "had to be produced by politics."[31] Ideology was the end, and politics was the means.

Silva makes a similar point but suggests that the promise of political impact induced intellectuals, at least before the military coup, to subordinate themselves to the political system. "Historically, the intelligentsia's supporting role towards the political parties and the state was due, moreover, to the technocrats' and intellectuals' conviction that they (i.e., the state and political parties) were the principal mechanisms for putting their plans for social reforms into practice." Silva's observation restates a point made much earlier by Tomás Moulian to the effect that those intellectuals who dominated leftist political parties during the 1960s were "secondary" or "passive" intellectuals. They simply adapted and distributed a discourse, he argues, whose essential principles were already formulated. They were neither critical nor creative. Instead, they were either "mere 'acclimators' of a product elaborated according to external canons, or they were 'men of faith' who had replaced hypotheses with beliefs."[32]

Intellectuals during this period ceded their critical and creative abilities to the priorities of political leaders. Indeed, the picture that many observers paint of the 1960s shows intellectuals closely attuned to politics but moving in lockstep with one or another grand and unassailable ideology. The Weberian distinction between the "political vocation" and the "academic vocation" had given way to the "committed intellectual" and the "committed university." As Lechner observed, "Between 1964 and 1973, social science studies progressively became more or less sophisticated justifications for conflicting political positions."[33]

This tendency by intellectuals to view politics merely as a means to impose a single ideological model takes several forms. Brunner refers to the "suppression of the past" to describe how intellectuals emphasized a utopian future to the detriment of established traditions and structures.[34] They saw history as little more than an ideological battleground, and the past as something to be overcome.

Viera-Gallo addresses this dimension more directly in terms of ends versus means: "In this eagerness, we did not pay attention to the problem of methods or means; we were interested in the ends. Even though we never proposed dictatorship as the proper path or instrument for achieving real democratization, in fact, by insisting only on objectives and giving them an absolute character, we contributed to weakening democratic practices."[35] His concern is with how commitment to a utopian end, when accompanied by a disregard for the means of getting there, causes democracy to be destroyed.

At issue here as well, perhaps, was the more generalized distrust of formal or bourgeois democracy that has historically accompanied socialist movements. The standard argument is that the bourgeoisie would never permit a democratically elected socialist government to carry out its legislative agenda, and therefore democratic elections should be seen as a means to power rather than an end in themselves. This "instrumental" approach to democracy was a common element in the rhetoric of the Chilean left.[36] It was less common among intellectuals, at least in any explicit form, but was certainly encouraged by the prevailing emphasis on utopian transformation, and disregard for existing values, traditions, and social structures.

Finally, Chilean intellectuals had a remarkable affinity for politics. Rather than confining themselves to the abstract and the esoteric, Chile's leading intellectuals focused on the major political issues of the day. They were concerned with how society was organized and where it was going. They expected to have an impact on politics. To be an intellectual, during this period, almost always meant being politically involved. "Sociologists," Brunner and Barrios note, "were not expected to publish; they were expected to transform the world."[37]

The extraordinary emphasis that Chilean intellectuals placed on politics was not altogether new. Intellectuals in Chile appear to have had for many years a close relationship with politics—much closer than have their counterparts elsewhere in Latin America. Edgardo Boeninger, a former university rector who directed a private research center during the mid-1980s and was named a minister in the new democracy, has pointed out that "the relation between politics and intellectuals has always been closer [here], and people have changed hats with great facility." Similarly, Alejandro Foxley has noted that, "in this country, the creation and elaboration of ideas always occupied a central place. The role of intellectuals was fundamental."[38]

The origins of this special relationship are less clear, however, and merit a more careful historical analysis than is possible here.[39] Observers suggest that Chile's principal political parties—the Liberals, Conservatives, Radicals, Christian Democrats, and Socialists—have been heavily influenced by intellectuals. (An exception is the Communist party, historically one of Chile's strongest parties but by most accounts virtually impervious to intellectuals.) The Christian Democratic party, for example, was founded by a group of intellectuals.[40] The Socialist party, in its several manifestations, has been strongly influenced by intellectuals. The traditional right-of-center parties in Chile have never had the anti-intellectual outlook that has characterized many such parties elsewhere in Latin America. And although intellectuals have only recently begun to play important roles in the parties of the right, observers regularly suggest that Chile's leading newspaper, *El Mercurio,* has traditionally provided the political right with an intellectual dimension. One explanation for this affinity is that Chile never developed the powerful regional *caudillos* so common in other Latin American countries and thus produced a different type of politician. Eugenio Tironi, a French-trained sociologist who was key in convincing Chile's opposition to use political opinion polling and focus groups in its campaigning, argues that Chilean politicians have traditionally been of a different type: "I think that the differences are not with the intellectuals, but with the politicians. . . . The Chilean politician is very distinct . . . not basically populist, nor a *caudillo,* nor . . . an autonomous class or caste,. . . . [but] rather—a more intellectual politician, with a certain professional formation, with a very close relationship to civil society."[41] Perhaps, as Tironi's comment implies, the longstanding strength of Chilean political parties has professionalized the role of politician and opened it to intellectual concerns.

Brunner, in a somewhat different vein, argues that the historically undifferentiated nature of Chilean elites has promoted overlaps among roles: "[We have had] a tradition of nonspecialized elites; a society little differentiated in the symbolic sphere, which means that politics and culture and art . . . overlap, . . . causing intellectuals to have a role in politics, and [causing] the political class, at the same time, to use as one of its criteria for legitimation the fact of being appreciated or not by intellectuals, and being near intellectuals—just as intellectuals, to legitimate themselves, have also used historically, and still use, the fact of being close or not to politicians, and of being recognized or not by politicians" (28 February 1991). In contrast with wealthier societies in Europe or North America which have developed more specialized social roles, Chilean elites are more likely to be called upon to stretch themselves across a variety of social roles. Thus academics are particularly likely to hold political positions at some point in their careers, and politicians to have come from the academy.

Taking yet a different tack, sociologist Javier Martínez, who played a key role in the 1988 plebiscite campaign, speculates that the traditional strength of the Chilean state helps explain the involvement of intellectuals in its activities: "Here there was a state that drew the best talent of the country toward its concerns, toward its institutions, not just toward public affairs [more generally]. . . . There must be a relation between this strong state that . . . set up this nation with such stable institutions, so strong with respect to society, and the fact that intellectuals here don't operate at the margins of institutions but operate inside them and in political life." Martínez sums up: "I think that the secret

. . . is simply that here there is an institutional strength that makes these two species of animals grow up together, and on certain occasions one influences the other."[42] The remarkably important role Chile's state has historically played in national affairs, according to this argument, has made it more attractive to intellectuals than in many other Latin American countries.

Another explanation is that the polarization of Chilean politics in the 1960s, and its increasing emphasis on ideology, created a stronger-than-normal demand by the political system for services that only intellectuals could provide. Compared to such countries as the United States or Brazil, where interest-group politics dominate, Chile's political culture, from at least 1960, has been, in the words of Brunner, "much more a true politics of ideology in which interest groups . . . are permanently faced with the brutal necessity of rationalizing themselves in ideological terms." That need to justify ideologically the demands of specific groups generated an emphasis on comprehensive ideological models. As Brunner continues: "Christian Democracy, just like the Popular Unity, just like the military regime, each with a great project for totally refounding society. . . . As long as society is like that, the role of intellectuals is necessarily going to be very strong because the intellectual is the specialist in the manipulation of great ideological models, much more so than the politician. And insofar as Chilean politics has been so sensitive to [those models], it is evident that intellectuals have always had a very decisive role" (28 February 1991). What is less clear, of course, is whether the traditionally ideological nature of Chilean politics caused intellectuals to involve themselves more in politics or was itself an effect of that involvement.

Whatever the explanation, power and intellect have had a long and close relationship in Chile. Politics has traditionally been not just a game of interests but also a game of ideas. That relationship strengthened during the 1960s, giving intellectuals a more important role in politics. When the Frei government assumed power in 1964, it incorporated substantial numbers of academic sociologists and economists as advisers. And more broadly, intellectual debate came increasingly to influence political behavior. As Foxley points out: "Politics during those years was done by a powerful 'political class' that penetrated social organizations, mobilizing them around vindictive objectives, with the goal of eventually taking power. Intellectuals exercised a powerful influence over [that process], feeding it ideologically and having notable success in defining the 'agenda' of problems and solutions that the political class would finally propose to the country."[43]

By 1970, with the election of Salvador Allende's Popular Unity government, the involvement of intellectuals in politics reached what was then a peak. The Allende government drew heavily upon the expertise of social scientists, hiring many and using others as advisers. "The weight of these revolutionary intellectuals, most of them 'organic' to their respective parties," according to Brunner and Barrios, "was felt in the communications media and in the central committees of the revolution. There was a popular government, a project for transition to socialism, and therefore an ample space for the ideological function of intellectuals and social analysts. Their word was listened to, taken into consideration; in short, valued within the ideological-political market as never before."[44]

The Breakdown of Democracy

Chile's democracy did not suddenly vanish in a hail of bullets when troops led by General Augusto Pinochet overthrew the government of Salvador Allende on 11 September 1973. It began to break down nearly two decades earlier with the erosion of traditional mechanisms and norms of political compromise. Until then, Chile's democratic system had been the envy of many other Latin American countries. Formal democracy had existed without interruption since 1932 and stretched all the way back, with only two brief exceptions, to 1830. By several measures, the evolution of democratic governance in Chile during the nineteenth century compared favorably with that of European countries.[45] The country had no recent, significant history of unconstitutional rule.

By the middle of the twentieth century, however, Chile's democratic continuity was becoming deceptive. The country's long history of constitutional rule masked a variety of shortcomings that increasingly pointed toward a breakdown. Electoral reforms and rising expectations were causing a sharp increase in political participation and placing new demands on the political system. (The number of voters, for example, grew nearly sixfold between 1957 and 1973.) Growing polarization among the country's political elites was steadily undermining traditional commitments to accommodation and compromise. And Chile's political center was eroding, becoming rigid, and no longer playing its traditional role as a broker within the country's fragmented and highly competitive party system. Although most of those problems were visible—and many were resolvable—they were generally ignored in the political debate of the time. The attractive but precarious nature of the system prompted one of the country's most distinguished historians to observe later that "in Chile stable democracy never existed. There existed, yes, a very perfect formal democracy that on September 11, 1973 fell like a house of cards, and disappeared suddenly without a trace."[46]

Some of the problems that afflicted Chile's democracy were structural. Chile's presidential system brought with it a rigidity that required flexible political elites in order to function properly. Because the political arena was sharply divided and increasingly competitive, Chilean presidents in modern times rarely represented more than a third of the electorate. Yet when no candidate achieved a simple majority of the votes in a presidential election, the Constitution required Congress to choose from among presidential candidates, rather than ordering a run-off election that could provide the winner with a popular mandate. In this way, of the last five presidents elected through 1970, only Eduardo Frei won by a simple majority of the popular vote; the rest were chosen by Congress, after receiving the largest minority of votes in presidential elections. Jorge Alessandri, for example, became president in 1958 with only 31.2 percent of the vote, and Salvador Allende became president in 1970 after receiving just 36.2 percent.[47]

Because presidents served fixed terms and could not be reelected, their accountability and legislative backing were limited. Constitutional provisions, however, often enabled them to act as if they possessed a broad mandate. Presidents could block legislation with support from just one-third plus one of the congressional delegates. They had few structural incentives for negotiation and compromise, reinforcing the stalemate and confrontation that so often characterize highly fragmented polities. The system depended heavily, therefore, on the disposition of political elites to seek alliances and accommodation with each other. Structural reforms that increased incentives for coalition building, or that substituted a parliamentary system, might have helped to moderate extreme positions and to nurture the consensus that did not arise naturally in the country's politics.[48]

Genaro Arriagada, one of Chile's most accomplished intellectual-politicians, has pointed out that the Constitution of 1925 in many ways "rewarded intransigence."[49] Parties could realistically aspire to win the presidency and gain access to broad governing power without making deals and developing stable coalitions. Thus party leaders tended to see electoral victory as a kind of once-and-for-all mandate. Once in power (even if, as in the case of Allende's Popular Unity government, without an absolute majority), they set about implementing their political agenda with little or no concern for accommodating other parties. The Christian Democrats, under Eduardo Frei, pursued their "revolution in liberty" as a "single party" (*partido único*), rejecting compromises with other groups. And the Popular Unity government of Salvador Allende subsequently bypassed legislative negotiation, relying instead on administrative fiat and legal loopholes to implement its "Chilean transition to socialism."

The country's political parties, although strong and representing the full spectrum of political opinion, were almost unregulated. Liberal rules on party formation and a proportional system of representation caused small parties to proliferate, to the detriment of larger, more stable groupings. Parties tended to be internally undemocratic, enabling leaders to operate independently from the rank and file. Lack of regulation led to unhealthy financial arrangements that sometimes included the inappropriate use of state funds for party purposes, and substantial secret funding from abroad. And Chilean political parties had been remarkably successful in penetrating the institutions of civil society, including student groups, professional associations, labor unions, and community organizations. Party representatives contested bitterly for control of these groups and then ran them almost as party subsidiaries. In this way, party leaders came increasingly to structure debate and influence decisions at all levels of society.[50]

In addition, a series of reforms that began in 1958 and sought to make government more efficient may have contributed to democratic breakdown. The measures, enacted over twelve years, limited the incentives for parties to strike preelectoral bargains with each other, strengthened executive control over the budgetary process, and restricted the ability of Congress to amend legislation and control patronage. Although they probably did make government less corrupt and more agile, they also reduced the scope of political bargaining and coalition building, and they enhanced the power available to a minority president.[51] Within a politically competitive and increasingly polarized setting, those changes made it even more difficult to achieve consensus.

But the most important problems were, as Moulian argues, "not structural, . . . but cultural, of the radicalization of the political elites." Between 1950 and 1970, Chilean politics underwent an extraordinary process of polarization that put the entire system in crisis and led eventually to breakdown. Increasingly, party leaders became more committed to their ideologies than to the democratic process. They promoted comprehensive, nonnegotiable solutions to social problems—what historian Mario Góngora has called *planificaciones globales*—that sought to transform society from the top down, without political alliances.[52]

The emergence of a Leninist left in 1955, of an uncompromising center in 1965, and of an antidemocratic right in the 1970s reflected new thinking across the political spectrum. Party leaders were increasingly placing ideological purity over traditional political bargaining and compromise, thereby undermining the trust and understanding that had enabled Chile's democracy to endure almost without interruption since 1830.

There is little evidence, however, that Chile's political polarization arose spontaneously from deep divisions in society. Chile was a relatively homogeneous country at midcentury, without sharp religious, ethnic, or geographic differences. Its income distribution was less skewed than that in most of the rest of Latin America, and it ranked among the most advanced in terms of education and health. Although Chile certainly had important class differences, support for each of the major political parties, with the exception of the Communists, came from across the spectrum of social classes rather than being concentrated in a single class.[53] Moreover, the limited empirical data available suggest that political radicalism was not common among the Chilean electorate.[54]

Instead, party leadership appears to have contributed fundamentally to the emergence of political polarization. This viewpoint is remarkably common among Chilean analysts. Valenzuela argues that party polarization was based substantially on "highly ideological political elites, in control of powerful party organizations, who structured the options of the electorate." Foxley speaks of parties focusing so heavily on ideology that they became distanced from the real demands of the people. Sociologist Manuel Antonio Garretón refers to the tendency of the traditional political class to "autonomize" itself (act independently) from its constituency, leading to high levels of ideology and polarization. Political scientist Juan Gabriel Valdés suggests a trend toward "party autism" in which leaders confuse ideology with reality, seeing levels of radicalism that did not exist and offering change for which there was little demand.[55]

Foxley compares the process to the Hirschmanian notion of "ideological escalation" in which the combination of competitive politics, growing radicalization, and the remarkably short path between intellectual creation and political proposals causes hastily conceived approaches to problems to become fundamental government policy.[56] Seeking to gain advantage in Chile's competitive political arena, and fueled by a growing taste for comprehensive, doctrinaire solutions, party leaders seized on the utopian schemes for social and economic transformation that had been developed by intellectuals. The highly institutionalized character of Chile's party system enabled leaders to transmit these steadily sharpened schemes to the mass level with relative success. And once in power, they turned them into policy. But the dynamic appears to have been top-down; the radical proposals for comprehensive change that dominated Chilean politics during the 1960s and the 1970s reflected fundamentally the polarization and conflict taking place among political elites. There is almost no evidence that they were responses to initiatives from the grass roots.

Significant polarization appeared first on the left and was probably exacerbated by a longstanding ambiguous position with respect to political democracy. Moulian notes that "the Chilean left, in its recent history, has thought of democracy in a double dimension: as a given and as an obstacle." Similarly, Walker refers to "the absence within the left, and especially within the Socialist party, of a clearly defined and articulated democratic socialism, that was consistent with the Allende program. The Chilean Socialist party, which in its origins had lived a markedly populist stage, characterized by an instrumental view of democracy, had evolved towards an unabashed Leninist posture, of frank and growing opposition to the institutions of representative democracy."[57]

The question of democracy had long been debated within the Socialist party. One of its founders, Eugenio González, fought vigorously for a democratic concept of socialism, but he and his supporters steadily lost ground to advocates of a more Leninist, insurrectional viewpoint. That viewpoint began to predominate in 1955, when the Popular Socialist party abandoned a conciliatory, multiclass strategy that sought gradual reform through alliances with the bourgeoisie for a "Workers' Front" approach that relied exclusively on the working class and its representatives to bring about socialism. According to the Workers' Front thesis, the bourgeoisie and petite bourgeoisie were too closely connected to the *latifundio* and big capitalists to be able to bring about fundamental socialist reforms. Alliances with centrist groups were therefore ruled out, leaving the Socialists and Communists to go it alone in transforming society. The nondemocratic approach became even more pronounced in 1967 when, during a party congress in Chillán, Socialist party leadership adopted a revolutionary line that saw democratic institutions as an obstacle to the establishment of socialism and sought to destroy the bourgeois state, replacing it with "popular power."[58]

The rise of class-based appeals was complemented by a growing emphasis on revolutionary, rather than gradual, social change. Here the Cuban Revolution played a crucial role. For some time, the left had debated the merits of the *vía pacífica* (usually meaning elections, and traditionally favored by Chile's Communist party) versus more radical, revolutionary change (increasingly advocated by the Socialist party). The apparent success of the Cuban Revolution profoundly influenced this debate, tipping the balance in favor of the revolutionary approach. The Cuban model "demonstrated that it was possible to 'skip stages' and begin to construct socialism now, having as an axis the working class and questioning thus the thesis of revolution by stages."[59] The growing salience of revolutionary approaches to social transformation is obvious in the 1961 declaration by Salomón Corbalán, Socialist party secretary general, on the meaning for Chile of the Cuban Revolution: "In our country, in accord with our reality, we must seek confrontation by the working class with the enemy class without promoting understanding or the *vía pacífica*" (139).

By contrast, the rise of democratic socialism in Europe had almost no impact on the Chilean left before 1973. As Walker notes, "Chilean socialism never paid significant attention to its European counterpart, except to denounce, in clearly pejorative terms, its 'social democratic' character" (127). Chile's Socialists looked instead to Latin America, and particularly to the region's populist movements, such as Peru's Aprismo. Thus they tended to stress nationalist, anti-imperialist and antioligarchic themes while neglecting, at best, the question of liberal democracy. Although they sought to incorporate the masses into politics, they paid little attention to the forms that incorporation might take.

To be sure, moderate, democratic elements survived on the left during the 1960s and 1970s and included among their ranks Salvador Allende. They were, however, unable to stem the growing tide of Leninism.[60] Allende's success in 1964, for example, in getting the Socialist party's Twentieth Congress to reject the insurrectional approach was only temporary. It prompted a group of young militants to resign and form the Revolutionary Left Movement (MIR) so as to "restore the revolutionary purity of Marxism in the face of the open treason of revisionism."[61] Allende's position then became untenable when the Communist and Socialist alliance that he headed lost the 1964 presidential elections to the Christian Democrats. This combination of principled defection and electoral defeat was decisive. The Socialists quickly rejected the "dead-end street of bourgeois democracy" and officially adopted Marxist-Leninism as their ideology (144). Walker summarizes this process: "While the democratic socialist concept contained in the *vía Allende* aspired to create the conditions for a socialist society through the gradual transformation of the state and the deepening of the existing democracy, acting within the limits of the constitution, the increasingly Leninist position adopted by the Socialist party led it slowly but steadily to propose the destruction of the bourgeois state and its substitution by so-called Popular Power" (169).

Polarization on the left was matched and exacerbated by hardening in Chile's political center. In the early 1960s, the Christian Democrats replaced the Radicals as the most important centrist party. The Radicals had long been known for their skills in negotiation and compromise and had traditionally played a crucial role in developing the consensus that Chile's democracy needed to function.[62] The Christian Democrats changed all that. They brought with them an ideological approach to politics, rejecting the Radicals' pragmatic deal making and coalition building in favor of a more consistent, principled stance. Instead of compromise, the Christian Democrats offered "authentic social-Christian politics," calculating that they could attract enough votes from the left and the right to govern. After impressive victories in presidential and congressional elections in 1964 and 1965, they set out on their "own path" to a "revolution in liberty," dealing with the opposition only when necessary. Chile's once-flexible political center had become rigid and ideological.[63]

In part, the Christian Democrats were reacting to the principled, revolutionary vision of the left by offering sweeping changes of their own. They sought to counter state socialism and "popular power" with economic reform and worker self-management, and thereby to remain competitive in the country's escalating electoral market. But their proposals constituted as well an effort to operationalize the Christian "communitarian" philosophy that had marked the party since its founding. And they reflected the trend toward doctrinaire, ideological positions that was coming to characterize Chile's political elites more generally.[64]

As Walker notes, the behavior of the Christian Democrats influenced decisively the radicalization of the left.[65] Leftist leaders saw the Christian Democrats as representing, in reformist guise, the ambitions of the United States and the interests of Chile's right. They also saw as dangerously close to their own agenda the populist appeals embodied in the Christian Democrats' communitarian philosophy, support for agrarian reform, and emphasis on "Chileanizing" copper production. And they were alienated by the Christian Democrats' rigid thinking and refusal to negotiate.

Thus the left, and the Socialists in particular, increasingly sought to counter the Christian Democrats by becoming even more radical. Elements favoring reform and political bargaining steadily lost ground to those favoring revolution and violence. The longstanding contradiction between Marxist-Leninist principles and liberal democratic practice was being resolved in favor of the Leninists. Two statements by political leaders make painfully clear the demise of traditional accommodationist norms: "Not for a million votes would I change a line of my program," said Christian Democratic party president Eduardo Frei in 1964; "We will deny the Christian Democrats salt and water," said Socialist party secretary general Aniceto Rodríguez in 1965.[66]

After 1964, however, the Christian Democrats never attracted enough voters to make their single-party strategy work. They were big losers in the 1969 congressional elections, getting only 30 percent of the vote compared with 42 percent in 1965. As the 1970 presidential elections approached, neither the left nor the right was willing to ally with the Christian Democrats, deciding instead to field their own candidates. The result was a minority presidency—leftist Unidad Popular candidate Salvador Allende won with only 36 percent of the vote—and the Christian Democrats came in last. They had failed to build a viable political center. Party allegiances remained spread across the political spectrum, polarization had increased, and the center had sacrificed its role as broker between left and right. Instead, conflict and intransigence became the hallmarks of Chilean politics.[67]

The government of Salvador Allende had little chance of resolving these difficulties. It was, as Valenzuela has noted, "a minority coalition dominated by Marxist parties dedicated to a fundamental transformation of that country's economic, social, and political structures."[68] It lacked the support to achieve its socialist agenda, and the will to settle for less. In order to satisfy the revolutionary left, it often bypassed parliamentary debate to adopt bold economic and social initiatives. It thereby confirmed the worst fears of the opposition, caused them to mobilize, and weakened their commitment to the democratic system. Efforts to resolve the growing political crisis in 1972 through a negotiated agreement broke down fundamentally because the government and the opposition could not trust each other and would not compromise. Party leaders progressively lost control of events, leading to political chaos and culminating in the military coup of 1973.

Political polarization, then, contributed heavily to Chile's democratic breakdown. Party leaders across the political spectrum came increasingly to value ideological purity over traditional political bargaining and compromise. Indeed, the very idea of politics as a mechanism for mediating conflict among different groups, and for regulating their access to power, fell into disrepute. Politics came increasingly to be seen in instrumental, utopian terms—as a tool for taking power and bringing about uncompromising social change.

3

Reinstitutionalization and Self-criticism: 1973-1982

There were really two worlds, two Chiles superimposed. Those superimposed Chiles had their own expressions. Opposition types read the newsmagazine Hoy, *listened to* Radio Cooperativa. *The other types read* El Mercurio, *watched the government TV channel, and frequented the salons of the Central Bank and the cocktails of the ceremonial Chile. And we, well, we frequented the cocktail parties of the more "open" embassies—the Italians, Germans, and the Dutch. Thus each had his own place. The big occasions for meeting were academic events or book launchings—the meetings of CED, of CIEPLAN, of ICHEH. They were opportunities for us to meet.*

—GENARO ARRIAGADA, 8 March 1991

A Period of Fundamental Change

The military takeover of power on 11 September 1973 marked a major turning point in Chilean history. In sharp contrast to the country's traditional commitment to democratic procedures and the rule of law, it established one of the most durable and autocratic dictatorships in Latin America. The military regime quickly declared a state of siege, suspended the Constitution, dissolved Congress, banned political parties, destroyed electoral registers, and imposed restrictions on the media. It set in motion a pattern of human rights violations that was to continue for more than a decade and included widespread torture, kidnappings, beatings, disappearances, and deaths. Although many politicians expected the military to return power to civilians soon after the coup, and despite General Pinochet's announcement that the military would hold power for just five years, the regime only reluctantly gave up power seventeen years later, after losing a nationwide plebiscite on Pinochet's continued rule.

The Pinochet regime had several fundamental characteristics. It was from the outset antipolitics. Reacting sharply to the political chaos and conflict of the Allende government, and to the more general bickering and *politiquería* that had long characterized Chilean democracy, it sought to eliminate politics—and especially politicians—from government for an extended period of time. Thus it instituted a government in which politicians had no role whatsoever. It replaced politics with administration, and politicians with technocrats. Decisions were made by administrators according to technical, professional criteria. As Pablo Baraona, twice minister of economic affairs in the military regime, stated: "The new democracy must be technified, so that the political system does not decide technical questions, but the technocracy has responsibility for using logical procedures to solve problems and to offer alternative solutions." The range of permissible decisions was defined in turn by the military junta. The result, in the words of Oscar Godoy, one of the country's most distinguished right-of-center political scientists, was "a military-technocratic alliance."[1]

Second, the regime was highly personalized, with power concentrated in the hands of Pinochet and a small circle of advisers, most of them military. Pinochet did not delegate significant power, nor did he develop a political party or movement that might provide a more permanent basis of support. Attempts to share power with established right-of-center parties were always half-hearted. Instead, the regime relied heavily on fear and favors to ensure order. Politics, for most of the regime's life, was never an issue.[2] Pinochet did not establish a bureaucratic-authoritarian regime like those that had emerged in Argentina and Brazil during the 1960s.

Third, the regime quickly moved from being temporary to being foundational in its objectives. In a conscious break with the past, it sought not just to depose Allende and restore order but to reshape fundamentally the relationship between the individual and state. Thus it eventually created, through the Constitution of 1980, a so-called protected democracy that concentrated power in the hands of the executive, provided for permanent military tutelage over government, and outlawed parties advocating "totalitarian" or "class warfare" viewpoints. And it established the region's most radical free-market economy. This was a kind of regime not seen in Chile for well over a century.[3]

Fourth, the coup produced a dissociation between the state and civil society. It created two Chiles: those who supported the military regime, and those who opposed it. The former were first-class citizens, with direct access to the state. They could hold government and university jobs, appear on television, and write in the newspapers. They were not in danger of having their offices searched or of being arrested, tortured, or made to disappear. The others were second-class citizens, with neither the privileges nor the protections available to supporters of the regime. As Genaro Arriagada vividly explains: "There was a dichotomy between an official country—orderly, efficient in certain aspects, in that the repression was very efficient, the military parades were fantastic, . . . they managed the Central Bank very well, . . . they had a beautiful economy to present to the international bankers. And on the other side, there was an 'underground' world that was also very spectacular, because foreign academics came and met people who did fantastic work here but had nothing to do with the state. . . . There were really two worlds, two Chiles superimposed."⁴ This disjuncture between the official Chile and the opposition Chile initially cut large groups of people adrift from traditional, legitimate institutions and roles in society.

The first decade of the Pinochet regime, then, was a time of great fear and great change. Most of those opposed to the regime faced sustained repression. For some that meant exile, arrest, torture, or even death; for others it meant unemployment, exclusion, or censorship. For all of the opposition it meant doubt and despair. The institutions of civil society were silenced, their leaders often exiled, jailed, or banished to remote villages. Political parties were banned, and labor unions broken up. Organized opposition was out of the question. The chief concern was survival.

For much of this period, two institutions dominated the scene: the armed forces and the Catholic church. The armed forces, through the military junta, were the regime. It was they who decided to reshape the country's economic and political institutions, enlisting the help of the "Chicago Boys" and a few conservative intellectuals, such as Jaime Guzmán. They made all important political decisions and controlled the appointment of civilians to government positions. A variety of political and economic groups supported them, providing advice and personnel, but none shared in the power. The armed forces ruled by themselves.

Initially, only the Catholic church could withstand the regime's repression. Responding to growing human rights violations, the church quickly became the principal symbol of active opposition. Its prestige, institutional strength, and moral force put it nearly beyond the reach of the military. The church was the only institution not required by the regime to request permission before holding meetings on its premises, or to subject its publications to censorship. Thus it was able to maintain its activities and add new ones when the other institutions of civil society had been dissolved or prevented from functioning normally.⁵

Throughout this period, the church used its legal and institutional structure to protect groups dangerously exposed to regime repression, and to carry out activities that were otherwise prohibited. It immediately took up the cause of human rights, participating first in an ecumenical Pro-Peace Committee to defend victims of human rights violations.

When government pressure forced the committee to disband, the church established its own internal organization, the Vicariate of Solidarity, to enable the same people to carry out the same functions. It also set up the Academy of Christian Humanism to serve as an institutional umbrella for the many talented groups of social scientists forced out of the country's universities. The Jesuit magazine *Mensaje* was for many years the only publication on the newsstands to publish critical work on contemporary national topics. Later, it was joined by *Análisis,* a weekly newsmagazine published by the academy that consistently featured dissident viewpoints.

For those who supported the military regime, however, this was a time of great challenge and activity. The regime's "foundational" agenda generated initiatives across the policy spectrum. Its overwhelming power meant that radical reforms could be introduced rapidly and without compromise. Thus the regime embarked on a concerted effort to transform the country's economic structure and social policy.[6]

The most far-reaching and dramatic of these transformations was economic. The regime enlisted a group of young, neoliberal technocrats—known as the Chicago Boys because they had been influenced by, and often trained at, the University of Chicago's Department of Economics—to "reconstruct" the economy after years of state control, macroeconomic disequilibria, and protectionism. The group immediately set out to implement radical economic policies that drastically reduced government spending, opened the economy to international competition, provided major incentives to private enterprise, and modernized private capital markets. Often experimental and occasionally inconsistent, the policies were criticized fiercely by opponents of the Pinochet regime and encountered significant, although less publicized, resistance from some of the regime's supporters as well. But they eventually struck pay dirt. Gross domestic product began to rise in 1976 and grew by more than 8 percent in each of the next three years.[7] Talk of a Chilean "economic miracle" began to grow.

In 1979, the regime announced that the reconstruction stage was completed and embarked on "seven modernizations" designed to refashion the relationship between the citizen and the state.[8] These initiatives sought to eliminate the monopoly power of organized labor, to privatize health care and social security arrangements, to promote a modern, export-oriented agriculture, to "transform" the judiciary, and to decentralize many government functions, particularly primary and secondary education, to the municipal level. Consistent with neoliberal principles, the modernizations all reflected a desire to move decision making on social services away from the central government, and toward individuals and markets.

In 1980, the regime sought to institutionalize its changes by establishing, through a plebiscite of questionable legality, an entirely new Constitution. The Constitution created a protected democracy that included a permanent tutelary role for the armed forces, a strong executive, a set of appointed senators to act as a brake to legislative excesses, and other restrictive measures. It also mandated a gradual transition to the new democracy which began with a plebiscite in 1988 and would end, depending on the results of the plebiscite, either in 1989 or 1997.

Whatever the outcome of these economic and social transformations (assessment would take several years), they constituted a radical experiment based on a systematic body of neoliberal thought that was new to Chile. For regime policymakers, these were revolutionary times. They intended to make great changes. The regime's labor minister, José Piñera, for example, took the seven modernizations idea directly from Mao Tse-tung's "four modernizations."[9] The 1980 Constitution was designated the "Constitution of Liberty" after the title of an influential book by neoliberal economist, Nobel laureate, and former Chicago professor Friedrich A. Hayek.[10] Born in violent reaction to the rigid utopian thinking that caused Chile's democracy to break down, the military regime proved every bit as revolutionary and absolutist as the leftist and centrist parties it replaced.

The coup caused a severe and sustained political and intellectual crisis. The traditional institutions and processes of democratic politics, such as Congress, elections, and free expression, were abolished. Political parties were made illegal; party leaders were intimidated through killings, exile, or jail; meetings and demonstrations were prohibited. Politicians could not publicly engage in politics and had no legitimate social role. A political vacuum was created.

The left initially bore the brunt of regime repression. Many leftist leaders were killed or arrested immediately after the coup. Most of those who survived either were expelled from the country or sought exile, fearful for their lives. The Socialist and Movement for Popular Unitary Action (MAPU) parties were virtually destroyed; most of their leadership spent the next decade or more in exile. Much of the Communist party soon went underground in an effort to survive.

The country's major centrist party, the Christian Democrats, also went underground, with many of its leaders in exile. The party's limited activities over the next decade were clandestine and illegal. Right-wing parties dissolved and worked through business organizations or through the government bureaucracy to achieve their goals. The myriad institutions of civil society, including neighborhood organizations, sports clubs, and professional associations, were prohibited from meeting or holding elections. The media was taken over, restructured, and tightly controlled. Overall, the political arena narrowed, became noncompetitive, and was monopolized by the state. A large segment of Chile's population had no political representation whatsoever.

At the same time, the universities were being purged, cutting many intellectuals loose from their traditional institutions and roles. Each of the country's eight universities was "intervened" by a military rector and "cleansed" of elements deemed antithetical to their proper functioning. Many professors were fired outright or were dismissed after academic witch hunts turned up their names. Others simply resigned in frustration. Some academics, perhaps hundreds, left the country out of fear or in search of employment. Many younger scholars, particularly in the social sciences, embarked on graduate study abroad, often with fellowships from foreign universities and donor institutions.[11]

The impact on dissident intellectuals in Chilean universities was devastating. Genaro Arriagada compared the measures to a neutron bomb that "saved the buildings but killed the spirit, at least in the social science area." He continued: "We lived in a brutal schizophrenia, because we frequented the best universities in the world, . . . however, in Chile we could not set foot in a single university" (8 March 1991). The university ceased to be a base of operations for much of the intelligentsia, leaving many intellectuals adrift and in search of alternatives.

The social sciences were hit particularly hard. The disciplines of sociology and political science almost disappeared from Chilean universities, and well-known centers for interdisciplinary social analysis, such as the Center for Studies of National Reality (CEREN) and the Center for Socioeconomic Studies (CESO) were closed. Those programs that remained were purged of their critical content, becoming exclusively professional and technical in their orientations. Work that emphasized structuralist perspectives, social movements, or conflict was eliminated. Interdisciplinary research centers were closed or reorganized.[12]

Economics at the universities suffered less than did the other social sciences but was cut back to a single neoclassical viewpoint. Marxist economics and political economy were ruled out. Structuralist approaches, Keynesian analysis, and economic history were discouraged. Economists identified with the left or the Christian Democratic party were fired or marginalized in favor of those sympathetic to the regime.

For dissident intellectuals and politicians alike, then, active opposition to the military regime was out of the question. Their chief priority was survival. Both groups had experienced professional failure, public repudiation, and official repression. They had been expelled from their traditional social roles and institutions. They faced an authoritarian government and a resurgent neoliberal ideology that completely excluded them. They could not oppose—or even criticize—the new conditions. They were in "complete occupational and intellectual orphanage" (Arriagada, 8 March 1991).

Preserving Dissident Thought: A New Institutional Framework

There was a crucial difference, however, between the plight of dissident politicians and that of intellectuals: politics was flatly prohibited, while research was, despite serious restrictions, generally legal. Unlike political criticism, academic analysis was not against the law. Thus displaced scholars could remain professionally active, providing they found a friendly institution and kept a low profile. That difference, and the intellectuals' successful efforts to exploit it, proved to have major consequences for Chilean politics over the next fifteen years.

Displaced scholars initially sought refuge in existing institutions not controlled by the military government. International and regional organizations with offices in Santiago, plus a few independent or church-based social research and action groups, temporarily absorbed many social scientists. Thus, for example, the Latin American Faculty of Social Sciences (FLACSO), the Center for Educational Research and Development (CIDE), and the United Nations' Latin American Demographic Center (CELADE) expanded to shelter some of those pushed out of universities. Foreign donor institutions often facilitated this process, providing funds for research fellowships and special programs.[13]

Some of these organizations changed permanently. FLACSO, for example, was forced to give up its highly regarded teaching program, which emphasized regional topics and drew students from many countries, and concentrate entirely on research. It incorporated several social scientists forced out of the Catholic University and began to focus almost exclusively on national issues. CIDE, which had been a relatively small institution in 1973, expanded its programs rapidly, taking advantage of the newly available talent and competing successfully for foreign funds.

But those arrangements had natural limits. International organizations based in Chile were not about to expand permanently, and the country had only three private social science research centers at the time of the coup: CIDE, the Latin American Institute for Doctrine and Social Studies (ILADES), and the Corporation for University Promotion (CPU).[14] Thus the existing institutional framework could not accommodate the new conditions, and scholars quickly began to seek new institutions and resources.

One of the early efforts to devise a more enduring response came from Claudio Orrego, an enormously talented intellectual and political leader who headed, at the time of the coup, the Christian Democratic party's Institute of Political Studies (IDEP). Surmising correctly that IDEP would be closed down by the military, he joined in 1974 with a small group of intellectuals to establish a new private institution that had neither party affiliations nor a controversial name: the Chilean Institute of Humanistic Studies (ICHEH). Their goal was to "keep democratic thought and a critical spirit alive among academic groups and social leaders" and to "carry out academic activities that would have political repercussions."[15] ICHEH operated almost entirely on funds provided by the West German Konrad Adenauer Foundation. Although it was always a small operation with only one full-time staff member, ICHEH was the first institutional response by Chile's politically involved intellectuals to the drastic restrictions on critical thought and discussion imposed by the new military government. It was the forerunner of the many private research centers that began appearing in the second half of the 1970s.

During its initial years, ICHEH was basically a publishing enterprise. It produced a series of monographs on the writings of democratic thinkers, on the social doctrine of the church, and on Christian Humanism, including, for example, the Nobel Prize address of Alexander Solzhenitsyn. It was perhaps best known, however, for a series of six books (known widely as the "yellow books" because of their bright covers) which Genaro Arriagada has dubbed Chile's first samizdat (8 March 1991). The books addressed issues that could generally not be discussed openly because of the strict censorship and violent repression that characterized the period. They were written (sometimes pseudonymously) by some of the country's leading dissident intellectuals and politicians and circulated privately in editions of two thousand, bypassing government censorship.[16] Perhaps the best-known volume was the first, published in 1976 and entitled *National Security and the Common Good,* which analyzed the "doctrine of national security" emerging in the armed forces of several Latin American countries and being used by the Chilean military to justify its repressive practices. That volume was instrumental in alerting leaders to the magnitude of the changes underway, and in focusing attention, as Brunner has noted (28 February 1991), on the hitherto overlooked potential of the armed forces for influencing broader governing ideologies.

ICHEH also established, under the church's legal framework and with funds from the Konrad Adenauer Foundation, the Center for Socioeconomic Research (CISEC). CISEC was led by Jesuit intellectual Mario Zañartu, who had a doctorate in economics from Columbia University and a reputation as a good manager. Its principal goal was to counter the regime's severe restrictions on press freedoms and its use of distorted information. By independently generating reliable data and analysis on topics of national concern, Zañartu has explained, it sought to "keep a critical spirit alive among social and political elites in the face of official efforts to deflect attention away from politics and towards making money" (19 December 1991).

To those ends it convened a team of opposition intellectuals and a few politicians to prepare regular reports on twenty-four thematic areas, including education, health, economic policy, agriculture, the media, legislation, foreign trade, public works, and the judiciary. The team prepared some fifteen to twenty reports annually between 1975 and 1979 and produced approximately six hundred mimeographed copies of each. It was a low-profile operation, conducted with great caution and using informal channels of distribution. Although the reports specifically stated that they were intended to help the Bishop's Conference design its pastoral programs, they were circulated as well to a broad range of dissident political leaders and professionals. (Many on the team would occupy top government posts when democracy returned nearly two decades later, including President Patricio Aylwin; Robert Zahler, president of the Central Bank; Alejandro Foxley, minister of finance; Andrés Sanfuentes, president of the Bank of the State; René Cortázar, minister of labor; José Pablo Arellano, director of the budget; and Francisco Cumplido, minister of justice.)

Another somewhat later response to the regime's severe restrictions on freedom of expression was the Group of Constitutional Studies, popularly known as the Group of 24. Established in 1978 by Christian Democratic politicians and lawyers to debate the regime's plans to establish a new constitution, the Group of 24 quickly became the only institutionalized expression of opposition political criticism outside the church. It met regularly to discuss the form a new constitution should take, and to debate the constitutional initiatives that were being developed separately by the military regime. It also addressed a variety of policy initiatives, including the merits of a parliamentary system, judicial reform, and limitations on the government's ability to intervene in the economy, that were to become central issues a decade later with the return of democratic rule. (Lawyer and intellectual Hugo Frühling characterizes the group as an "important intellectual step forward" because it addressed those issues so early.)[17]

The Group of 24 was also significant because it was one of the early instances of rapprochement between the Christian Democrats and the left. Frühling was the only figure from the left who attended the inaugural session at the Hotel Las Acacias in Santiago. Gradually, however, representatives from the Christian Left, Socialist, and MAPU parties became regular participants and began the slow process of establishing a dialogue with the Christian Democrats. That dialogue would lead, over the next decade, to the Democratic Alliance in 1983, to the National Accord for the Transition to Full Democracy in 1985, and to the thirteen-party Concertación that engineered the victory over Pinochet in the plebiscite of 1988.

The Group of 24 had an additional benefit: it gave the left, which was the most severely repressed portion of the political spectrum, its only public outlet for criticism of the military regime. At the time, not even the personal declarations of leftist politicians could be quoted in the Chilean press. Through the Group of 24, and within the framework of formal constitutional debate, the left was able to reestablish a limited voice in public affairs.

Perhaps the most interesting aspect of the Group of 24, however, was that it constituted, as Edgardo Boeninger has pointed out, the first instance in which opposition political figures used the cover of research to meet publicly to address political issues (29 January 1991). Although the Group of 24 was basically the initiative of Christian Democratic politicians (former party president Patricio Aylwin was one of its principal organizers), its official purpose was to carry out analyses and studies of constitutional issues. It sought a high public profile, issuing declarations and seeking press coverage for its criticisms of the regime's proposed constitutional reform. It included from the outset such centrist intellectuals as Boeninger (the only nonlawyer among the original twenty-four participants) and drew in major intellectuals from the left, such as sociologists Eugenio Tironi and Manuel Antonio Garretón. The combination of opposition politicians and intellectuals working in the same institution to analyze and debate political issues, but often from different traditions and with different objectives, first appeared clearly in the Group of 24. It established a precedent for the new and complex relationship between intellectuals and politicians that would become so common, and so crucial, to the opposition's strategy over the next decade.

ICHEH, CISEC, and the Group of 24 were all pioneering efforts to address the severe limitations on political and intellectual freedoms imposed by the military regime. They reflected the opposition's enormous determination to remain politically active despite the considerable personal risk associated with doing so. They were part of a lengthy series of experiments that the opposition carried out after the coup—reshaping existing institutions, establishing new ones, and testing new activities—in an attempt to thwart the regime's restrictions on politics, critical thought, and freedom of expression. They demonstrated that in-country opposition to the Pinochet regime, at least at the intellectual level, was possible.

Yet none of these early efforts was designed to replace permanently the institutions and activities that the military regime had either abolished or taken over as its own. They were stopgap measures, intended to address specific problems over a limited period of time. None provided full-time employment for the significant numbers of opposition professionals who had been displaced from university and government positions. None offered the institutional infrastructure—security, salaries, space, secretarial assistance, professional interchange, financing, and international contacts—essential to survival over the longer term. Although courageous and remarkably effective, they were essentially short-term experiments that prepared the ground for later initiatives.

Only the dissident intellectuals, and particularly the social scientists, managed to produce an enduring solution to the new conditions. Determined to remain active in their country and in their professions, they eventually established a whole new institutional framework for intellectual activities: a network of private social science research centers. When the coup took place, the country had only three such centers; by 1988 it had, by one count, forty-nine of them employing 664 professionals, 134 of whom had done graduate work in Europe or the United States. They were publishing more than twenty periodical journals or bulletins and had produced hundreds of academic books. By contrast, only some two hundred social scientists were carrying out research at Chilean universities in 1988.[18]

The Chilean centers were not unique. Rather, they were part of a broader trend toward private social science research institutions that took shape throughout South America during the late 1970s. Such institutions, rare in Latin America before 1965, by 1990 had become the principal locus of social science research in most Latin American countries. Many were founded by academics forced out of university and government positions by the authoritarian governments that came to dominate the region after 1965. Others were established in reaction to the bureaucratic strictures of local universities and their inability to provide adequate conditions for good research.[19]

In Chile, however, social science research had been firmly based in universities before the 1973 military coup. Thus the new institutions marked a fundamental departure from the past. Most were completely separate from traditional intellectual institutions—unconnected even with private universities—and depended at the outset on the church or some other existing institution for legal status. They were initially ignored by the media and excluded by the universities. Bookstores refused to sell their publications. Their funds came entirely from abroad, provided by foreign donors and development assistance organizations seeking to ameliorate repression by the military regime.[20] Their second-class status, and the possibility of government harassment, led them at first to keep a very low profile.

The Catholic church played a critically important role in developing the new centers. Under the leadership of Cardinal Raúl Silva Henríquez, archbishop of Santiago, the church established the Academy of Christian Humanism in late 1975 to act as an institutional umbrella for academic groups cut adrift from their traditional institutions. The cardinal described the academy's task as "intellectual work, intended to promote research, development and communication of the social and humanistic sciences."[21] He set up a pluralistic board of directors that included former university rectors, distinguished academics, and ecclesiastical figures who, because they were obviously not leftists, would not provoke military authorities. Among them were Edgardo Boeninger, Fernando Monckeberg, Enrique D'Etigny, and Father Raúl Hasbún.[22]

Church support was crucial, providing legal status otherwise unavailable from the government, and freedom to hold meetings and publish documents. For many years, private institutions in postcoup Chile could not hold public meetings without prior permission from the military government. The church, however, argued successfully that its spiritual vocation and legal status exempted it from such laws, much as diplomats are immune from the dictates of local authorities. Thus institutions organically associated with the church, like the academy, could organize public events when other private institutions could not. The prestige and authority of the church, and especially of Cardinal Silva, provided an important measure of political protection as well.

The cardinal did not, however, attempt to limit the academy to church dogma or programs. Duncan Livingston, the academy's executive secretary during its formative years, observed that the new institution was not intended to be "an instrument for advancing [the church's] own objectives, but simply a space where Chileans who were persecuted or otherwise in danger could develop intellectual activities because those activities were valuable in themselves" (14 January 1992). That approach, consonant with Chile's traditionally strong respect for intellectual activity, led the church to refrain from trying to control the specific contents of academy programs, and to tolerate the presence of a remarkably broad range of viewpoints.

At the same time, most groups affiliated with the academy understood that limits existed. Political activism was generally out of bounds because it might provoke serious reprisals by the military government. And blatant attacks on church values could not be tolerated, in part because they might erode crucial support by the bishops for the cardinal's position. Thus intellectuals adopted an operating principle that sought to balance their need for protection with their fear of control: "Not so far away that you freeze; not so close that you burn" (Livingston, 14 January 1992). The result was an unspoken agreement in which the church respected the principle of intellectual freedom, and intellectuals affiliated with the academy respected church values.[23]

The academy also constituted an early step in the rapprochement between the Christian Democrats and the left. Initial impetus for establishing the academy came simultaneously from two politically different groups: one comprised centrist academics (including Ricardo Jordan and Jesuit Renato Poblete) and was led by former rector of the University of Chile, Edgardo Boeninger; the other comprised left-of-center academics (including Humberto Vega and Manuel Antonio Garretón) and was led by former academic vice-rector of the Catholic University of Valparaíso, Duncan Livingston. Although both groups valued academic inquiry and intellectual freedom, they differed substantially on politics. Thus they were sometimes reluctant collaborators, particularly as the academy grew in size and importance. Their academic partnership, however, fostered political dialogue. One early example was a two-month, semiclandestine seminar that sought specifically to promote discussion between Christian Democratic and leftist, chiefly MAPU, party leaders. That seminar was one of the first systematic discussions between centrist and leftist political leaders after the coup and reportedly led to significant advances in understanding between the two groups.[24] More generally, opposition intellectuals from sharply different political traditions learned to work together in the academy's many programs.

From an initial three-project, six-researcher program funded by the Ford Foundation, the academy came to encompass six research programs and two semiautonomous institutions employing over three hundred persons, two-thirds of them researchers. The programs included research on human rights, agrarian development, labor economics, political attitudes and development, and education and comprised principally researchers who were prohibited, for political reasons, from teaching in the country's universities.[25] Many were among the leading Chilean specialists in their respective fields. In 1979, when the military regime withdrew from the international treaty that provided legal status to FLACSO, the academy provided, after considerable debate, the legal status that FLACSO needed to continue operating in the country.[26] Similarly, when Chilean members of the Mexico-based Institute of Latin American Transnational Studies (ILET) returned from exile, they did so under the academy's legal-institutional umbrella. By 1988, groups affiliated with the academy had published nearly 150 books and constituted the greatest single concentration of opposition social science talent in the country.[27] The academy had evolved from a small group concerned with preserving academic freedom to a major center of dissident debate and discussion on social issues.

Moreover, the academy provided stimulus and a context for public affairs activity at a time when opposition intellectuals were barred from public life. Its October 1977 seminar, "Social Sciences and National Reality," constituted the first occasion after the military takeover that dissident academics were able publicly to meet and discuss national issues. Beginning in 1978 it organized a series of "study circles" around broad professional areas (health, economics, journalism, education, philosophy, agriculture, etc.) that regularly convened many of the opposition's leading specialists for critical, public debate in their respective fields. The circles tended to mirror the country's principal dissident academic and public affairs groups, giving them a common forum and a public voice not otherwise available.[28] They thereby appropriated functions no longer carried out by the country's traditionally activist professional associations (*colegios profesionales*). Indeed, some of the study circles (in medicine, education, sociology, and architecture, for example) provided the core leadership for professional associations that emerged after the military government eased its restrictions.[29] And many of the participants went on to assume top government positions when democracy returned more than a decade later.

The church was not the only locus of new, private social science research centers. Completely autonomous centers also began to appear. The going was much tougher outside the institutional umbrella of the church, however. The government refused for many years to grant appropriate legal status to institutions formed by opposition academics, forcing some to operate without legal status, or to incorporate as for-profit partnerships rather than as nonprofit educational institutions. (These restrictions also affected support from foreign donors, who often had difficulty funding groups that lacked legal status and preferred groups with nonprofit status.) They were subject, as well, to all the restrictions of the military dictatorship and lacked the political protection provided by the church. These completely autonomous centers were thus slow to emerge, coming into their own only during the 1980s.

One of the earliest and most successful was the Corporation for Latin American Economic Research (CIEPLAN), established in 1976 by a gifted group of economists led by Alejandro Foxley. Many of CIEPLAN's staff had worked together at the Catholic University since 1970 as the Center for National Planning Studies (CEPLAN) but found themselves, after the coup, increasingly isolated and harassed by university authorities. Through careful maneuvering, they managed to secure nonprofit legal status without attracting the regime's attention. Then, with funding from foreign donors, they set up a new, private institution that went on to become one of Latin America's leading sources of economic research.[30] Reflecting the precarious conditions confronting private opposition groups, however, CIEPLAN formed a prestigious international advisory committee to provide some measure of political protection. They also established, with assistance from former Colombian finance minister Rodrigo Botero, a separate legal status in Colombia, giving them a refuge should they be forced to leave Chile.

Another pioneer was the Center for Economic and Social Studies (VECTOR), established by elements of the Socialist party explicitly to analyze social and political problems, and to promote a broader dialogue across the opposition political spectrum. VECTOR was one of the earliest systematic efforts to combine social scientists and politicians and was better known for its conferences than for its research. It was also the only academic center that experienced serious regime violence. In 1984 its quarters were searched, its directors arrested, and one of its researchers relegated to a small village in the south of the country.[31]

During the 1980s, many completely autonomous centers were established, representing a new generation of scholars returning from study abroad or from exile, such as the Center for Social Studies and Education (SUR) and the Latin American Center for Research on Political Economy (CLEPI). Some of the returnees were employed temporarily at the already-established centers while they organized new institutions. One center that eventually played an important role in promoting opposition dialogue was the Center for Development Studies (CED), founded in 1981 by Christian Democratic leader and former minister of foreign affairs Gabriel Valdés. By the mid-1980s, then, private research centers had become a major new element in Chilean academic life.

In comparison to private research centers emerging elsewhere in Latin America, the Chilean centers had several distinctive characteristics. They were, as Brunner and Barrios point out, more numerous and more likely to be organized around a specific topic, such as women, labor economics, or peasant development, rather than an entire discipline. Also, they were more likely to include a distinct "political-cultural" perspective. Each tended to have a single, relatively cohesive political viewpoint, reflecting the traditional weight of ideology in Chilean social science, and the traditional tendency of Chilean institutions to organize around political subcultures.[32] Thus the new centers, like university faculties and programs before the coup, tended to represent single, relatively cohesive political positions rather than to recruit staff from across the entire opposition political spectrum.

The Chilean centers had some other noteworthy characteristics. They adopted an open style of operation that facilitated ties with non-academic groups, and particularly with politicians. The very isolation and marginalization that affected the entire opposition may well have promoted greater openness. All sectors of the opposition shared a sense of failure, a feeling of vulnerability, and a need to understand the new conditions. The political parties saw the centers as in some sense their own and accorded them credibility. Thus at least some of the natural distance between academics and social actors was erased, making new relationships possible. As Sergio Bitar suggests, "We are not talking about NGOs [nongovernmental organizations] in which ten researchers gathered to talk among themselves. . . . [There was] a strong interaction with broader sectors and especially with political parties. . . . Thus they were catalysts, they were convokers" (16 January 1991). Despite their considerable academic credentials, Chile's new private research centers were not ivory-tower institutions.

This openness was a result as well of the centers' including people with prior political experience and concerns among their staff. CIE-PLAN's founder, Alejandro Foxley, for example, left a post in the government's planning office for a research position at the Catholic University when Salvador Allende was elected president. Humberto Vega directed the Allende government's budget office before founding the Program of Labor Economics (PET) at the Academy of Christian Humanism. FLACSO sociologist Tomás Moulian had been one of the founders of the MAPU party. Javier Martínez, one of the key researchers at SUR, was the regional director of the MAPU party in Valparaíso before the coup, while heading up the Catholic University of Valparaíso's Institute of Social Studies. The extraordinary politicization that occurred during the 1960s had sharpened the political sensitivity of most academics and prompted many, particularly social scientists, to become politically active. After the coup, the fact that the opposition was barred from political and government activity forced many politicians with academic training to seek employment in the academy. Thus the centers typically comprised an uncommon and potent mix of academics with strong political concerns, and politicians with strong academic backgrounds.

The character of their staffs caused the centers to orient their work toward real-world problems. Research topics included the causes of the military coup, the nature of the new authoritarian state that followed it, and the changes in social structure and composition the new regime was bringing about. The centers analyzed in great detail the government's sectoral policies, particularly its economic and social programs. They developed a whole series of research specialties, many of them new to the country, including international affairs, urban social movements, political theory, civil-military relations, agrarian social structure, the sociology of culture, and the status of women.[33]

As time went by, they also turned their attention to democracy, and to the problem of democratic transition. This interest in democracy, as Lechner has pointed out, came with a measure of irony: "Paradoxically, Chilean political science, established as an empirical science during a democratic regime, made democracy its central focus of reflection only under a dictatorship." Before the coup, most social scientists focused on social, not political, development. It was only after the military junta sought to eliminate politics and politicians from government that Chilean social scientists began to take politics seriously. The result was an impressive body of research that encompassed democratic theory, political parties, electoral systems, and the role of civil society under democratic rule. The focus on democracy led to an expanding network of analysts within and without Latin America who exchanged information and analyses and frequently met to discuss transition experience and strategies. Some of those activities were deliberately promoted by such institutions as the Buenos Aires–based Latin American Council of Social Sciences (CLACSO). Others grew out of relationships Chilean social scientists had previously established through graduate study abroad and participation in multinational research projects. The rich store of knowledge and insight that emerged from these exchanges was gradually translated to political actors through meetings, publications, and informal conversations.[34]

Although all the Chilean institutions were established by highly trained social scientists, and analysts tend to refer to them as "think tanks," they were in fact quite diverse. Some were predominantly academic, carrying out basic research and publishing in prestigious international journals. Others had a more applied focus, using research to address concrete policy issues, and disseminating results in forms more accessible to policymakers. Still others provided practical information, technical assistance, and political advice to social movements. By the late 1980s, research and action programs often existed side by side in many of the centers.

Virtually all private research centers, however, shared a growing set of contacts with social actors. Prompted by the major changes underway in society, intellectuals began in the mid-1970s to reach out, often under the auspices of the church, to university students, labor leaders, professional associations, and community groups. Some established programs of meetings and publications designed for social actors. Others embarked on action-research projects that sought practical solutions to the problems of the urban poor. Still others undertook participatory research that enlisted representatives from such sectors as women or peasants in analyzing their problems and devising broad policy solutions.[35] These efforts complemented work by a much larger set of nonacademic, private voluntary organizations working with the poor.[36] Although rooted in research, they became channels for providing information, technical assistance, and training.

They grew, as well, into a widespread network of social communication. Although impact here is difficult to demonstrate, the "ten years of invisible work" these groups carried out was important in helping revitalize Chile's civil society. Their efforts took place, as Brunner suggests, "in a practically silent, invisible, and nonspectacular way. But they established the communicational, ideological, cultural, and, in part, political infrastructure that enabled later . . . a whole civil society [to spring] up again with relative force. . . . Without those ten years of work, the resurgence [of civil society] would probably have been much weaker, narrower, and slower" (28 February 1991).

Dissident intellectuals also enjoyed strong support from foreign academics and academic institutions. Scholars from Europe, Canada, and the United States visited Chile regularly throughout the 1970s and 1980s, bringing with them information, ideas, and encouragement. Universities as diverse as Stanford, Stockholm, Notre Dame, Duke, California–San Diego, and Oxford offered fellowships for graduate students, visiting professorships for senior scholars, and opportunities to publish. The latest in social science research flowed steadily into Chile throughout the dictatorship via exchange agreements with foreign universities and research centers. Nonuniversity centers, such as the Latin American Program of the Woodrow Wilson International Center for Scholars (in Washington) and the Center for Inter-American Relations (in New York) organized conferences and speaking opportunities that enabled Chilean scholars to travel and meet with their counterparts abroad. These activities—extraordinary in size and diversity—constituted external havens and catalysts for reflection and networking. They helped intellectuals develop a new agenda and ethos. Although marginalized in their own country, Chile's dissident intellectuals remained firmly connected to the global academic mainstream, thanks in part to the determined efforts of the foreign academic community.

Moreover, the opposition private research centers received their funding almost entirely from foreign sources. A broad array of public and private donors from Europe and North America supported the new research centers throughout the seventeen years of military dictatorship. The process began with emergency measures for displaced social scientists shortly after the 1973 military coup, evolved into core support for the private research centers that emerged a few years later, and expanded into a formidable mix of program and institutional assistance during the 1980s. Foreign donors helped dissident social scientists remain professionally active in Chile rather than having to abandon academic pursuits or seek academic employment abroad. They provided hundreds of fellowships for master's and doctoral study in Europe or North America. They provided the seed capital for the initiatives of a few social scientists that became a vast new network of private research centers. And they provided those centers, over a decade or more, with the sustained assistance necessary to grow and produce.[37] For much of this period, there was no domestic funding for dissident intellectuals.[38] Without these foreign donors active over nearly two decades, the centers might not have existed.

The motivations of foreign donors varied considerably. Some sought simply to build and maintain Chilean capacity to carry out high-quality social science research. Their assumption was that good research and training were an essential base for policy choices, even though the timing and shape of their impact could not be predicted. Others took a more instrumental approach, supporting only research that would (at least in their view) directly help resolve specific, immediate problems. Still others had a more broadly political motive, seeking to keep critical, independent thought alive in Chile during the dictatorship, and to nurture policy expertise for a future democratic regime. Most donors were motivated by some combination of these factors. A broad array of donors, however, many of them incensed by the repression of the Pinochet regime, were disposed to support the critical, high-quality research being produced by Chile's talented social scientists.

Major donors included the Ford Foundation, the Canadian International Research Center (IDRC), and the Swedish Agency for Research Cooperation with Developing Countries (SAREC). The Ford Foundation provided start-up assistance to many of the centers in the 1970s, including CIEPLAN, the Academy of Christian Humanism, PET, and PIIE. It continued its funding throughout the 1980s, averaging over $800,000 annually in Chile grants between 1980 and 1988. For at least part of the 1980s, Chile was the largest Latin American recipient of funds from SAREC and IDRC.

Donors providing smaller but still significant amounts to the research centers included the Inter-American Foundation, the Tinker Foundation, several European governments, and the European Economic Community. France's Mitterand government provided substantial support for CERC at the Academy of Christian Humanism. The Dutch government supported a variety of Chilean nongovernmental organizations, many of them research oriented. The German political foundations, principally the Friedrich Ebert, Friedrich Nauman, and Konrad Adenauer foundations, occasionally included support for research within their Chilean programs.[39] Thus even a conservative estimate would suggest that an annual average of some $1 million in foreign funds flowed to Chilean private research centers between 1975 and 1980, and an annual average of $3 million between 1980 and 1988.

The massive, postcoup foreign support that flowed to Chile's private research centers was not entirely new, however. In some sense it was a logical extension of aid provided during the 1960s, when a variety of foreign donors undertook a sustained and substantial effort to strengthen social science teaching and research. Many of the social scientists who established and populated private research centers after the coup had acquired their graduate training and research experience through those early programs. Some of the donors who funded the private research centers after the coup had worked in Chile for many years and were incensed when academic programs that were just coming up to speed in the early 1970s were dismantled by the military authorities. Thus a human resource base was already in place for postcoup donors to build on. And several donors had already established programs and relationships with Chilean intellectuals. Foreign funding for Chile's private research centers in the late 1970s and 1980s, therefore, was significantly facilitated by historical precedent: a broad effort by foreign funders over many years to establish modern social sciences in a developing country.

The need to raise money in a competitive, international donors' market had important implications for the emerging private research centers. As a group, foreign donors tended to value science more than ideology, and technocratic issues over theory. They also tended to tie continued support to evaluations of work accomplished. Thus research had to be justified in new terms, done well, completed on time, and published. International standards became more relevant. Researchers were subjected, in Brunner's words, to "three Anglo-Saxon formulas: 'publish or perish,' 'no nonsense' and 'accountability.'"[40] Chile's academy, like its economy, had been thrown open to international competition.

Thus the output of the centers was generally of good-to-high quality, often constituting the best such work being done in the country, and sometimes the best in the region. But it was also different. The emphases on ideology and on revolution that had become common in Chilean social science during the 1960s diminished as scholars began to reevaluate their traditional approaches. Other emphases—more purely scientific or directly policy oriented—took their place. Analysis became more dispassionate, specialized, and empirically based. Researchers returned to the values that had initially accompanied the institutionalization of scientific research in Chilean universities during the 1960s. The result was a new style of social science, more autonomous from political ideology. As one observer, musing over these changes, put it: "Intellectuals went from being ideologues to being analysts."[41]

Some portion of this shift was a result of the centers drawing their support almost entirely from international donors, who tended to favor empirical, applied studies over work on theory or ideology. But a more important factor was the trauma occasioned by the breakdown of democracy and the repression of military rule. As Lechner notes: "The 1973 coup signified an existential experience that radically transformed life. We had thought that our debates were no more than words, and found, to our horror, people being accused, tortured and killed for their ideas. We experienced the fear of violence and our own impotence in the face of its arbitrariness and impunity. Political-ideological conflict was replaced by war, and we experienced a loss of security—not only physical and economic, but also the loss of certainties, of symbolic reference points, of social influence and collective power—all that vital world, including the democratic order, that we had taken for granted."[42] Faced with the dramatic failure of old approaches, dissident intellectuals began exploring new ones.

The dynamic of activities at the centers was different from that of precoup Chile. The shift was, in the words of Genaro Arriagada, from the traditional university, "where you spent four years producing a book, or one year producing a twenty-five-page paper," to "the most cruel free market of competition for projects. . . . You had to have an implacable rigor to produce, because you had to fulfill obligations to the Konrad Adenauer [Foundation], to the Ford Foundation, to ECLA, to the University of whatever, and so the Chilean intellectual world became terrifically productive, terrific because you had to . . . spend four months doing this project and certify that you had finished it to that foundation, because you had to fit with this other, and then spend three months in Canada, and then return and then . . . and so forth" (8 March 1991). New standards of productivity began to appear.

The new centers' administrative arrangements were also different from those of precoup institutions. Seeking to maximize scarce funds, they became leaner and more efficient. The private centers experimented with different approaches to organization, administration, data gathering, computation, and publishing. Staffing decisions became more closely tied to talent, training, and output. Salaries and tenure depended on funding. The evaluation of results came to play a more important role. Again, Arriagada describes the change: "In contrast with what used to happen in the University of Chile, where if you had a project you could take three weeks, three months, or three years, because the university, when all was said and done, would always pay you—you could always go at the end of the month and get your paycheck—in contrast here they said to you, 'Look, this is a project for which we have $4,000, and we've calculated that we can give you $800 for four months, and that leaves us with $800 for overhead, so are you interested in these four months?' You knew that at the end of those four months the grant was over, and if you took longer you had two options—either not turn in the work, in which case that source would be closed to you forever—or turn it in, in which case they would be ready for the next project. So, the productivity of Chilean social scientists under these implacable laws rose to incredible levels" (8 March 1991).

Over time, the private research centers transcended their origins in the military junta's cleansing of mainstream academic institutions. They became a new kind of academic infrastructure that, although outside the official system, provided dissident intellectuals with their basic professional needs: an institutional framework, funds, colleagues, standing, and access to local organizations. They also provided a link between local scholars and the foreign intellectual community, many of whose members refused to collaborate with the universities or the government. They were extraordinarily productive, generating a torrent of academic publications, seminars, short-term training programs, and international consultancies. They became the most dynamic segment of their country's social science—a kind of informal university.

The new centers also became, during the decade after the military coup, the exclusive locus of critical, independent thought in Chile. They were regularly, and seriously, referred to as "the catacombs," evoking an image of dark, secret places where the persecuted labored to preserve their beliefs.[43] They constituted "spaces of liberty" where dissident intellectuals barred from universities, government, and the media could meet, work, and exchange ideas. They preserved intellectual diversity, nurtured criticism, and kept at work a whole generation of talented thinkers who might otherwise have emigrated or left the academy entirely. Having been banished from the mainstream, the dissident intellectuals took the mainstream with them.

Transforming Dissident Thought

Even as they preserved dissident thought, however, intellectuals at the private research centers also began to transform it. Politics in Chile had traditionally emphasized ideology, and thus the coup generated an intellectual, as well as a political, crisis. It represented not just the failure of interests but also the failure of ideas. Opposition politicians and intellectuals alike wanted to understand why their ideas had failed, and what that meant for the future.

Intellectuals were particularly able to address such questions. They had the institutions and funds necessary to carry out research. They were well versed in ideology and political analysis. Moreover, the trauma of failure and repression hit intellectuals hard, generating a collective sense of responsibility and considerable soul searching. They were overwhelmed by the breakdown of democratic government and aghast at the repression that followed. They needed to understand what went wrong, why, and what that implied for the future. They also faced few alternatives. Politics was illegal, teaching at universities was out of the question, and criticism of the new regime was dangerous. One of the few options available to dissident intellectuals was to keep their heads down and do research. Thus they began to examine critically the dissident thought they were preserving.

In assessing their impact, however, it is important to understand the restrictions placed on political activity by the Pinochet regime. Political parties were suspended immediately after the coup and then summarily dissolved. For the next decade, political parties—left, right, and center— were entirely illegal. They could not lawfully own property, hold meetings, choose leaders, or issue statements.

The response of several opposition parties, most notably the Christian Democrats and Communists, was to go underground. But that strategy was dangerous, given the regime's repressive apparatus and determination to stifle traditional politics. Dissident politicians were routinely harassed, arrested, and exiled. Torture, even death, were very real prospects for those associated with the left. Politicians could act as politicians only by breaking the law and incurring significant risk. Formal political activity thus almost came to a halt during the balance of the

1970s. There was no opposition debate on political strategy; there was only dissidence.[44]

Dissident intellectuals faced significantly better conditions. Their profession had not been outlawed. They were able to secure enough foreign funding to establish private institutions and to resume professional activities. Their academic vocation permitted them to address topics that politicians could address only at significant risk. Although they were forced to maintain a low profile, they possessed the core resources necessary to survive and produce. Social science was generally legal; politics was not.

Thus intellectuals began to examine the causes of the defeat, churning out studies on the Allende government and its downfall. Much of this exercise constituted a self-analysis. Traditional beliefs and political positions were challenged. It was a period of "radical self-criticism" and "extraordinarily sincere dialogue." The trauma and rethinking were greatest on the left, which found its very existence at issue and was forced to confront the longstanding contradiction between its revolutionary rhetoric and its reformist practices. But the trauma extended across the political spectrum to encompass as well Christian Democratic intellectuals who had opposed Allende. Overall, Chile's intellectuals embarked on a decade-long "learning process" that was to reshape political thought and rejuvenate civil society.[45]

Initially, they carried out purely academic analysis on the breakdown of the Popular Unity government and its immediate aftermath. The focus was on what had happened, and why. Later it shifted to understanding the nature of the new regime and the changes taking place in the country. As Garretón points out, however, there was no strategic political debate during this period.[46] Emphasis was on understanding past failures and present realities. The work of the centers comprised almost exclusively documentation, analysis, and explanation—academic activities that intellectuals undertake anywhere in the world.

The private research centers were also prevented, until at least 1978, from communicating their work to a broader public. Dissident intellectuals were barred from government and university positions and had almost no access to the media. They were subject to censorship and distributed their publications quietly through informal networks of interested individuals. Moreover, there was little incentive for engaging in public outreach. Not being noticed was the best way of staying out of trouble.

Indeed, virtually their only audience for nearly a decade was a political and professional elite. As Brunner suggests, between 1973 and 1983 "no one except the political class was aware of, or read, what Chilean intellectuals were producing, at least inside the country" (28 February 1991). Only a relatively small group of well-educated opposition politicians and professionals paid attention to the intellectuals' work. They did so in part because of their traditional ties with intellectuals, and their interest in the issues intellectuals were addressing. But another major factor was the near monopoly that intellectuals had on political analysis and discussion. They were doing work that could not really be pursued elsewhere. Intellectuals presided over one of the few "spaces of liberty" open to the opposition.

That gave intellectuals resources that politicians lacked. They possessed institutions, funds, and freedom to operate; politicians could legally possess none of these. As Boeninger explains: "Donors were not so free as to finance just anyone who, under the label of an intellectual, was doing political work. The Ford Foundation was a clear example. It had certain parameters—it had a great sympathy for democracy, but it could not finance people just because they had a political label. That, from the beginning, gave practical importance to intellectuals, it gave them a presence. They offered shelter to the politicians. It produced a very important relationship" (29 January 1991). Intellectual activity had been empowered with respect to political activity. The constraints of dictatorship and foreign assistance had combined to accentuate the traditional relationship between intellectuals and politicians, and to shift the balance of power in favor of intellectuals.

Thus there began to develop a complex and ultimately very important relationship between dissident intellectuals based at private research centers and politicians. During the worst years of political repression, the academic centers constituted a kind of sanctuary for the political opposition, providing a place where it could meet, come to terms with its failures, and rethink its politics. The centers imposed an academic framework on politicians, inviting them to seminars and sending them publications. Sometimes they even provided employment, contracting academically qualified politicians to write research papers. Intellectuals who later would enter politics were based at these centers, carrying out research on politically relevant issues. Some intellectuals also held leadership positions in the clandestine parties.

There emerged what participants repeatedly characterize as "a kind of strange mixture of political intellectuals" (Bitar, 16 January 1991) composed of "intellectuals who take up politics and politicians who for the first time reflect from a more doctrinal perspective on great state issues."[47] Lacking legitimate meeting places, politicians gravitated slowly toward the private research centers. Lacking an audience, dissident intellectuals gravitated slowly toward their political counterparts. The process was not formal, deliberate, or structured. It simply happened, fueled by tradition, talent, common concerns, and the comparative advantages that intellectuals had under the dictatorship. A new relationship formed and began to ferment.

Several examples help illuminate the growing interpenetration of political and intellectual roles. Ricardo Lagos, a Ph.D. in economics from Duke University who founded the Party for Democracy (PPD) in 1987, chaired the board of a private research center, VECTOR, during the 1980s. Ricardo Núñez, who became president of the renewed Socialist party in the late 1980s, carried out research at various centers after his return from exile in 1981. Enrique Correa, one of the founders of the MAPU party, worked at several church-related centers during the 1980s. Ricardo Solari, a member of the central committee of the Socialist party's Almeyda branch, spent much of the 1980s working at SUR on labor programs. Angel Flisfisch, a Michigan-trained political scientist and FLACSO senior researcher, was a member of the Socialist party's central committee during much of the 1980s, as was his colleague at FLACSO, sociologist Manuel Antonio Garretón. Alejandro Foxley, who founded CIEPLAN in 1976 and headed it until 1989, became a key figure in the Christian Democratic party during the 1980s. Increasingly, academics and politicians were sharing roles.

One of the first manifestations of this new relationship between politics and the academy took the form of technical criticism. Careful, empirical studies by centers like PIIE, PET, and the Agrarian Research Group (GIA) gradually established a stock of solid data on the impact of regime policies in such areas as education, urban poverty, and rural development. Opposition figures, political and intellectual, began using this growing body of technical analysis to mount accurate and effective criticism of regime policies.

Indeed, until approximately 1980 the opposition could publicly criticize the regime only on technical grounds. Political criticism was dangerous and unlikely to be picked up by the media even if attempted. Technical criticism, however, particularly on economic policy, was occasionally tolerated. As one opposition economist observed: "Clearly, the most acceptable criticism was economic. Thus the political debate quickly became a debate over economic policy. And that converted many of us into protagonists in that debate, as much because there was a technical base for our comments as for the issues we had chosen."[48]

Intellectual-politician Ricardo Lagos describes how intellectuals and media alike turned the limited space available for technical analysis into political debate. "In a dictatorship, not everyone can speak. . . . Thus the intellectual is someone who can begin to talk about themes that are forbidden to the 'political' class and does it from his own 'scientific' perspective. In Chile the first public debate began much more in the economic area than the political area. People debated economic policy. . . . I remember vividly the first time they interviewed me in the magazine *COSAS*. It was already 1981, but it was as an economist, in the sense of someone being interviewed supposedly because of what he knew. Yet there was an element of complicity in the interview, because they knew they were interviewing someone who was openly in opposition. It was clearly a game in which intellectuals participated understanding that certain words could not be said. This game went on."[49]

In 1978, for example, CIEPLAN scored a major breakthrough when its careful and devastating criticism of the regime's consumer price index was picked up by several newspapers and newsmagazines, marking the first public debate between the regime and the opposition, an event of fundamental political significance. It diminished the credibility of a technocratic military regime that had otherwise seemed invincible. It established that the opposition had not only survived but could challenge the regime's vaunted economic technocrats. And it constituted an important symbolic victory for an opposition that otherwise felt it had no way to speak out. In Brunner's words: "The fact that a group of respected technicians could show that technically the CPI [Consumer Price Index] had been manipulated and yet were not immediately persecuted for doing it certainly had an important effect over the next few years" (28 February 1991). Yet the debate was based exclusively on highly technical research that took years to complete and that only a few experts really understood. Science could speak when politics could not.[50]

Over time, then, the private research centers became one of the few places where some semblance of opposition political discussion could be carried out. As one leading academic-politician noted, "The only permissible places or ways of addressing political problems required putting on an intellectual hat" (Boeninger, 29 January 1991). Because politicians could not act, another observed, "the word became part of action" (Bitar, 16 January 1991). Yet another commented: "Anxious party leaders, with no significant capacity to influence events, lived in a constant process of discussion, reflection. . . . Thus many of them—the MAPU, the UP [Popular Unity] parties, the Socialist parties (particularly the non-orthodox sectors) and the Christian Democrats—gave the centers a privileged position in discussing and exchanging opinions. . . . It's no coincidence that Gabriel Valdés, for example, was president of the Center for Development Studies, or that Foxley was president of CIEPLAN, . . . or that the Institute for the New Chile, based in Amsterdam, was [led by] Jorge Arrate, or that Heraldo Muñoz had his own center,

PROSPEL [Latin American Foreign Policy Monitoring Program]. It's no coincidence that FLACSO had a Brunner or a Flisfisch, et cetera. There developed an intermediation between formal academic institutions and political groups" (Núñez, 18 March 1991).[51]

Between 1973 and 1983, the principal, and often only, road to opposition politics in Chile ran through the academy. Political parties were illegal and in disarray. Dissident intellectuals alone possessed the funds, institutions, and relative freedom to address seriously the most important political issue of the day: the collapse of the democratic regime. Their comparative advantage vis-à-vis politicians enabled them to expand into the political vacuum created by the military regime. The private research centers slowly became a source of new political thinking and discourse. Politics in Chile became intellectualized.

Making the Left Democratic

By far the most important transformation in opposition political thought wrought by intellectuals during this period was the establishment of an explicitly democratic socialism in the mainstream of Chile's left. Chilean socialism before 1973 stressed revolutionary change and was characterized, as Walker points out, "by . . . a permanent ambiguity about, if not a frank questioning of, the institutions of representative democracy."[52] The left did not warmly embrace democracy during the 1960s and 1970s; the democratic socialism that had emerged in Europe had not yet taken root in Chile.

That reality changed after the coup because the trauma of failure and repression sparked a long, complex process of renewal in leftist thought. In the words of one participant: "The military coup prompted, . . . particularly on the left, a process of review . . . of what they had done well, and especially of what they had done wrong, because, definitively, that led to the failure."[53] The process was fed by exposure, through exile or study abroad, to democratic socialism in Western Europe and to the increasingly evident failure of the socialist societies of Central and Eastern Europe. Although its pace varied substantially among parties, it was basically a systematic review of political theory and practice, led by a "new intelligentsia of the left," that reshaped the positions of party leaders.[54] When it reached fruition, around 1985, a fundamental change had occurred: the Chilean left, and particularly the Socialist party, had become broadly democratic. That change made possible the emergence of a unified opposition in early 1988 and contributed fundamentally to Pinochet's defeat in the plebiscite later that year.

The process itself comprised more than a decade of soul-searching on fundamental political principles. Initially, two issues dominated debate: the "causes of the defeat" and the nature of the new dictatorship. One early explanation by Socialist party stalwarts was that the left had not been "sufficiently Leninist" and should have prepared militarily to accept the "inevitable" conflict.[55] That contention, however, reaffirming a traditional, radical-left viewpoint, sparked an extended discussion on basic party principles. Critics, instead of explaining events in terms of defeat at the hands of a traitorous military, emphasized the failure of the Popular Unity government to generate majority support for its agenda. They began to question the role of ideology, of charismatic leaders, and of the state. And they challenged conventional wisdom on democracy and social change.

The renewal process was complex, involving many twists and turns. As Walker points out, it did not begin with the question of democracy, focusing instead on more pressing issues such as human rights. The political left was by far the most persecuted segment of society after the coup, suffering a disproportionate share of arrests, beatings, disappearances, and deaths. Direct experience with systematic and brutal violations of human rights sensitized the left to their source—authoritarianism—and to the importance of preserving and protecting those rights. That led it, gradually, to see democracy in a different light—as a guarantor of human rights—and to appreciate the need to resist all forms of authoritarianism.[56]

But the rejection of authoritarianism brought up a more basic issue: the question of political forms. Important segments of Chile's left had traditionally discounted formal democracy as a bourgeois notion and contrasted it with a more profound democracy, usually one based on the dictatorship of the proletariat. With the experience of repression, that position steadily lost ground. The potential of democratic forms, and not just their deficiencies, came into view. Walker explains: "In this sense, the authoritarian experience caused the set of norms and procedures commonly associated with 'formal' democracy (universal suffrage, alternation in power, separation of powers, habeus corpus, the rule of law, among others) to be valued to their full extent" (176).

The shift here was fundamental, from an essentially instrumental approach that viewed democracy only as a means to the greater objective of socialism, to an approach that valued democracy as an end in itself, regardless of its social and economic policy consequences. It meant rejecting revolution as the path to social change and replacing it with democratic reform. It meant abandoning class as the principal basis for political organization and acknowledging the legitimate interests of diverse social groups. It meant seeking "the creation of a democratic national culture rather than an emancipatory project geared toward a particular social sector."[57] The result was a new, explicitly democratic socialism. Although many points remained unclarified, and not everyone agreed on every point, the socialist mainstream became unequivocally democratic.

Thus a radically different line of thinking emerged within the Socialist party. It caused the party to split in 1979, producing a short-lived reformist faction led by former party secretary general Carlos Altamirano. The new approach then fostered the "Socialist Convergence," a confluence of leftist politicians and intellectuals around antiauthoritarian, prodemocratic ideas. The Convergence became the nucleus of a new socialist position, generating spirited discussion on three continents, copious documentation, and a series of agreements on political principles. It proposed a "triple rupture" with traditional socialist beliefs: their emphasis on ideology; their emphasis on the left rather than the nation; and, most importantly, their "ambiguity regarding political democracy."[58] Late in 1983, major strands of the renewed left formally established a new Socialist party. In 1984 they elected Carlos Briones as their first president. In 1985, the principal remaining renewed groups were incorporated. A new party had been born; a new, explicitly democratic left had emerged.

Intellectuals were crucially important at every step of this process. They led the criticism of orthodox party positions, helped establish the Socialist Convergence, produced most of the analysis and documents that fed discussions, convened interested parties, participated directly in the debates, and helped launch the renewed Socialist party. As Brunner points out: "Intellectuals set in motion a process of renewal through multiple instances in which they began to meet, first among themselves and later with [those] leftist politicians more attuned to themes of renewal and criticism of the traditional left, and they began to develop this kind of reflection and action" (28 February 1991).

They did not, of course, act alone. Politicians were intimately involved, particularly at the levels of debate, planning, and negotiation. But they seldom operated independently of intellectuals. Many of them, in fact, were intellectuals. When asked to name those intellectuals who had influenced the leaders of the Socialist party, one politician (himself with training in philosophy) responded: "Almost all of them are intellectuals."[59] Intellectuals often held formal positions in the parties or served as continuous, informal advisers. Many key socialist politicians, such as Ricardo Lagos, Jorge Arrate, and Ricardo Núñez, had done graduate work abroad in the social sciences and had been practicing academics in Chile.[60] Heraldo Muñoz, himself an intellectual who participated actively in socialist politics, observes: "What is interesting is that in this movement there appear very strongly . . . not the old leaders whose base was in labor or in the party organization but, rather, intellectual figures like Ricardo Lagos, . . . Eugenio Tironi, . . . Manuel Antonio Garretón, . . . Angel Flisfisch. . . . There were politicians as well, but there was concentrated in the intellectuals a capacity for creation and leadership" (19 August 1991). In Chile's socialist renewal, the distinction between intellectuals and politicians was often unclear. Instead of being separate, the political and intellectual realms were interpenetrated.

Some examples help clarify the extraordinarily central role intellectuals occupied. The single most influential organ for debate on the renewal process was the journal *Chile-América,* founded in Rome by a group of exiles that included such prominent intellectuals as José Antonio Viera-Gallo, Julio Silva, Jorge Arrate, and José Miguel Insulza. Arrate also helped establish another group influential in the renewal process—the Institute for the New Chile—in the Netherlands and became secretary general of the renewed Socialist party in 1989. Viera-Gallo later became the president of Chile's Chamber of Deputies.

In Chile, two academic research centers—FLACSO and SUR— were central to the renewal process. In the words of Christian Democratic leader Edgardo Boeninger: "The leaders of renewed socialism were inspired basically by ideas coming out of FLACSO. Thus intellectuals had an enormous influence on politics" (29 January 1991). FLACSO senior researchers Angel Flisfisch and Manuel Antonio Garretón served on the Socialist party's central committee during much of this period. They, along with two other senior FLACSO staff members, Tomás Moulian and José Joaquín Brunner, produced some of the most influential documents critiquing traditional leftist positions and arguing in favor of change. Intellectuals based at SUR, particularly Eugenio Tironi and Javier Martínez, were also key contributors to the debates.[61]

Many founders of the Socialist Convergence were distinguished intellectuals. They included, in addition to those just mentioned, Ricardo Lagos (later minister of education), Heraldo Muñoz (later ambassador to the Organization of American States), Juan Gabriel Valdés (later ambassador to Spain), Jaime Estévez (later elected to the Chamber of Deputies), Luis Maira (later a vice-president of the Socialist party), Carlos Portales (later director of foreign policy in the ministry of foreign relations), Alvaro García (later subdirector of the ministry of planning), and Sergio Bitar (later a vice-president of the Party for Democracy). Convergence founders also included two of Latin America's most accomplished social scientists—Enzo Faletto and Aníbal Pinto—and two well-known intellectuals from the radical Revolutionary Left Movement (MIR)—Carlos Ominami (later minister of economic affairs) and Gonzalo D. Martner (later subsecretary for regional development in the ministry of interior).[62]

The process was contentious and often painful. A major struggle was under way between proponents of traditional and renewed leftist thought involving deeply established principles with emotional, as well as intellectual, dimensions. Here the heavy concentration of intellectuals on the side of change appears to have been crucial. Heraldo Muñoz continues: "This renewed sector that was perhaps a minority in terms of the quantity of militants compared with the other sector, where the presence of intellectuals in its leadership was minimal, became successful . . . because it imposed the ideas, [because of] . . . its capacity to articulate new socialist thinking, a new socialist image—more pragmatic, more realistic, more in tune with popular sentiment. . . . I believe that that presence of intellectuals, that capacity for vision, permitted us to end up being the principal force" (19 August 1991).

The fundamental change was to shift the center of leftist political thought away from revolution, where it had been in the 1960s, and toward democracy, where it ended up in the 1980s.[63] That process was fueled both by the exile experience, particularly with European social democracy, and by critical thinking within the country, but it always had a strong intellectual base. As Bitar notes: "A political-intellectual influence from exile, and a reproduction of that thesis inside the country by . . . intellectual elements, were permeating political leadership" (16 January 1991). Another accomplished intellectual, Javier Martínez, argues that "the Socialist party completely changed its discourse because a group of intellectuals—sociologists, philosophers, historians—in part echoing the European discussion but basically taking seriously the problem of democracy, began to question the bases of Marxist-Leninist thought and began to build a new version of leftist politics for the country" (6 March 1991).

Making the Center Flexible

Underlying the transformation in thinking by the left were broader changes that encompassed intellectuals at the center of the political spectrum. Although centrist intellectuals, principally Christian Democrats, felt less directly defeated by the coup, they were nonetheless appalled at its repressive consequences and impelled to examine its causes. Moreover, they were increasingly implicated by the junta's attacks. As the new regime shifted from a temporary to a foundational character, it broadened its target to include liberal democracy in general and traditional ways of doing politics in particular. It sought to eliminate politics, at least temporarily, from Chilean life, and to replace politicians with administrators and technocrats. And it moved to establish a new, protected democracy that significantly limited legislative autonomy and provided for permanent military tutelage over political affairs. Thus Chile's political center, which objected to human rights violations and continued military rule, increasingly became the focus of regime repression. The trauma that so profoundly affected the intellectual left spread across the center as well.

Chile's political center, however, differed significantly from its left. The center was already committed to democracy and had less to rethink. Its principles were not so fundamentally challenged by the failure of the Allende government and the military takeover. As Garretón points out, "A Christian Democrat did not have to make a switch in his metaphysical structure. A leftist, in contrast, had to [consider] giving up Marxist-Leninism."[64] The Christian Democrats were criticized more for their ideological rigidity before the coup than for the content of their beliefs. They were charged with abandoning the center's traditional role as a broker within the country's fragmented and highly competitive party system and trying instead to govern alone. Thus the center faced a different task. It had to rethink its political strategies and behavior more than its basic political beliefs.

The political center was also stronger and more coherent than the left. The Christian Democratic party, which dominated the center, remained a formidable political force after the coup. Despite the military regime's restrictions, it retained impressive levels of unity, organization, and leadership. Thus it presented centrist intellectuals with a more vigorous and less demoralized party apparatus. In contrast to the left, where intellectuals might achieve a virtual corner on party decision making, Christian Democratic intellectuals were, in the words of one observer, "a kind of cream on top of the milk" (E. Correa, 8 March 1991). They had to contend with a much stronger institutional context; Christian Democratic politicians were harder to influence.

Centrist intellectuals nonetheless embarked on their own extended effort to "rethink the country," critiquing political strategies and examining national needs. As with the left, the process was long and complex. It focused initially on conduct during the Frei and Allende governments, and then on the nature of the new dictatorship. The central concerns were determining what had gone wrong and what the new regime was like. Over time, intellectuals developed those concerns into a compelling critique of Christian Democratic behavior before the coup, and a well-founded denunciation of the military regime.

Because the Christian Democratic party remained a relatively strong force, however, the efforts of centrist intellectuals were more often a part of broader party initiatives. This was particularly the case before the death of former president Eduardo Frei in early 1982. By 1977, Frei appears to have begun systematically moving the party away from the hegemonic go-it-alone strategy it followed during the 1960s and toward an emphasis on flexibility and coalition building.[65] One result was a seminal 1977 party document, *Una Patria para Todos,* written by the party's most distinguished intellectual, Jaime Castillo. That document emphasized the common plight of the Chilean people ("We are united in suffering, in failure and also in hope") and called for a "National Movement for Democratic Restoration" that would "respect the rights of political parties" and "cultivate the spirit of national reconciliation." It was, according to one party leader, Mariano Fernández, a "crystallization of the Christian Democratic agreement to promote unity."[66]

The party hierarchy's new stance appears to have been responsible for two of the most visible intellectual initiatives taken by the political center during the first decade after the coup.[67] The Group of 24, established in 1978 to critique the military regime's proposals for a new constitution, was composed at the outset almost entirely of Christian Democratic party officials and only later came to incorporate a broad range of more purely intellectual figures, such as Eugenio Tironi and Manuel Antonio Garretón. Similarly, the Center for Development Studies (CED), which would eventually play a major role in developing consensus on transition strategy and posttransition policy, was established in 1981 by former foreign minister Gabriel Valdés, rather than by a group of academics.[68] Planning his return to Chile after a decade with the United Nations in New York, Valdés was determined to form a group that would be "academic in form, but political in content, that could contemplate from the outset a clear rapprochement with socialist and related sectors . . . and among politicians and intellectuals from different traditions."[69] Clearly, Christian Democratic party officials were taking the initiative to bring intellectuals into political discussions.

Often, as well, centrist intellectuals carried out their work in close contact with intellectuals on the left, a major change for Chile's intellectual community. Before the coup, intellectuals had banded into highly polarized groups. Under dictatorship, however, they began to behave differently. The early initiatives of the Academy of Christian Humanism, for example, deliberately sought to bring together scholars from across the spectrum of opposition viewpoints. Several seminars outside the country, such as the 1980 conference in Bellagio, Italy, organized by the public affairs program of the New York–based Center for Inter-American Relations, convened intellectual and political figures from across the opposition. Intellectuals at CIEPLAN and CED developed fluid relations with counterparts at FLACSO, SUR, and ILET. A new style of operation, characterized by contact and debate between centrist and leftist intellectuals, developed and eventually spilled over into the political sphere. Brunner suggests that this growing dialogue among intellectuals facilitated subsequent political dialogue between the Christian Democrats and the Socialists by creating "a sense of convergence and coming together among distinct currents of thought that had been very separate prior to 1973" (28 February 1991). The *camino único* of the Christian Democrats was giving way to *concertación.*

Another distinctive aspect of the impact centrist intellectuals had on politics was the dominant role played by economists. Whereas on the left sociologists and political scientists were key, in the center economists had the greatest intellectual impact. This was so in part because, for the center, economic policy was a more contentious issue than were fundamental political beliefs. During the 1960s, the Christian Democrats had adopted a relatively utopian approach to economic policy, based on the writings of Jacques Maritain and Catholic social doctrine. That approach, sometimes referred to as "communitarian economy," emphasized (rather vaguely) modifying the structure of property through "worker-controlled enterprises" and other new forms that reconciled the conflict between labor and capital.[70] The inadequacies of that approach, along with the radical economic reforms introduced by the military regime and the striking technical expertise of the Chicago Boys, presented the Christian Democrats with a major challenge. They had to demonstrate they could run the economy with as much technical skill as the Chicago Boys, but with greater equity. They needed a new approach to economic policy.

Not surprisingly, then, one of the intellectual groups that most influenced thinking in the political center—CIEPLAN—was staffed principally by economists. Under the leadership of Alejandro Foxley, CIEPLAN provided new ideas where the center needed them most: on economic policy. It helped the Christian Democrats transform their "revolution in liberty" into a pragmatic combination of competitive markets, investment in human resources, and macroeconomic responsibility. It thereby countered the technical expertise of the Chicago Boys by offering a technocracy of the center.[71] Although it played a less important role in changing fundamental political beliefs and strategies than did such research centers as FLACSO and SUR on the left, CIEPLAN provided a guarantee that, if the center returned to power, the economy would be managed according to modern technical principles.

Nonetheless, CIEPLAN played a more purely intellectual role than did several other influential centrist groups. It was first and foremost a research organization, established and run by academics rather than by political leaders. It had no formal ties to the Christian Democratic party, and its influence on party positions was principally the result of the quality of its work and participation in party affairs by several staff members. Although it made deliberate efforts to reach out to social actors and to promote discussion beyond the academic community, it placed less emphasis on those activities than did other centers, such as CED and the Group of 24. CIEPLAN's chief function was to create ideas.

Moreover, CIEPLAN tended to go beyond technical economics to incorporate a political economy dimension into its work. Its staff always included at least a few political scientists and sociologists and was sensitive to the political and social dimensions of economic behavior. Foxley, for example, took a special interest in questions of political thought and social policy. He produced some of the most devastating criticism of the behavior of intellectuals, and of Christian Democrats, during the 1960s. He also developed a thoughtful and broad blueprint for democratic governance in the 1990s. Another CIEPLAN staff member, Ignacio Walker, wrote perhaps the most definitive account of the complex post-coup renewal in leftist political thinking. CIEPLAN consistently went beyond narrowly technocratic concerns to address broader intellectual issues.[72]

Efforts at CIEPLAN to reshape economic policy and to establish a broader critique of centrist political thinking were complemented initially by the activities of the Group of 24 and ICHEH, and later by CED and CERC. The research centers presided over an exercise that was fundamentally intellectual, marked by profound reflection on outlooks and ideologies. Through research, debate, conferences, and publications, they engaged political leaders in analyzing the democratic breakdown and in criticizing traditional politics. Although centrist intellectuals were less critically influential than their counterparts on the left, they nonetheless were instrumental in reshaping political thinking. A new set of values and principles began to appear. Ideology and utopia were giving way to democracy as the fundamental basis for political agreements.

What emerged eventually was a transformation of the political center that was comparable to, although less dramatic than, changes occurring on the left. A "new social-Christian intellectual culture" began to take shape.[73] The doctrinaire ethos that had dominated Christian Democratic thinking during the 1960s steadily gave way to more accommodationist attitudes. Previously discredited concepts, such as compromise, coalition building, pragmatism, pluralism, moderation, and ambiguity, were revalued. Emphasis shifted away from ideology and utopia, and toward diversity and democracy. Gradually, the political center became flexible once again.

Intellectualizing Politics

During the ten years that followed the 1973 military takeover of government, then, opposition intellectuals preserved dissident thought by establishing a network of new, private research centers and transformed it through a systematic critique of past political beliefs and behavior. They thereby began to acquire political, as well as intellectual, influence. The distinction between intellectual and political leadership had begun to blur. As one observer noted: "Political elites tended to become completely confounded with intellectual elites. Intellectuals became the bearers of politics, and politics was done through intellectual, academic activity."[74] Politics had been intellectualized.

But their political roles now were different. They were no longer the "affirmers of ideology" or "men of faith" that Foxley and Moulian found so common among intellectuals before the coup.[75] Instead they had become critics, analysts, and innovators—foxes rather than hedgehogs. With politics illegal and civil society fragmented, intellectuals presided over one of the few locales where opposition leaders could gather to discuss political issues. They became an important source of information and analysis. They helped politicians understand the causes of democratic breakdown, and they introduced new ideas into political debate. They were fundamental in helping the left become broadly democratic and in making the center flexible once again. They began to act upon the political system rather than to simply carry out its wishes.

Those were important achievements. Without an explicitly democratic left and an accommodationist center, the opposition could not have fashioned, almost a decade later, the coalition that defeated Pinochet in the 1988 plebiscite. Instead, voters would have been presented with a traditionally fragmented opposition that fit all too well Pinochet's dire prediction of chaos and conflict should he lose. The plebiscite, which the opposition won by a margin of 12 percent, might well have been lost.

Nonetheless, intellectuals functioned during this period almost exclusively as academics. Their activities were typical of intellectuals anywhere in the world—data gathering, analysis, writing, and debate. But because they now had an audience composed of political actors, their academic product eventually had enormous political significance. As one politician observed: "If you analyze the Chilean transition from 1988 to

1990, you will understand little—mainly the formalities of the process. But if you analyze from 1988 backwards, at least nine years to 1979, you will almost certainly find in all the political formulations that circulated around the academic centers . . . the formulations that later materialized in 1988 and 1989, in the Concertación" (Núñez, 18 March 1991). Their impact was neither immediate nor direct. As an intellectual explained: "Intellectuals took a set of initiatives that . . . were multiple, small, decentralized, relatively invisible, usually indirect . . . but . . . helped constitute a network of social and cultural communication among intellectuals and politicians that only translated into political action long after that network had long since fully permeated the political parties, the unions" (Brunner, 28 February 1991). The impact of intellectuals on politics during the decade after the coup occurred almost entirely at the level of ideas.

At least until 1980, then, in-country opposition politics principally took the form of intellectual analysis. The private research centers were virtually the only game in town. Politics, having been outlawed, took refuge in the academy. And the academy, having been empowered, expanded into the political vacuum. But it was not so much that Chilean intellectuals became political during the decade after the coup. Rather, Chilean politics became intellectual.

Convergence and Reenvisoning the Future: 1983-1986

[We had] . . . a political class frankly atomized and very disarticulated, . . . clearly divided by profound fault lines. Until that moment they had been completely incapable of establishing even simple relationships among themselves. That is, the problem wasn't that debate was highly polarized, the problem was that there simply were no relationships. There were, in the strict sense, parallel worlds, never converging. Between figures of the time, a Pablo Baraona or people linked to economic teams and officialist economic worlds, Pinochetistas and, on the other side, Christian Democrats, Socialists, et cetera, . . . there simply was no relation.
— ANGEL FLISFISCH, 17 January 1991

You must at least know what path to follow. Even if you can't follow it, it's important to know where the path is. . . . I think that [intellectuals] appropriated a function of political parties with respect to strategic conceptualization, a vision of society, a vision of the path. And that was very useful. . . . I am absolutely convinced that the type of transition that we had—the type of government we have—would not have been at all the same without the existence of these private research centers.
— SERGIO BITAR, 16 January 1991

By 1983, the military regime of General Augusto Pinochet had transformed Chile's economy and society, restructuring the economy along neoliberal, free-market lines and reshaping social policy by reducing the role of the state and enhancing that of markets and the private sector. It had imposed, through a plebiscite of dubious legality, a Constitution that gave it formal legitimacy and set a timetable for a return to a protected democratic government. To be sure, the regime continued to be sharply repressive, and the democracy it promised was circumscribed, many years off, and accompanied by strict military supervision. But it had completed its foundational stage and had begun a slow, grudging march toward civilian rule.[1]

Between 1983 and 1986, the opposition began to come alive and look to the future. Political parties cautiously raised their heads as some activities became, if not legal, at least sporadically tolerated. They initiated a strategic debate over how best to confront the dictatorship. Civil society reemerged as community groups, professional associations, and student organizations stepped up their activity. Opposition intellectuals and professionals began occasionally to appear in the press. A sense of change, even optimism, was in the air.

The opposition's high hopes stemmed from a massive banking failure in 1982 that plunged the economy into recession and set off widespread demonstrations against the military government. Those events galvanized the opposition: for the first time in nearly a decade, the regime seemed vulnerable. Political and social leaders resumed public activity, demanding that Pinochet resign, a provisional government be established, the Constitution redrawn, and free elections held. Their optimism proved to be short-lived, however. The regime met force with more force and skillfully drew the opposition into fruitless talks. Then, when massive clandestine arms caches were discovered, and an attempt by the extreme left to assassinate Pinochet failed, the regime declared martial law, stepped up repression, and retreated into its bunkers. As the demonstrations languished, the opposition grew frustrated and depressed. Its efforts to force the regime from power had failed.[2]

Opposition intellectuals began during this period to have more direct political impact. They continued to carry out primarily academic work but shifted their focus from political thought to political strategy. They used their credibility and expertise to participate directly in the incipient political debate. In doing so, they made major contributions in two areas: restoring the mutual trust and understanding that had been missing from Chilean politics for two decades, and providing strategic vision and policy analysis for the reemerging political parties. By late 1986, opposition intellectuals had transformed their academic roles well beyond those traditionally associated with the ivory tower. Soon some of them would begin to transcend those roles and become political actors.

The Early 1980s: Context and Crises

By the early 1980s, the Pinochet regime had instituted a set of radical social and economic reforms. Under the direction of the neoliberal Chicago Boys, it had completely restructured the economy, eliminating the bulk of government subsidies, reducing tariffs and import restrictions, and subjecting most economic activity to free and competitive markets. It had sharply reduced the economic functions of the state and significantly expanded those of the private sector.

Judged by some indicators, those policies had been remarkably successful. Gross domestic product and real wages had risen steadily over five years. The country had drastically reduced inflation and had eliminated its fiscal deficit. Foreign investment had surged, and nontraditional exports had more than tripled from the mid-1970s. Several negative factors—continued high unemployment, a trade deficit, rising foreign debt, low domestic investment, and increasingly unequal distribution of income—were generally discounted. Policymakers talked about Chile's economic "boom" and confidently expected even greater gains over the next several years.

The regime had also imposed a new Constitution that provided much-needed political legitimacy and established a procedure and timetable for a return to a protected democracy. And it had carried out a series of "modernizations" that converted its neoliberal principles into radical policy reforms. This was a period of triumph: the regime looked stronger than ever, and the country, many thought, was on the threshold of development.[3]

Dissident intellectuals had also accomplished a great deal. Not only had they survived, they had succeeded in establishing a large and vigorous network of alternative institutions that provided them with stable employment, professional interchange, and significant visibility. They had become productive, efficient, and well connected to their peers in Europe and the United States. They had, for the most part, come to terms with the failures of the past and fashioned a new way of political thinking. They had become more specialized, empirical, and technocratic. The overwhelming emphasis on ideology that had characterized them in the 1960s had given way to instrumental and policy concerns.

The new political outlooks emerging among dissident intellectuals were the product of many factors. Chile's private research centers, in part because their funding came from abroad, had strong ties to centers elsewhere in Latin America, in Canada and the United States, and throughout Europe. Their staffs had regular contact with foreign scholars and occasionally carried out research with them. They attended international conferences and were well aware of the major ideological shifts such as Thatcherism, *glasnost*, and *perestroika* that were taking place abroad. Many received fellowships to pursue graduate degrees in Europe and North America.

Intellectuals living in exile had been subjected to even greater stimuli. Most leftist political leaders and many intellectuals were in exile until at least 1984, typically in such countries as Sweden, France, the Netherlands, Italy, Venezuela, and Mexico. Many deliberately went to such Communist-bloc countries as the Soviet Union, East Germany, and Rumania, which had traditionally maintained strong ties with the Chilean left. Some of those subsequently decided to resettle in Western Europe.[4] For nearly a decade, they experienced directly the capitalist democracies of Western Europe, and the "real" socialism of Eastern Europe or the USSR—something that had seldom occurred before. They were exposed to the debate over Eurocommunism, read Gramsci, and developed direct relationships with European social democratic parties. They also experienced firsthand the political repression and economic stagnation that characterized Communist-bloc countries, and the declining power of those regimes. Many who had in the past scorned European social democracy began to take it seriously. Many others, appalled at conditions in Eastern Europe, began to seek a new approach.

The exile experience had a major impact on dissident intellectuals. They initiated a profound debate on political principles that eventually led them to embrace European social democracy and many fundamental elements of free-market capitalism. Much of that debate was conducted in the journal *Chile-América,* which was edited in Rome by José Antonio Viera-Gallo and became, during the late 1970s and early 1980s, the leading forum for Chile's Socialists. That debate had a major impact. "Rome is what most marked me," said Socialist intellectual Jorge Arrate. "It was the great influence on us, just as the Cuban Revolution and the Allende government had been before."[5] By the early 1980s, when exiles again began to be allowed to return to Chile, they brought with them a new appreciation for democracy and a new approach to economic growth.

Chile's intellectuals, whether resident inside or outside the country, had been exposed to the great changes that were sweeping the world. More than in the past, they were connected to colleagues abroad, aware of new developments and moved in response to reinterpret their own thinking. Dissident intellectuals had become part of a European and North American community of scholars; their thinking had become internationalized.

Nonetheless, the country, and particularly the political system, still faced a daunting legacy of conflict and repression that kept groups apart and hampered debate. The conflicts of the past thirty years—between Catholics and non-Catholics, revolutionaries and reformists, opponents and supporters of Pinochet—had, in the words of one observer, "an enormous symbolic weight" that made forging coalitions in the 1970s "unthinkable" (Martínez, 6 March 1991). As Brunner notes, the divisions were based not just on ideology but on dramatic events that had occurred in the recent past: "You must remember that the Popular Unity government had been toppled, in part, by Christian Democratic mobilization, and that the Allende government, and the parties of the Popular Unity, had been completely intolerant with respect to the Christian Democrats, generating political enmity and enormous cynicism" (28 February 1991).

Those differences began to soften as democracy and pluralism came to dominate party agendas across the political spectrum in the 1980s. But tremendous psychological and interpersonal barriers remained, and Chile's political firmament was highly fragmented. Politicians from different factions tended to distrust each other and were not accustomed to working together. Indeed, they often had no contact whatsoever, operating in political subcultures that had almost no real overlap. Thus the "parallel worlds" that Flisfisch refers to in the chapter epigraph.

In addition, the opposition, in sharp contrast to the military government, had no coherent agenda for the future. A strategic debate had not begun, and there was agreement only on some vague concept of democracy.[6] Yet the only real prospect for a transition to democracy was that established by the Constitution of 1980. Under its provisions, Pinochet, by winning a plebiscite scheduled for 1989, could stay on as president until 1997, presiding over a protected democracy that provided only minimal space for opposition influence in government. Few in the opposition thought that the plebiscite would be fair, or that they could defeat Pinochet if it were. Moreover, they had consistently repudiated the Constitution of 1980 and the transition it mandated, because it embodied an authoritarian concept of democracy and had been imposed through an unfair plebiscite. The opposition thus overwhelmingly rejected the democratic transition planned by the military regime but had no transition strategy of its own.

The political mood began to change fundamentally when a major economic crisis took shape in 1982. The first sign came on 4 April when the country's leading newspaper, El Mercurio, ran an editorial criticizing the government's economic policy. Such criticism was unheard of, and the paper's editor, Arturo Fontaine Aldunate, was persuaded to resign shortly thereafter and sent off to be ambassador to Argentina. El Mercurio had been a staunch supporter of the Pinochet regime and was often referred to, with considerable seriousness, as the leading political party on the right. Its criticisms, therefore, could only have been prompted by a major problem.

In the second half of 1982 Chile's banking system failed, the consequence of flawed macroeconomic policies and lax government supervision of the banks. By early 1983 the banking sector was insolvent, and the government had to step in and take over most of the banks. The result was a "financial earthquake." The stock market crashed, mutual funds went bankrupt, and a significant proportion of national wealth was lost. The economy quickly went into recession. Unemployment rose to over 30 percent (49 percent in Santiago's construction sector), and Gross Domestic Product fell by 21.3 percent. Pinochet's economy, after several years of success, suddenly seemed a failure.[7]

These events had great political significance. They suggested, for the first time since the military takeover of government in 1973, that the regime was vulnerable. They also cost the regime significant support. Many people from all social levels were seriously hurt by the deep recession that followed. They included wealthy business leaders, former high regime officials, and common citizens whose savings were wiped out. The military government had always relied on three factors to limit critics: (1) painful memories of the conflict and chaos that preceded the coup; (2) fear of government repression; and (3) a successful, expanding economy. The financial crisis of 1982 eliminated one of those three pillars of support and left the regime trembling atop the other two.

The reaction was not long in coming. On 11 May 1983 the Confederation of Copper Workers (CTC), the country's largest labor federation, staged a "symbolic protest" against the regime and its policies. Originally conceived as a national strike and later modified into a less ambitious national protest, it came at the behest of Rodolfo Seguel, newly elected president of the National Workers' Command (CNT) and a political unknown.[8] Scheduled despite the skepticism of some labor leaders and many politicians, it was a rousing and surprising success.

The day began relatively quietly, with only limited absenteeism and a few incidents. Even by midafternoon, there was no sign of significant public response. But at 8 P.M. people began banging pots and pans across Santiago. Automobiles surged into the streets blowing their horns. Throughout the city, including middle- and upper-class neighborhoods traditionally dominated by supporters of the military regime, a major and unprecedented public protest broke out. Chile had lost its fear of repression and had begun to speak out.

A few days later the government closed down the chief opposition radio station, Radio Cooperativa, and initiated the first massive *allanamientos,* or sweeps, through lower-class neighborhoods, rounding up and arresting large numbers. Pinochet made an angry speech accusing politicians of acting through the unions to cause trouble. The newly elected president of the Supreme Court, Rafael Retamal, however, had opined that the protests were legal. Seguel quickly announced a second protest for 14 June sponsored by the unions. Thus began a cycle of monthly protests and strikes that would continue for more than three years.[9]

Both the government and the opposition were caught off guard. Opposition political leaders had felt serious doubts about the planned event; many labor leaders had shared them. Few had expected the social organizations to move on their own, without direction from the political parties. They had underestimated the "resurrection of civil society" that was under way.[10] The myriad institutions of civil society commonly referred to in Chile as the *bases*—unions, community organizations, professional associations, student groups—moved ahead of the politicians. They provided the channels that were initially essential to convert broad discontent into systematic, targeted protest.

A new period had dawned, and a psychological threshold had been crossed. The protests that began on 11 May 1983 sparked a growing wave of open resistance that changed the opposition and the regime alike.[11] The experience of "losing one's fear" and publicly defying the regime was for many a kind of declaration of independence. It fed on deep feelings of resentment and powerlessness built up over nearly a decade. Many believed that the fall of the regime was imminent—perhaps just a matter of weeks. The song "*Y va a caer*" (He's going to fall) was on everyone's lips. After ten years of repression and humiliation, the opposition desperately wanted it to be true.

Opposition Strategy: Social Mobilization

The spectacular success of the initial protests took opposition politicians by surprise. They had not expected this "eruption of politics into public space" and were not prepared to capitalize on it.[12] Until then they had focused their efforts on surviving, understanding past failures, and criticizing the Pinochet regime. Now an unexpected opportunity had appeared. For the first time since the coup, they began to think seriously about transition strategy.

They reacted quickly. Within two months, the Christian Democrats had publicly assumed leadership of the protests in defiance of the regime's ban on party activity. By August, a group of center and center-left politicians, led by Christian Democratic party president Gabriel Valdés, had formed the Democratic Alliance (AD), calling for Pinochet's resignation, a provisional government, and a constituent assembly.[13] Two years later, the leaders of eleven opposition parties, led by Sergio Molina, who had been minister of finance under Frei; Fernando Léniz, who had held the same position under Pinochet; and José Zabala, a Christian Democratic businessman, signed the National Accord for

Transition to Full Democracy (AN), calling for open elections and compromise on several sensitive issues. The agreement was historic, marking the first alliance in over two decades between the Socialists and the Christian Democrats and the first formal opposition agreement that included significant former supporters of Pinochet. What began as a reaction by labor leaders to economic disaster became a call by political parties, "Democracy Now."

With these events, an opposition strategy emerged that was to persist, in its fundamental elements, until early 1988. The strategy was consistently rupturist in character. It rejected the mechanisms for transition established by the Constitution of 1980, demanding instead that the regime turn over power immediately, either through a provisional government or direct elections. It vowed to pressure the regime through "social mobilization" (usually defined as peaceful street demonstrations large enough to destabilize the government) until it gave in.[14]

But the opposition's approach was from the beginning, as Walker suggests, a "contradictory double strategy."[15] The Democratic Alliance envisioned a two-step process in which massive peaceful demonstrations would convince the military to withdraw its support for Pinochet and negotiate a transition to democracy. Much of the orthodox left, however, was dismayed by the moderate character of that stance and quickly took a different tack. In September 1983, three major leftist groups—the Communist party, the Almeyda wing of the Socialist party, and the Revolutionary Left Movement (MIR)—formed the Popular Democratic Movement (MDP). The MDP adopted a more explicitly insurrectional approach, opposing any dialogue with the regime and maintaining that "all forms of resistance" to the dictatorship were legitimate. It supported the growing armed confrontation being carried out by the Manuel Rodríguez Patriotic Front (FPMR) to spark a "national mass insurrection." In contrast to the explicitly political, reformist strategy of the Democratic Alliance, the MDP's strategy was increasingly military and revolutionary.[16]

For both groups, the emphasis on social mobilization was based on several assumptions about the regime: that it had little popular support, that its neoliberal economic model would fail because it discriminated cruelly against the poor, and that discontent was broad and deep enough to generate massive and sustained public demonstrations against the regime.[17] The opposition believed, as Brunner points out, that the economic model "was condemned to failure because it was socially discriminatory, because it was based on high foreign debt, because it brutally divided the country into a rich minority and a poor majority, because it lacked its own dynamism, et cetera . . . The economic critique basically said, 'Keep pushing with the mobilization because in this country there's so much poverty and so much misery that the economic model is so condemned to failure that, even if it takes a while, we can't lose'" (28 February 1991). Only repression, it seemed, kept the regime in power.

There was, in fact, initially little debate over the basic elements and assumptions of the mobilization strategy. Intellectuals and politicians alike tended to believe that the only way to confront the regime was through social mobilization. In some measure, that belief may have been born out of the extraordinary psychological significance of dramatic public protests for an opposition that had suffered so much and for so long. The idea that Pinochet might finally be forced from power was almost painfully attractive, and protesting was a kind of collective catharsis.

It may also have been true, as Socialist leader Ricardo Núñez suggests, that the spontaneous, grass-roots origins of the initial protests established a dynamic that political leaders felt they must follow: "There was a qualitative change with the outbreak of the protests . . . in which influence shifted away from the professional and academic political leadership and toward social organizations and party cadres—the process became 'massified'" (18 March 1991). Another way to interpret Núñez's observation, however, is in terms of an impassioned resurgence in party activity after so many years of paralysis and repression. For nearly a decade, party cadres had been relegated to the sidelines, while politics became essentially an intellectual endeavor. With the outbreak of mass protests, they suddenly had an opportunity once again to act, and they seized it, thrusting aside intellectuals and sometimes even top party leadership. Midlevel party activists and grass-roots leaders took over, following their traditional political instincts and assumptions. An editorial published in early 1986 by APSI, one of the chief opposition newsmagazines, captures the fervor that gripped opposition thinking: "This is the year, Pinochet is the obstacle, only mobilization will overcome him."[18] Once again, political parties were calling the shots in opposition politics.

Whatever the explanation, few cared initially to criticize the mobilization strategy. Even when no less a personage than former Christian Democratic party president Patricio Aylwin suggested, in a 1984 seminar sponsored by ICHEH, that the opposition put aside its reservations about the legitimacy of the 1980 Constitution and explore ways to work within it, his words had almost no impact on opposition strategy.[19] As one observer recalls, his suggestion was "enormously criticized within the Christian Democratic Party and, obviously, by the rest of the opposition."[20] Aylwin did not persist and went along with the mobilization approach. His instincts would later, of course, prove to have been correct.

The assumption that the regime was unpopular and weak led opposition leaders to believe they could elicit enough social protest to disrupt normal governance and force the military to negotiate an immediate transition to democracy. In the words of Gabriel Valdés, then president of the Christian Democratic party: "We saw that [mobilization] process growing, creating difficulties for Pinochet, which strengthened our conviction that Pinochet was going to enter into negotiations, and after each protest or before each protest we called to Pinochet and the armed forces that we were democratic and wanted to dialogue." Thus they supported an ongoing series of *protestas* that persisted until late 1986 and included massive demonstrations, general strikes, and the banging of pots and pans by opposition supporters in front of their houses at preestablished evening hours. They also presented a series of proposals to the military, which typically demanded Pinochet's resignation, a provisional government, and a constituent assembly. They specifically rejected the regime's 1980 Constitution.[21] Opposition strategy, in short, was consistently rupturist: it sought to alter the mechanisms and timetable the regime had established for transition to civilian rule.

Faced with the growing wave of protests, the regime bought time, hinting it might compromise on the transition to civilian rule. Pinochet appointed, in August 1983, a respected ex–National Party politician, Sergio Onofre Jarpa, as minister of interior and authorized him to negotiate with the Democratic Alliance. He also took bold steps to resolve the financial crisis, naming a young technocrat, Hernán Büchi, as his new finance minister. Talks with the opposition soon broke down, for neither side was willing to give ground. By then, however, the regime had regrouped and stiffened its resolve. On 6 November 1984 Pinochet declared a state of siege, and the regime redoubled its repressive efforts. A stalemate had been reached. Violence had once again overwhelmed Chile's fragile political arena.

Over the next several years, Chile became a battleground, as regime and opposition fought it out through protests, arrests, kidnappings, torture, and bombings. The almost-monthly protests continued through 1986 and met harsh, armed repression that killed hundreds and jailed thousands. Government troops routinely raided poor neighborhoods and sent leftist leaders off to detention in remote villages. The opposition persisted in its belief that only massive public demonstrations would cause the regime to compromise on its plans for transition to civilian rule. Pinochet and the armed forces consistently refused to back down.

They were determined to avoid the reprisals meted out against the Argentine military after that country returned to civilian rule in 1983, and they made clear their willingness to use any level of force necessary to maintain order. More isolated kinds of violence also became commonplace. Communists were found with their throats slit. Army officers were assassinated by leftist terrorists. During the demonstration in 1986, a military patrol sprinkled gasoline on two youthful protesters and set them afire.

The regime's uncompromising use of repression succeeded. Instead of growing and spreading through the country, the protests and demonstrations peaked in late 1983 and then began to decline. Sociologist Javier Martínez describes the process: "From September 1983 the character of the protests began increasingly to be defined in terms of the social sectors that were protesting. The city's marginal groups began taking over, and the middle class began to disappear from the mobilization. That . . . clearly marked the strategy's failure as a national strategy of democratic construction." Even though people would continue to turn out (several hundred thousand demonstrated peacefully in favor of the Democratic Alliance in late 1985), and violence would grow, not many had the stomach for insurrection or civil war. Thus, for at least some sectors of the opposition, according to Martínez, the protests shifted from being an opportunity to being a burden: "In 1984 people began already to talk not of *calling* for protests, but rather of *passing* the protests . . . the big discussion among political leaders was whether we passed them well or not. It was like passing an exam. Instead of being a challenge to the regime, [the protests] began to be almost a challenge to the opposition—to see whether they would be able to muster a protest or not" (6 March 1991).

By early 1986, with the protest movement waning and the National Accord on hold, the opposition established the Assembly of Civility, a coalition of professional associations and other civic organizations designed to emphasize the broad, grass-roots nature of support for an immediate transition to democracy. The Assembly's "Demand for Chile," however, differed little from the demands of the National Accord and was met by renewed repression from the military regime. Increasingly, the moderate opposition found itself drawn toward violence, accompanied by elements of the far left that knew a good deal more about agitation and protests than it did. In Arriagada's words: "The democratic opposition had become trapped between the repression of Pinochet and the lunacy of the Manuel Rodríguez Patriotic Front and the Communist party" (8 March 1991).

The opposition was left in disarray, dismayed at its inability to move the regime and appalled at the violent forces apparently building on the left. "We sank," said one analyst, "into total depression at the end of '86 because everything had failed—the Communist strategy and the non-Communist strategy" (Walker, 7 March 1991). Christian Democratic party president Gabriel Valdés expressed the concern of many opposition leaders: "We thought that our Democratic Alliance, . . . which was formed by people who were absolutely democratic, might be overtaken by the MDP . . . and the Communists, who had always violently attacked us. Then came the attempt to assassinate Pinochet, which produced a great commotion and made us see that we might go into civil war or a totally uncontrolled situation" (1 March 1991). Having demanded "Democracy Now," the democratic opposition instead found itself facing violent conflict between the military and the far left.[22]

The opposition failed principally because it misjudged the situation, "underestimating the regime's strength, and overestimating its own." As Garretón points out, the opposition based its thinking on a "classic insurrectional model" that assumed it could apply sufficient force to make minimal governance impossible, bring the regime to its knees, and negotiate a surrender of power.[23] Its belief was based on several assumptions: (1) that the regime was conservative in the sense of seeking to retain the powers and privileges of a traditional elite in the face of demands by the poor; (2) that it stayed in power only through repression; and (3) that its economic policy was broadly unpopular and doomed to failure. That kind of regime was inherently vulnerable, and the economic collapse had tipped the balance toward breakdown. Unfortunately, most of those assumptions proved to be false.

Moreover, the opposition never really agreed on objectives or strategies. It comprised instead a tacit, uneasy alliance between two groups: a centrist, basically middle-class coalition that favored nonviolent means to achieve pluralist democracy; and a traditional leftist coalition oriented toward the urban poor and willing to use violence to achieve socialist revolution. The first group, dominated by the Democratic Alliance (AD), favored negotiations with the regime and rejected violence; the second, dominated by the Democratic Popular Movement (MDP), refused to negotiate and was willing to risk broader, armed confrontation. As it turned out, these two approaches were not compatible. Increasingly, the moderate opposition found itself caught between the repressive measures of Pinochet and the revolutionary violence of the far left.

Finally, the opposition failed to appreciate the regime's commitment to its "new institutionality" and the military's cohesiveness and loyalty to Pinochet. By demanding what was in effect an unconditional surrender and expecting social mobilization to force negotiations, the opposition placed a bet it could not win. The call for Pinochet's resignation, a provisional government, and a constituent assembly was unacceptable to the military and did not generate enough social mobilization to change the military's mind.[24] Even the more moderate demands of the National Accord in late 1985 were categorically rejected. The strategy may even have been, as Walker suggests, counterproductive, causing the military to close ranks around Pinochet in the presence of a perceived threat to the armed forces as a whole.[25] As a result, the military retreated into its bunkers while the demonstrators wore themselves out.

To be sure, the mobilization strategy produced some successes. By losing its fear of the regime, the opposition passed a psychological milestone that was essential for successful confrontations later on. It also established new zones of autonomy, in terms of public expression and political activity, that the regime was never able completely to revoke. It began the process of talks across party lines that would culminate in the Concertación of 1988. And its efforts helped revive the political and social forces that had lain dormant for nearly a decade, causing them to dispute the regime's legitimacy and raising the costs of its continued rule. These were important achievements and correspond well to Stepan's prescriptions for democratic opposition movements in authoritarian regimes.[26]

But, following Stepan's prescriptions further, the opposition failed to create a credible democratic alternative. Virtually no transition to democracy in recent history had followed the path implied by the opposition's mobilization strategy. Fundamental realities, including the nature of the regime, opposition disunity, and the kind of democratic process to follow, had not been addressed. The military was not prepared to surrender. Many elements on the left, particularly the Communist party, had no intention of negotiating and preferred a fully insurrectional strategy, even if that meant civil war.[27] There was, in Stepan's terms, no agreement on a "formula for the conduct of democratic contestation."[28]

The Birth of the Intellectual-Politician

As regime repression eased and political space appeared, opposition intellectuals deliberately began to take on more political roles. Their activities—research, teaching, publication, and debate—remained essentially academic. But their focus shifted from the past to the present and future, and from political thought to emerging questions of political strategy. They began taking systematic steps to address concrete political problems, such as opposition unity, the realities of transition politics, and posttransition policy, that the regime's difficulties and its own transition timetable brought to the fore. They also began deliberately to reach beyond the academic world to influence *la clase política*—politicians, social actors, and professionals. They thereby went beyond the classic role of intellectuals as producers of knowledge to become articulators between the world of ideas and civil society.

They did so in large part because other elements of civil society, particularly political parties, remained weak, divided, and disorganized. After a decade of precarious, clandestine existence, Chile's political parties were ill equipped to carry out their traditional representational and contestational functions. They were still legally banned and thus could not openly meet, choose leaders, and debate issues. Many parties were little more than clusters of traditional leaders with no demonstrable base and only limited contact with their presumed constituencies. Some politicians, indeed, had only recently returned from exile.[29] Their ability to gauge citizen preferences, devise strategy, and mobilize support was often suspect at best.

Leftist parties in general were still recovering from the repression they had suffered at the hands of the dictatorship. Many leaders had been exiled; some had been killed. The trauma of defeat also set in motion an extended debate over principles and organization that had only recently begun to coalesce into new groupings. The renewed Socialist party, for example, was only founded in October 1983 and elected its first president, Carlos Briones, in 1984. The Christian Democrats had only recently (and clandestinely) elected a new president, Gabriel Valdés, after the death of Eduardo Frei. All right-wing parties had voluntarily disbanded during the 1970s and were just beginning to reorganize. Ricardo Núñez, who later became president of the renewed Socialist party, describes conditions: "In general the parties were decimated. Clear, sharply defined party structures did not exist. All the parties were small *cúpulas*, or groups of leaders, who tried to maintain a degree of national presence, but with little national transcendence. Neither the Communist party, nor the divided Socialist party, nor other sectors of the left—not even the Christian Democrats, who had a formal president, Gabriel Valdés—could say that they had a . . . capacity to lead the great processes that Chile was living" (18 March 1991).

The government had systematically fragmented the labor movement and fiercely resisted efforts to form labor confederations.[30] A significant exception, of course, was the church, which continued vigorously to oppose the regime despite the appointment of a new, more conservative, archbishop. But the institutions of civil society more generally, although gaining strength, continued to be atomized, disorganized, and proscribed.

Other institutions that had traditionally provided a link between politics and civil society remained severely constrained. The universities were still under direct or indirect government control. Television was totally dominated by the regime. Other media (radio, newspapers, and magazines) faced serious limits and sanctions. Ricardo Lagos, one of the most prominent intellectual-politicians on the left, describes the obstacles to speaking out that remained even after a decade of dictatorship: "In 1983, for example, I remember the first time that the government TV channel interviewed me regarding the Democratic Alliance. I said, 'I'm not making declarations to the government channel because you will edit what I say, and I don't know how it will come out.' The journalist said, 'You understand, sir, that on the government channel no one can talk for more than thirty seconds. I must edit what you say.' And I said to him: 'In that case, you ask me a question and I will answer in thirty seconds, but whatever I say gets aired.' He consulted with his superiors and responded, 'I accept, but on two conditions: you cannot say the word "dictatorship," and you cannot refer to the president of the Republic in inadequate terms.' I accepted and did not use the word "dictatorship," and referred to Pinochet as General Pinochet."[31]

Opposition intellectuals, by contrast, possessed formal legitimacy, strong institutions, secure funding, broad analytical experience, and substantial credibility developed over nearly a decade of productive work. And unlike most politicians, who remained deeply divided by past conflicts, intellectuals talked to each other fairly regularly. They shared a conceptual base, a literature, a technical language, and a commitment to science. They participated in the same seminars and conferences. Through years spent addressing similar topics they had developed a professional network that, as Tironi notes, "simultaneously exerted influence on the Christian Democrats through Boeninger, for example, or through a Foxley, and . . . on the Socialist party through Lagos, through an Arrate, or a Núñez or . . . Vodanovic." In the face of party competition, they had the capacity to work across party lines. They understood each other and could work together. They constituted, in Tironi's words, a "precursor to the Concertación" that would occur among opposition political parties several years later (20 March 1991).

Opposition intellectuals possessed another advantage. A decade of political repression had severely limited dialogue among opposition groups and fragmented social relations. That gave research centers, as Foxley notes, uncommon power: "The dictatorship atomized social life. . . . For many years there were no places to meet, and it was very difficult to exchange important experiences with anyone. Thus any place where you could gather was . . . highly valued. The research centers became meeting places almost like a social club. And since those inviting were intellectuals, it gave us greater power to convene people than we would have had under normal conditions."[32]

Similarly, Ricardo Núñez suggests that party leadership—under pressure, with almost no capacity for significant influence, and constantly involved in soul-searching—"gave the academic centers a privileged role in discussion and interchange among themselves, and with other sectors, including those linked to the dictatorship." So much so, according to Núñez, that "practically all the important meetings of political parties took place in direct connection with institutions linked with the Church or the Academy of Christian Humanism, with FLACSO, with CED, et cetera—all of them . . . because those centers wanted an active link with political leaders, because many political leaders also worked directly in these centers, and because [they] were parties whose intellectuals for a long time now had rejected the alternative of violent change and armed struggle" (18 March 1991).

Just how many meetings of which parties took place at academic centers is hard to assess. Clearly, however, the boundaries between politics and the academy were blurring even further, and trespassing across those boundaries was growing. Thus the research centers began to carry out functions that, in more normal times, would have been carried out by other, explicitly political, institutions. Opposition intellectuals moved even further beyond their traditional function as producers of knowledge, to take on as well the task of building bridges between the world of ideas and political actors.

Chief among the new activities intellectuals undertook were seminars, conferences, workshops, debates, and discussions on issues related to democratic transition and consolidation. These events were organized almost exclusively by private research centers in response to the greater freedom that accompanied the regime's difficulties and the sudden demand for information. Most were exercises in forward planning. They convened leaders from the democratic opposition, and occasionally even supporters of the regime, to discuss transition issues and the shape of policy under a democratic regime. They also attracted leaders from nonpolitical institutions, including professional associations, unions, student organizations, and community groups. Their extraordinary impact, however, often extended well beyond strategy and policy: by bringing together political actors who otherwise almost never met, they began to restore the mutual trust and understanding that had been missing from Chilean politics for more than two decades.

The activities were generally academic in nature. They included seminars, conferences, short courses, and off-the-record discussions. Organized by intellectuals, usually around previously prepared academic papers and presentations by researchers, they often combined theoretical ideas with empirical data to analyze specific policy issues. They addressed topics ranging from democratic theory to municipal reform, producing a vast collection of documents and publications. Thus they did not violate the regime's continued ban on political activity.

But the activities were also uniformly political in their significance. They presented policy alternatives and encouraged participants to debate them. In the absence of a parliament and the other institutions of democratic rule, they provided almost the only arena for systematic discussion of many political and social policy issues. As the principal meeting place for Chile's democratic opposition, they offered one of the few locales where the opposition and supporters of the regime could exchange ideas systematically and informally. As Brunner notes, these activities "permitted intellectuals and politicians to begin generating a common conversation, a common analytical framework, a diagnosis of what was happening, and permitted intellectuals to transmit all that they had been accumulating and writing more directly and rapidly" (28 February 1991).

Over the next three years, efforts by the academic centers to address democratic transition issues mushroomed. Virtually every private research center sponsored events and participated in those organized by others. Some, such as CERC and FLACSO, focused principally on academics, convening university professors and advanced students around topics that could not easily be addressed within the universities. Others, such as VECTOR, targeted the leaders of nonacademic institutions such as political parties, professional associations, labor unions, and community groups. The Catholic University of Chile organized a particularly successful conference in 1986 that brought international experts together with Chilean politicians and academics to discuss democratic governance. Some institutions, such as PIIE, GIA, CIDE, and PET, emphasized specific policy sectors, inviting educators or health-care professionals to discuss policy issues that would have to be faced when democracy returned. Others targeted sensitive topics, such as labor relations, the role of the military, and human rights. All sought to apply the resources of the academy to promoting and smoothing the transition to democracy. Their efforts would be felt at many different levels over the next several years.

Influential Research Centers: FLACSO, CIEPLAN, CEP, and CED

The efforts and impact of several institutions particularly stand out. The Latin American Faculty of the Social Sciences (FLACSO), for example, was easily one of the most influential institutions but was also the most purely academic. Its talented senior staff, led by José Joaquín Brunner, Angel Flisfisch, Manuel Antonio Garretón, Norbert Lechner, and Tomás Moulian, had helped it become a regional leader in work on political theory and comparative politics during the decade after the coup. FLACSO was also the academic institution that most influenced the renewal of leftist political thinking in Chile during the late 1970s and early 1980s. Many of its staff members were leaders of the Socialist Convergence that argued forcefully and successfully for the emergence of a democratic socialism into the mainstream of Chile's left. It had become a major intellectual presence on the left of Chile's political spectrum.

During the mid-1980s, FLACSO began more systematically to reach out beyond the academic cloisters and address issues related to democratic transition. In 1984, for example, it established an ongoing research workshop on the armed forces and democracy. It organized, with the University of Chile's student federation (FECH), a series of courses on current events for labor leaders and students. It sponsored workshops in various provincial cities, often in collaboration with other academic centers, on such topics as agrarian reform, the evaluation of social projects, and the evolution of the state. FLACSO brought together regularly a group of young historians interested in the social and political history of Chile's *clases populares*. It organized a two-year training program for young researchers that produced at least sixty graduates, many of whom would eventually take positions in the new democratic government. It organized a series of specialized courses on survey research techniques, just as political opinion studies were beginning to appear on the national scene. At a time when the broader social science community, particularly young professionals and those based at universities, still faced serious limits on their work, FLACSO provided an important impetus and framework for addressing emerging social and political issues.

FLACSO's political impact, however, extended well beyond the formal events it organized. FLACSO's senior staff included some of the most distinguished left-of-center political theorists in the country. Their publications were regularly noted by political leaders and often reviewed in the press. As political space opened up, they were increasingly in demand for interviews and op-ed articles, even in the proregime media. They participated regularly and prominently in the activities organized by other centers that targeted political actors more directly. They began to speak out forcefully on issues related to transition strategy. Two of the senior staff, Flisfisch and Garretón, were members of the Socialist party's central committee, and several others had close ties with party leaders. Much of FLACSO's senior staff, in fact, either participated directly in internal party debates or informally counseled politicians who did. Indeed, many of FLACSO's staff members were prototypal political-intellectuals who moved easily back and forth between the academy and politics.

Another academic institution that played a major role during this period was the Corporation for Latin American Economic Research (CIEPLAN). During the mid-1980s, CIEPLAN became particularly concerned about the legacy of the military regime's approach to economic policy-making. Under the military regime, Chile had been subjected to a rigid, top-down style of economic policy-making that relied on a higher rationality for justification and brooked no objections. That approach clearly was not compatible with democratic governance, and CIEPLAN feared that it had created pent-up resentment that would make it difficult to devise and implement responsible economic policy once democracy returned. As a CIEPLAN document stated: "The isolation and silence of key social actors—who have been subjected to radical changes in economic and social relations—converts society into a kind of 'black box,' whose changes and situations are not adequately known, making it particularly difficult to foresee its future behavior." Intellectuals, CIEPLAN argued, had a special responsibility in this case: "Everyone knows of the propensity of intellectuals in Chile to propose voluntaristic schemes about what is desirable and rational for society without considering what concrete social actors think and want. This makes necessary a more systematic effort to detect what has happened with those actors and tune in to the real problem agenda that they envision and give priority." Thus CIEPLAN sought "a different form of public policy-making," which it called "concerted development," that emphasized building consensus among social and economic actors on key policy issues.[33]

To those ends, CIEPLAN established an innovative program of "community dialogues" designed to put economists in direct contact with important sectors of society throughout the country. They sought both to sensitize economists to the priorities and views of a broad array of social actors, and to communicate to those actors information and arguments that might enhance their understanding of modern economic policy-making. Staff members organized an ongoing series of visits to provincial cities throughout the country. They met with local governments, business leaders, political party officials, community groups, labor organizations, journalists, students, and university faculty. They heard about local problems, and the local impact of national economic policy. And they presented their own policy views.

The dialogues program paid special attention to the country's principal labor organizations. CIEPLAN was concerned about the potential for labor unrest once democracy returned and sought to help labor leaders develop bargaining positions that addressed their needs without jeopardizing economic growth. Led by MIT-trained economist René Cortázar, CIEPLAN organized short courses, seminars, and informal discussions on general economic policy for labor groups around the country. They began regularly to advise the country's principal labor confederation on economic affairs and promoted, with limited success, direct contacts between business and labor leaders. Several years later, when democracy returned and Cortázar became minister of labor, he successfully negotiated an agreement between business and labor that permitted a significant reform in labor legislation.

CIEPLAN also organized, as part of the dialogues program, short courses on economic policy for university students, professors, and journalists. And it produced, in addition to its regular academic publications, a new magazine, *Revista de CIEPLAN,* written for a broad, policy-concerned audience. The *Revista* presented CIEPLAN's views on current social and policy issues and was distributed to social and political leaders throughout the country.

One result of these activities was to give CIEPLAN staff current, reliable information on what was going on in Chile and how a broad array of social actors felt about it. The program took them out of their offices and into repeated, direct contact with groups affected by economic policy. It complemented their theoretical models and statistical data with fresh, qualitative information on how the country was changing. They talked to people; people talked to them. It was, as one senior staff member put it, "a way of connecting ourselves to the real world" (O. Muñoz, 27 August 1991).

Another result was to enable CIEPLAN to begin outlining an economic policy that could command broad legitimacy and still maintain economic growth under a democratic regime. Through seminars, workshops, and informal discussions carried out over several years, CIEPLAN staff were able to explain policy alternatives to a broad range of social actors, and to generate serious discussion about them. They thereby sharpened their sense of how different sectors felt and became increasingly able to gauge the potential for consensus and to develop and refine realistic policy proposals. The experience improved the quality of their policy proposals and enhanced their credibility vis-à-vis other policy-making groups. For an institution that, a few years later, was to provide the core of the new democracy's economic team, that experience was extraordinarily important.

The broad wave of discussions on transition issues that emerged around 1984 encompassed parts of the political right as well. Here, however, there was a good deal less activity. Much of the right still supported the Pinochet regime and saw no need to plan for anything other than the slow transition to a protected democracy envisioned by the 1980 Constitution. And right-wing private research centers were scarce, as most right-of-center intellectuals had been able to remain in the universities.

An important exception, however, was the Center for Public Studies (CEP), virtually the only right-of-center think tank to emerge during the 1980s. CEP had been founded in 1980 by a group of economists and business leaders seeking to broaden the legitimacy of neoconservative political and economic thinking by distancing it from the military regime. Fully independent of the government, CEP relied on local business groups and foreign donors for support. It was a serious intellectual enterprise, convening top scholars and policymakers to discuss political, economic, and social issues. CEP's quarterly journal, *Estudios Públicos*, became the leading source of conservative and neoconservative social thought, publishing translations of such figures as Michael Novack, Friedrich Hayek, Samuel Huntington, and Milton Friedman, along with articles by respected local academics on political philosophy and social policy. Beginning in 1986, CEP also became one of the country's most respected sources of political opinion polls, playing an important role in providing reliable information to political leaders. Its combination of intellect, neoconservative principles, and interdisciplinary scope was new to the academic scene. It was a manifestation of the modern right that was emerging in Chile.

Under the direction of Arturo Fontaine Talavera, CEP organized seminars and conferences on topics that ranged from the transition to democracy in Spain to the role of the private firm in a democracy. It hosted presentations by distinguished foreigners and teamed local right-wing intellectuals with their counterparts from CIEPLAN, FLACSO, and other centers identified with the opposition to Pinochet. CEP's initiatives were particularly important because they constituted one of the few early opportunities for intellectual leaders from the opposition to express their views directly to leaders from the right. Among the opposition figures invited to speak at CEP functions in 1984 and 1985, for example, were Angel Flisfisch (FLACSO), Patricio Meller (CIEPLAN), Eugenio Tironi (SUR), and Francisco Cumplido (later minister of justice in the Aylwin government). CEP staff members and associates also participated regularly in the activities organized by other private centers around Santiago. In this way, CEP helped to establish the identity and legitimacy of a democratic right, and to generate a dialogue with center and left intellectuals.

Perhaps the most active and broadly effective institution working on the topic of democratic transition during this period was the Center for Development Studies (CED). Founded in 1981 by former foreign minister Gabriel Valdés, CED was conceived as an open, pluralist center that could explore alternative approaches to Chile's development. It responded to a broader shift away from the globalizing political ideologies of the sixties in favor of more empirical, policy-centered intellectual approaches. The early thinking that led to CED was almost certainly influenced as well by the decision of Christian Democratic leadership in the late 1970s to drop its single-party stance and return to coalition politics. Valdés brought together a core group of intellectuals and professionals, all of them identified with (but not officials of) the Christian Democratic party, and secured funding from a variety of European governments and foundations.

Although research was at CED's core, policy was its principal concern. The idea that Pinochet would soon fall was widely shared, and CED wanted to have a policy package ready for the democratic government that would replace him. Over the next several years, first under Valdés and then under economist Ernesto Tironi, CED's work had a strong development thrust, focusing on policy options in such areas as municipal government, poverty alleviation, and industrial promotion. CED's objectives were never exclusively academic, however; it sought from the beginning to develop, through analysis, personal contact, and debate, political consensus on social and economic policy. And Valdés's original commitment to pluralism bore fruit. Despite its Christian Democratic origins, CED came to be seen as open and receptive to viewpoints from across Chile's democratic political spectrum.

In 1985 Edgardo Boeninger, an economist who had been rector of the University of Chile when the coup occurred in 1973, became CED's director. Boeninger had worked part time at CED since its founding, but his move to director marked a significant departure for the institution. Although long identified with the Christian Democrats, he had never previously been a member of the party. Thus he was not associated with the party's rigid and uncompromising past and could talk easily with political leaders of all stripes. And, although firmly identified with the world of ideas, chiefly as an academic leader, he had not participated in the great ideological debates of the 1960s. In the eyes of most observers, Boeninger's strength was more in articulating ideas than in creating them. As Garretón put it: "His great advantage is that he's an empty page, . . . so if you and I have a disagreement, we go talk with him. On this empty page, you write the letter *a* and I write the letter *b*. He then decides how *a* and *b* fit together, and what the page means" (8 March

1991). Many saw Boeninger principally as a political engineer who ex-
celled at devising workable combinations of ideas and people.

Boeninger brought with him a different emphasis. He doubted that
the antigovernment protests under way would bring down the regime
and thus saw as less urgent the need to devise a policy package for a new
democratic government. He was convinced, however, that Chile's fundamental political problem was the lack of trust among social and political actors, and that reestablishing that trust was a prerequisite to
reestablishing democratic rule. Thus his priority was to "re-establish
confidence among people, organized groups, political parties and social
actors" through "coexistence, dialogue and encounter." Boeninger felt
it urgent to "reconstruct the political and social fabric" so badly worn
by years of polarization, conflict and repression.[34]

CED's evolution toward political dialogue had in fact begun before
Boeninger took over. At first, CED's activities attracted primarily independent professionals and academics with Christian Democratic or
center-left viewpoints. Soon moderate Socialists began to take part,
along with Christian Democrats more closely affiliated with the party.
Then persons representing center-right and liberal positions began participating. Although CED always had difficulty in attracting supporters
of the military regime, it was more successful than any other opposition
center group and became the country's leading, and most consistently
plural, setting for policy dialogue.

The decision to focus less on devising policy and more on promoting
dialogue was nonetheless significant. Chilean society had been atomized.
The ideological divisions of the 1960s and 1970s had been exacerbated
by the killings, disappearances, torture, exile, arrests, firings, and count-
less other injustices perpetrated by the Pinochet regime. Not only did
members of different political factions disagree, they seldom even talked.
Indeed, some found it difficult to be together in the same room. And
because political activity was illegal, they had few occasions to overcome
their differences. Chile continued to be, as Constable and Valenzuela
have pointed out, a "nation of enemies."[35]

Under Boeninger's direction, CED gradually shifted from being the
source of an alternative program of government to being a place where
leaders from diverse political and social groups could meet and exchange
ideas. Its emphasis moved away from policy and toward personal relations. The process of meeting and establishing trust became more important than achieving specific policy outcomes. That did not mean that
substantive issues were dropped. Indeed, the meetings featured some of
the country's most accomplished intellectuals and were firmly based on

careful analysis and empirical data. But substance became the occasion that permitted broader and much-needed dialogue among social groups to take place.

The keystone of CED's dialogue efforts was a large program called "Political Concertation, National Project, and Democracy." The program ran for nearly three years, beginning in 1984, and attracted funding from a variety of foreign sources. As Boeninger states, developing dialogue and trust took priority over specific policy outcomes: "If we reached conclusions that were relevant in themselves, stupendous; but what was fundamental was reconstructing the political fabric."[36] Its four subprojects—on economics, politics, reaching agreement (*concertación*) and young leaders—illustrate the varied and creative approaches to outreach that intellectuals tried between 1983 and 1986.

The first, and possibly the most important, of these was the subproject on economics, which demonstrated particularly well a significant aspect of CED's emerging methodology: bringing people from opposing camps together to exchange views in an informal, nonthreatening environment. Rather than criticize existing policies or try to come up with an alternative, CED commissioned economic position papers from three traditionally incompatible lines of thinking: the Christian Democrats, the left, and the right. The participants then met regularly to present and discuss their views. Through these debates, they were able to confirm for themselves, in a low-key, academic environment, how each group really thought. Later on, the project evolved into more specific topics, such as private property, income distribution, and economic policy-making.

A second subproject, entitled "Political Conditions for a Stable Democracy," emphasized political issues. Here the goal was to convene academics and social actors to discuss issues vital to Chile's efforts to reestablish a stable democracy. CED designated a politically diverse executive committee to ensure that conflicting views were represented and to avoid charges of political favoritism. The members included Boeninger (from the center), Angel Flisfisch (a FLACSO political scientist from the left), and Juan Yrarrázaval (a center-right lawyer and political scientist).

The committee then chose ten topics that constituted real, and usually contentious, dilemmas in Chile's transition to democracy.[37] Each was developed by a core group of academic specialists through carefully prepared papers that drew on theory and empirical data. The papers were presented at ongoing workshops that brought together some of the country's principal political leaders—the presidents of political parties and other political personalities—of all the political hues. Through these discussions, participants were expected to broaden and deepen their understanding of democratic governance, come to understand and trust each other, and explore areas of consensus regarding a future democratic system.

Several other activities evolved from the economic and political dialogues. CED organized a series of "exercises in concertation" that brought opposition labor leaders together to discuss the general theme of democratic transition, followed by more specific topics, such as relations with business enterprises, the role of unions, and labor legislation. An innovative element here was the incorporation of experiences from other countries. CED brought to Chile several European experts in labor legislation and organized a two-week visit to Europe for a group of labor leaders, business leaders, and academic specialists. The toughest aspect of this initiative was convening business and labor leaders for talks on labor legislation. Those meetings produced few substantive advances during a year and a half but, in Boeninger's words, "broke the ice" (60).

CED also made a concerted effort to incorporate the most difficult yet crucial actor in reconstructing the social fabric: the military. CED began by inviting retired officers to attend workshops focusing on political democracy. Progress was slow, but eventually some sixteen retired generals, admirals, and other representatives of the armed forces participated. That initiative later expanded into an ongoing CED project that succeeded, by 1989, in developing regular conversations between politicians and active military officers on civil-military relations.

Finally, CED targeted young political leaders emerging in the political parties and in student federations. CED used themes and speakers transplanted from the other workshops to stimulate debate between politically diverse groups of young political leaders and their older counterparts. Those activities began later and met with less success, chiefly because the political world was by then shifting its attention to the upcoming plebiscite and losing interest in the seminar format.

Through this set of activities CED evolved into the country's leading link between the world of ideas and political actors. It was, as Brunner observes, "the most important motor synthesizing all the work of various prior years—a synthesis that was intellectual, but at the same time political-intellectual—involving politicians and intellectuals. . . . Although other centers contributed to that task, CED clearly played the most important role" (28 February 1991). By combining political balance, openness, and a commitment to understanding diverse viewpoints, CED was extraordinarily successful in putting intellectuals in touch with social actors and building bridges among Chile's fragmented political community.

The Impact of Private Research Centers

What impact did these activities by private research centers have? Visibility and activity, after all, do not guarantee influence. Did the efforts by intellectuals to reach beyond their traditional function as producers of knowledge, to become articulators between the world of ideas and political actors, make any difference? Did the broad wave of seminars, conferences, publications, workshops, debates, and discussions promote and facilitate the transition to democracy? Definitive answers to such questions are inevitably problematic. The relationship between cause and effect is seldom straight and narrow; when it tries to connect ideas with political behavior, it becomes particularly labyrinthine. Nonetheless, the facts at hand, and the judgments of those involved, suggest that intellectuals had a major impact in two broad areas: helping the newly stirring opposition political forces overcome their bitter divisions, and providing them with strategic vision.

One of the most important contributions intellectuals made during this period was not intellectual at all, but psychological. Whatever their substantive impact, the hundreds of seminars and workshops on transition issues that research centers organized helped restore the mutual trust and understanding missing for so long from Chilean politics. Those activities brought academics and social actors of diverse political beliefs together regularly and in informal circumstances. Most of the sessions emphasized scientific understanding rather than political competition. Some were off the record. They brought together people who almost never met and enabled them to voice ideas, face-to-face, on policy issues that they otherwise did not discuss.

The CED program "Political Concertation, National Project, and Democracy" provides a particularly vivid example of how intellectuals helped foster personal relationships across Chile's political spectrum. For Angel Flisfisch, who helped coordinate the CED program, the chief result was to create a "climate of sociability" in which "people began to serve as bridges between their respective worlds, connecting with mediators from other worlds. . . . All the relevant public personalities paraded through CED's workshops," he said, "from Jaime Guzmán and Sergio Fernández to Patricio Hales of the Communist party. There was . . . a dialogue . . . framed in terms of civilized relationships about the crucial themes of the transition. . . . The principal [result] was to establish relations of sociability that were a kind of prerequisite for any later agreement."[38] People came to understand and even to trust each other. They developed personal relationships.

Another prominent politician, Hernán Vodanovic, emphasized the personal contacts among political leaders, and particularly among socialists, that the CED program facilitated: "It was a very plural setting that sought to integrate Christian Democrats and Socialists, whose combination was the key to structuring a unified opposition. . . . The seminars and all those initiatives organized by intellectuals helped the socialist world get to know itself more intimately, come closer together, because the conflict among socialists was very strong, . . . and the only way for people from different socialist factions to talk was in the heat of a seminar. . . . [Elsewhere,] they only fought; they slandered each other."[39]

Yet another participant, Heraldo Muñoz, suggested that the seminars and workshops contributed significantly to later agreements on the rules of democratic procedure: "These dialogues, which were fundamentally intellectual at one point, gradually acquired aspects of political reconciliation. I refer, for example, to the workshop on political analysis that took place at CED under the direction of Edgardo Boeninger, himself an intellectual, whose participants were well chosen from the distinct political currents, . . . but who participated as individuals, even though everyone realized that they brought with them a genuine expression of their respective parties. The intellectual dialogue—there were even prepared documents—was a series of reflections about political science but always focused on Chile and on the future possibilities for returning to democracy. I think that helped prepare the path so that, based on those discussions, or collaterally with those discussions, party leaders began reaching agreement on basic rules" (19 April 1991).

By promoting personal contact in low-key settings, the events caused the "parallel worlds" of Chilean politics to begin converging. They brought political actors together in a way that had not occurred for many years. They attracted, in the words of Sergio Molina, "articulators of thought" who "met, got to know each other, and discussed." "Those debates were very important," he said, "because they kept destroying myths and prejudices."[40] Manuel Antonio Garretón, reflecting on the CED program, offered a more trenchant comment: "It made the Christian Democrats realize that the Socialists, at least at the technical level, weren't brutes; and made the left realize that the Christian Democrats weren't fascists" (8 March 1991).

Given the bitterness and division that had characterized Chilean politics for more than two decades, this was a major achievement. It bridged gaps that were as much psychological as substantive. It began to reconstruct relationships of trust and mutual understanding that had broken down in the 1960s and 1970s and were essential to democratic government. By creating a "climate of sociability," the research centers' activities helped "reconstruct the political and social fabric"—conditions that were crucial to establishing the Concertación early in 1988 and that led to the plebiscite victory later that year.

In addition to building trust among the newly stirring political forces, intellectuals also helped provide them with strategic vision. Between 1984 and 1987, opposition intellectuals played a major role in furnishing *la clase política*—politicians, social actors, professionals—with information, analysis, and criticism. Intellectuals dominated the social and economic policy debate and were an important factor in the debate on political strategy. Their efforts, in the words of Alejandro Foxley, "had a decisive influence on an elite from the political parties, businesses, labor unions—an elite that was quite reduced in numbers but was very influential in the key decisions that were taken in the period immediately prior to the plebiscite" (14 March 1991).

Here the contributions of intellectuals derived directly from their traditional strengths as analysts and interpreters of events. What was different was their impact on social actors. The protests in 1983 had taken the opposition by surprise. Political parties were still illegal and disorganized. No strategic debate was underway. With no shared vision of what postauthoritarian policy should look like, the opposition needed information and analysis. Intellectuals responded by reaching out to political and social actors, initiating a long process of dialogue and learning. They thereby managed to project their ordinary analyses and interpretations in extraordinary ways. Intellectuals provided political leaders with strategic vision in four general areas: (1) understanding how society had changed under the military regime; (2) rethinking democratic transition and governance; (3) criticizing the social mobilization strategy; and (4) developing consensus regarding post-authoritarian policy.

Understanding the Transformations Under Way

An early and important result of the intellectuals' efforts was helping the opposition understand the military regime and the changes it was bringing about in Chilean society. Not surprisingly, both intellectuals and politicians started from an overwhelmingly critical posture. Much of the opposition tended initially to dismiss the regime as conservative or even fascist, dedicated to defending the interests of a traditional economic elite and able to maintain power only through repression. For many years, they regularly condemned the regime as politically authoritarian, economically reactionary, and highly unpopular.

That appraisal began to evolve and become more nuanced, however, as researchers completed a variety of empirical studies exploring the distinctive features of the military regime and assessing its impact. Carried out by many different centers over a decade or more, the studies addressed topics ranging from the regime's ideology and supporters to its impact on agricultural productivity, education, fiscal policy, social stratification, foreign trade, health care, and administrative reform. The scientific character of the studies often strengthened the opposition's attacks on the regime but also provided an important counter to opposition prejudices and misperceptions. By the mid-1980s, the studies had created an up-to-date body of empirical analysis that transformed opposition political thinking.[41]

One result was a growing realization that the Pinochet regime diverged radically from the stereotypical Latin American military government—that it was not conservative in the traditional sense but sought instead "a profound and revolutionary transformation of Chilean society" (J. J. Brunner, 28 February 1991). The accumulating analyses demonstrated, for example, that economic liberalization negatively affected some members of the very oligarchy that presumably supported the military regime. They also showed that the regime did not rule entirely through repression but possessed as well the capacity to mobilize significant support from quite diverse sectors of society. Often, the sources of that support had little to do with traditional political ideologies. The studies suggested that many conventional assumptions and categories had to be abandoned—that the Pinochet regime had created a new set of conditions.

Brunner describes the role played by these academic analyses: "All the initial publications of people like Garretón, Tironi, Lechner, [and] me on the fact that the regime was not purely a repressive military regime, with a fascist, conservative, oligarchic character, but . . . was a foundational, modernizing regime, with a capacity to mobilize sectors besides those favoring violence . . . are documents that, read today, seem awfully primitive. . . . But they opened up a whole new issue. . . . They showed that the regime in fact had to be analyzed differently than we thought during the first few years after '73, that it could not be analyzed as merely a fascist regime" (28 February 1991).

For example, an extensive study by Javier Martínez and Eugenio Tironi (both sociologists at SUR) directly challenged the assumption held by many politicians and social activists that Santiago's shanty dwellers were ready to bring down the Pinochet regime through collective public demonstrations. They argued that economic reform and political repression had produced major changes among the urban poor, weakening the class basis for social mobilization. Blue-collar and salaried workers had become a much smaller proportion of the labor force, and union membership had declined drastically. The urban poor had split into diverse segments that related differently to society. They were too fragmented to constitute an effective social movement, particularly if violence and possible loss of employment were involved.[42]

Moreover, the researchers found that the urban poor were more interested in participating in government than in bringing it down and replacing it with something radically different. They rejected street violence, preferring social order and peaceful dialogue with the government. The conditions for a revolt against the established order simply did not exist. "The revolutionary and communitarian logics that have thus far dominated the shanty-dwellers' movement," Tironi concluded, "are totally 'out of synch' with the views that predominate among ordinary shanty dwellers, and have seriously limited that movement."[43]

The work of Tironi and Martínez constituted a strong critique of conventional wisdom regarding the political potential of Santiago's shanty dwellers. Their analysis, suggests Brunner, "had a great influence in showing that, by 1985, we were facing a new kind of society and consequently needed a new kind of political thought and political strategy and had to rethink the old categories we used to criticize the economy and the policies of the military regime" (28 February 1991).

Although these were academic studies, their results and implications nonetheless reached political and social actors. They constituted grist for the new wave of seminars and workshops being organized by the academic centers. They were often mentioned in Chile's newspapers and newsmagazines, particularly when their conclusions had significant political implications. And, of course, some of the same academics who carried out these studies also participated, directly or indirectly, in the internal debates of political parties.[44] As a leader of what then was the more orthodox wing of the Socialists, Ricardo Solari observes: "Without that debate, we would have gone blind into everything that happened after. . . . So we had the option of confronting the new picture on the basis of prejudice or instinct, versus confronting it trying to understand what was happening."[45]

Once again, Brunner's comments help capture an extraordinarily complex dynamic: "Well, there were seven years of people reading. . . . I don't think that many people read, but these things got mentioned in seminars, people commented, someone who had read said, in a group where there were lots of politicians: 'But some intellectuals are saying these other things . . . ,' and 'Garretón said that the regime was foundational . . . ,' and these things got discussed, despite the fact that almost no one had read the study. If just one person had read it, that was enough so that fifteen guys from the political directorate of the Christian Democratic party were talking about these things." Politicians did not always welcome the conclusions intellectuals were drawing. Again, Brunner: "I remember, for example, a Gabriel Valdés [then president of the Christian Democratic party] absolutely furious with us because of the things we were publishing, telling us that the academy in this country definitely understood nothing, and that the policy should be social mobilization. Here there had been no modernization, here we had to confront a repressive, reactionary dictatorship, et cetera."[46]

But angry responses often demonstrated that the messages intellectuals were sending were getting through to political actors. By carefully documenting the changes under way in the country, intellectuals established an important empirical base for opposition policy. They produced findings that were often both counterintuitive and compelling, thereby helping offset the isolation and misperceptions that afflicted political actors. Gradually, and sometimes despite strong resistance, they set the stage for a broader critique of the opposition's transition strategy. And their analyses would prove especially valuable several years later, as politicians debated how to confront the regime in elections.

Rethinking Democratic Transition and Governance

The wave of meetings and seminars organized in the mid-1980s also explicitly addressed questions of democratic transition and consolidation. Several research centers organized such events, particularly FLACSO, CIEPLAN, SUR, and the Catholic University's Institute of Political Science. Some sought to illuminate the problems facing Chile by relating them to broader academic debate on democratization. Others brought representatives from countries that had recently shifted from dictatorship to democracy, such as Peru, Argentina, and Brazil, to discuss their experience. In the process, they systematically exposed politicians to contemporary social science thinking on establishing democratic rule.

Here, CED was the clear leader, especially effective in bringing recent theory and experience in democratic transition to the attention of political actors and in generating intelligent debate. Through papers and structured discussion, participants were exposed to the work of such academics as O'Donnell, Schmitter, Stepan, and Dahl and to the experience of such countries as Brazil, Argentina, Greece, Spain, Portugal, and Italy in establishing and consolidating democracy. They discussed alternative approaches to political competition, the merits of different constitutional regimes, and the importance of democratic procedures, developing a broader comparative framework for understanding Chile's problems. And because sensitive topics were lifted out of the conflict and ideology that had surrounded them for several decades and posed in scientific terms, they were easier to discuss.

It is difficult, of course, to determine just how that information affected participants. Boeninger argues that CED's workshop "Transition Scenarios and Strategies," which brought party leaders and academics together to discuss how Chile might best achieve a transition to democracy, had a major impact. It was instrumental in convincing participants that the transition would only occur through elections, and that the opposition should therefore stop trying to force Pinochet's resignation through social protests and seize the opportunity offered by the Constitution of 1980 for a plebiscite on his continued rule. "This conclusion, which we reached at CED," argues Boeninger, "influenced the decisions that the parties took."[47] That strategy, considered political heresy between 1980 and 1987, was adopted in early 1988 by the newly created opposition Concertación, and led to the plebiscite victory.

On the other hand, one of the coordinators of CED's program, Angel Flisfisch, suggests that the workshop's impact was less direct, simply placing on the table ideas and options for politicians to consider: "Before 1986 you will find work, papers, from these seminars and activities saying that these two options exist and lead to radically different transition scenarios. The great majority of the papers tended to emphasize or favor the second scenario—the nonconfrontational, negotiated approach. They were influenced by O'Donnell, by Schmitter, through all the transition literature being produced in the United States. They all said that, but I think that the only thing the papers did was place those ideas in being. It's not that there was an impact on political leadership—that you persuaded them what the correct path was. I don't think it was like that. I think that they always maintained a certain scepticism with respect to those analyses. The politician's view is that, fine, that's analysis, but life is more complex; it runs on other rails. . . . It's not that they were persuaded, but that the ideas were there as an element they could use if other developments caused them to choose . . . a pacted, negotiated, political transition that included neither violence nor social mobilization. . . . It was a labor of conceptualization" (17 January 1991).

Both interpretations—persuasion and conceptualization—are plausible. The relationship between cause and effect is complex in politics. Even politicians don't always know exactly what led them to choose one option over another. Making political actors aware of the argument for an option is certainly different from persuading them to choose it, but both are important. Systematically laying out the logic and implications of alternative paths helps people make better decisions. It enriches their understanding of events and provides a stronger base for the decisions they eventually take. And in the process, they may well be tilted toward an option they would not otherwise have chosen—or only have chosen much later. Information and understanding make a difference. Whether the result was persuasion or conceptualization, the CED workshops systematically exposed participants to sophisticated information on democratic institutions and processes over a substantial period of time. The participants paid attention, and many of them learned. In the words of Social Democratic party vice-president Mario Papi: "We had a long period of learning. I believe—and we often laughed about it—that we had never theorized so much about democracy and about transition, as we did under dictatorship." And those discussions, he points out, were often reported widely in the press. "Journalists would arrive and listen to the debates and . . . report what was said. . . . That was unprecedented. . . . These were not really political meetings; they tried to analyze everything from an academic perspective. . . . Never had [the intellectuals] gotten so much press—the newspapers printed this, the radio taped that, and later transmitted special programs explaining how a party coalition should function, . . . the role of the opposition in a democracy, presidential regimes, parliamentary regimes. . . . And these things were transmitted just as today they transmit political debates" (7 March 1991). Absent traditional political activity, social science became news.

Criticizing the Social Mobilization Strategy

During this period intellectuals also played a significant role as direct critics of opposition political strategy. The most important manifestation of this function was their impact on debate over the social mobilization strategy. The outbreak of systematic public protests against the regime in May 1983 and their evolution into an essentially rupturist political strategy that relied heavily on social mobilization was immensely popular among opposition political and social leaders. After suffering years of repression, the opposition found the prospect that Pinochet might finally be forced from power irresistible and the protests deeply satisfying. Most believed that the military dictatorship was thoroughly illegitimate and could be overthrown.

Speaking of this period, Edgardo Boeninger recalls the conviction that prevailed among the opposition: "The chant that was popular— 'He's going to fall'—reflected the center's attitude that [Pinochet] would fall in the next protests, or those immediately after . . . or if he didn't fall next month, we'd see what was necessary. It was all very simple, like in cowboy movies—the good guys just keep punching the bad guys" (29 January 1991). Many, particularly those on the left, resisted even the idea of negotiations regarding a transfer of power. Thus a maximalist strategy that demanded some form of surrender by the regime and deployed massive social mobilization to obtain it was hard to resist. Many intellectuals shared that vision. The sentiments expressed by Alejandro Foxley were initially common among opposition intellectuals: "I was for the protests and social mobilization, and against Pinochet's timetable. . . . Discussion about tactics to defeat Pinochet had nothing whatsoever to do with whether one's thinking was renewed or not" (14 March 1991).

Moreover, the alternative—participating in the referendum on Pinochet's continued rule established by the 1980 Constitution—was for many unacceptable. They felt it would constitute de facto recognition of the Constitution's legitimacy and doubted that any election administered by the military regime would be fair. Experience with the 1980 referendum on the new Constitution, which was held without the guarantees that have traditionally accompanied free and fair elections in Chile, had been deeply disappointing. The opposition's decision to contest that election was seen by many as a tactical error, having contributed some measure of legitimacy to a fundamentally rigged election. That experience weighed heavily on opposition politicians and made them reluctant to participate again in elections organized and administered by the military regime. Thus the insistence on "Democracy Now."

Unfortunately, however, the opposition's strategy—social mobilization linked to calls for the military to negotiate a transition different from that established by the 1980 Constitution—was not working. The opposition's various proposals, including the Alianza Democrática in August 1983, the Acuerdo Nacional in August 1985, and the Demanda de Chile in April 1986, led to nothing. At first the regime used negotiations to stall for time; then it refused to negotiate at all. Pinochet's flat rebuff when Archbishop Francisco Fresno tried to discuss the Acuerdo Nacional during a twenty-minute Christmas Eve meeting in 1985 ("No, no, we'd best turn the page") was the most categorical expression of the regime's unyielding position.[48] The push of social mobilization and the pull of opposition offers to negotiate, even when combined, were not enough to draw the military into serious talks.

Further, the protests were losing broad support. The enthusiasm that greeted them in May 1983 began to ebb, particularly in the face of massive and systematic regime repression. "It was more a process of extinction than a decision to terminate that approach," suggests Javier Martínez. "I would almost argue that the maximum protest was in September '83 and, nonetheless, the protests continued until October '85. . . . That inertia, that continued each time with protests of lesser intensity, showed that there was not, at that time, an alternative strategy—that this thing kept on because, so to speak, that was how you did opposition" (6 March 1991). Much of the labor movement withdrew its formal participation after the regime fired nearly two thousand striking copper workers in June 1983. The middle sectors began to withdraw soon after, in response to the violence that accompanied the protests or to the growing role of the hard-left Popular Democratic Movement (MDP) in the labor movement, or simply because they did not believe the protests would work.[49]

As the middle class withdrew its participation, urban marginal groups, accompanied by extremist, proviolence elements, began to dominate the protests. Students, shantytown youths, and the urban unemployed became preponderant elements. Gradually, and almost imperceptibly to political leadership, the protests lost their broad, grass-roots support. And the regime became increasingly free to concentrate its repression on poor neighborhoods.

Equally serious, the leadership of the protests was split both on methods and on ultimate objectives. The Democratic Alliance saw the protests as a form of social pressure that would bring the regime to the negotiating table. The MDP, however, saw them as a path to mass insurrection, designed to topple the regime without negotiations. As Arriagada points out, both sides promoted social mobilization without recognizing the difference between the social mobilization practiced by Gandhi in India and that practiced by Trotsky and Lenin in Russia in 1917 (4).

Beginning as early as 1984, there appear to have been serious private doubts among a few opposition political leaders regarding the social mobilization strategy. As Martínez observes: "I remember conversations in which [Gabriel Valdés] suggested that the most probable result would be participation in the plebiscite, but that social mobilization was essential because it helped forge a majority for the plebiscite, in case it came to that." But politicians were very reluctant to criticize the mobilization approach. They had taken responsibility for organizing and promoting the protests. And they had for several years flatly and emotionally rejected the only alternative: the Constitution of 1980, and the transition scenario it established. They were deeply and publicly committed to forcing the regime to change its plans. As Martínez notes: "It would have been viewed as very shameless for opposition leaders to say all that, and then say 'We're going to participate in the plebiscite'" (6 March 1991). The opposition had painted itself into a corner.

An anecdote recounted by Genaro Arriagada, who then headed the leading opposition radio station, Radio Cooperativa, illustrates how surprising and difficult to accept the dwindling support for the protests was: "We had a program on the radio . . . called the Cooperativa's computer that involved a small public opinion survey of two hundred cases to show what the public thought on health, unemployment, et cetera. . . . Well, around 1985 when the regime lifted the state of siege, we commissioned a poll on how people felt about it. At that time, the program had two parts. First, a journalist . . . asked people on the street what they thought, and then we presented the results of the survey done the previous week. . . . This time I ran into the journalist the morning of the broadcast and she said, 'Hey, I had bad luck. . . . Everyone I interviewed turned out to be a fascist. . . . Most of them favored the state of siege.' Then the poll results arrived and indicated that the majority of the country, especially in the popular sectors, had been in agreement with declaring the state of siege. . . . We concluded that the country was tired of the protests and having their neighborhoods be the scene of confrontations between the police and youngsters who were burning tires, and that what they wanted was for someone to impose order" (8 March 1991).[50]

And indeed, opposition leaders persistently maintained their rupturist stance until well into 1987. In January 1986, for example, Christian Democratic leader Claudio Huepe reaffirmed that the Democratic Alliance's fundamental strategy was to "exercise maximum possible pressure so as to get the armed forces to negotiate."[51] That same month, Sergio Molina was compelled to declare the National Accord in recess, principally because the center and left majority parties would not agree to a proposal by the right-of-center members to suspend social mobilization activities for ninety days in an effort to get negotiations with the regime started.[52] In May, Socialist leader Ricardo Lagos declared that "there is no incompatibility between a political solution and social mobilization."[53] Most opposition leaders insisted, at least publicly, that forcing the military from power was the objective, and social mobilization the instrument.

In 1986, however, public criticism of the mobilization strategy began to appear, and much of it came from intellectuals. As Arriagada notes: "From the intellectual world, a very interesting critique of the protests began. There were articles, internal party documents—by Boeninger, me, Brunner—articles that analyzed the protests . . . and by 1986 there was a fundamental affirmation that [the protests] wouldn't work" (8 March 1991). Brunner similarly stresses the efforts of intellectuals connected with political parties: "In reality it was people from the Socialist party, like Flisfisch, Vodanovic, Garretón, and others, who initially, in 1985 and 1986, suggested that the strategy was absolutely condemned to failure. . . . Those were the people who first said: 'This society is not totally repressive, and this economic model is not a total failure. . . .

Look at all those new, modern plantings of grapes for export up in the North.' At that time, when someone said such things, people looked at him as if he were absolutely crazy" (28 February 1991).

The intellectual critique of opposition strategy took many forms. Initially, it was low profile and occurred behind the scenes. Intellectuals continued to hold a near monopoly on opposition seminars and conferences. The widespread sense that change was imminent increased the demand by political actors for information and analysis. The CED workshop "Transition Scenarios and Strategies," which began in 1986, systematically exposed opposition leaders to academic thinking on democratic transitions, and to the experience of other countries. Other centers also addressed the question of transition, sometimes bringing to Chile academics and politicians from countries that had successfully moved from dictatorship to democracy. (One of the most visible and successful such workshops was organized by the Catholic University of Chile in 1986.) Many intellectuals regularly discussed strategy questions informally with party leaders; some participated formally in internal party debates. A few intellectuals managed to address transition issues in the press, through interviews and short articles. A discussion—typically low-key and with academic overtones—slowly began to develop among intellectuals and politicians about transition strategy. That discussion was increasingly critical of the social mobilization approach.

The role played by intellectuals changed fundamentally, however, on 26 September 1986, just after the discovery of arms caches in the north and the assassination attempt on Pinochet. One of the country's most distinguished sociologists, José Joaquín Brunner, leaked to a leading pro-government newspaper, *La Segunda,* a six-page memorandum he had written criticizing opposition strategy and calling for a new approach. Brunner's memorandum, which had been circulated the previous week to opposition leaders, sharply criticized the social mobilization strategy and proposed cutting ties with the hard-left MDP, shifting emphasis from conflict to negotiations, and recognizing the conditions for transition established by the 1980 Constitution.

Brunner's act was a political bombshell. The right immediately congratulated him for taking a position they agreed with. Opposition politicians reacted with dismay, repudiating Brunner's views publicly and criticizing him angrily in private. Socialist leaders said he should not have discussed publicly issues that were the topic of internal party debate. Two close colleagues, Angel Flisfisch and Manuel Antonio Garretón, subsequently appeared in the same newspaper supporting his right to speak out but disagreeing with several of his conclusions. Leaders across the opposition were indignant. As Eugenio Tironi recalls, however, their reactions were often "suspiciously emotional." Brunner was criticized, first, as an intellectual daring to opine publicly on a fundamentally political issue ("Intellectuals should stick to their business, and we'll stick to ours"); and second, as Tironi explains, because his act was "a kind of betrayal of the martyrs who had fallen in the protests" (20 March 1991). None of the criticisms comprised an effective counterargument. But Brunner was, as one opposition intellectual put it later, "a kind of Lone Ranger in this story."[54]

Nonetheless, the tide had turned. Brunner's critique sparked a sustained debate, much of it in the press, over the wisdom of the opposition's social mobilization approach. His voice was soon joined by those of other intellectuals, including particularly Garretón and Flisfisch. A month later Edgardo Boeninger sent a twenty-four-page letter to Christian Democratic party leaders making many of the same points Brunner made and recommending a new approach. Socialist leaders—particularly the party secretary general Ricardo Núñez—began to distance themselves more explicitly from the "all forms of struggle" position espoused by the MDP, and to emphasize instead "political solutions."[55] By early 1987, even the MDP had begun to reject violence and call for national reconciliation. The social mobilization strategy had been effectively and publicly discredited.

Brunner's memorandum was the most dramatic step in an extended intellectual critique that significantly influenced political strategy. Through activities that were, for the most part, academic—data gathering, analysis, debate, and publication—intellectuals articulated a conviction that politicians were already coming to feel but found exceedingly difficult to accept. Brunner explains: "I think that intellectuals initially helped show the Chilean political class that it was on a difficult political path, . . . that it was playing a game—forcible overthrow—for which it had neither experience, nor tradition, nor knowledge, nor means. . . . And it showed them that there was another political game which they already knew how to play—the game of negotiation, mobilizing political symbols, publicly criticizing a regime, joining efforts, forging coalitions" (28 March 1991). They acted, in Juan Gabriel Valdés's words, as "sharpshooters," cutting through emotional positions with a few well-chosen ideas (29 May 1991).

Boeninger, commenting on the role played by intellectuals during this period, suggests that they "placed into question the thesis that social mobilization would end the dictatorship" and then began to add "other, more theoretical reflections . . . that said, basically, 'Look, if you want democracy, what kind of scenario [historically] leads to democracy? . . . that guerrillas have seldom led to democracy, . . . that what leads to democracy is an electoral process.' Then the problem became how can we design an electoral scenario. And that was when social and political leaders began to realize that the plebiscite established by the Constitution was approaching, and to look much more closely at its implications. Then, from the academic research centers, there emerged the vision that this created an opportunity, . . . that it was possible to construct a scenario . . . that would give us a chance, and that otherwise we had no chance at all" (29 January 1991).

Similarly, Social Democratic leader Mario Papi argues that intellectuals made politicians realize "that politics had a certain logic and that we had to return to conducting politics in classical terms, that it was not intelligent to throw ourselves headlong against the dictatorship because that was their approach. Intellectuals enlightened a political class that . . . had become tremendously disoriented" (7 Maarch 1991). In short, intellectuals helped convince politicians to shift their focus from the barricades to the ballot box.

Brunner's decision to speak out, however, was qualitatively different from the other activities of intellectuals. It represented, as Foxley suggests, a "departure from conventional wisdom" that was probably more important symbolically than analytically. It initially scandalized opposition leaders, but it "produced a greater space of liberty." "More than legitimizing an idea, it legitimized an attitude" that comprised "looking at the whole range of possible alternatives and saying what one thought" (14 March 1991). In Chilean politics, where discourse was traditionally conditioned by rigid, preestablished codes, and where one never departed from conventional wisdom because doing so was too risky, that was a major shift. It demonstrated dramatically that the past did not have to weigh so heavily on the present, that molds could be broken. Brunner said, as one Socialist leader put it, "what many thought but no one dared to say openly."[56]

Brunner's act was also more political than intellectual, a deliberate shift from academic analysis to political proposition. It typified a broader change under way in the roles being played by opposition intellectuals. Intellectuals were beginning to edge out of the academy and take on functions that were more purely political. Some began speaking out publicly on political issues and participating more directly in party affairs; a few even began seeking political leadership. They started to transcend the academy and operate more deliberately in the political arena. Over the next two years, that trend would become much more pronounced.

Developing a Postauthoritarian Policy Consensus

Intellectuals also played more purely technocratic roles during this period. As conviction grew that democracy was approaching, attention turned increasingly to the policy choices that a democratic transition would bring. The staff of most academic centers already had a thematic focus—on education, health, or rural development, for example—and had conducted research on those topics for many years. One center, CED, had been established in 1981 principally to develop a policy package for the new democratic government. Around 1984, the centers began to concentrate more deliberately on the implications of their work for future policy. Through seminars and workshops, intellectuals helped initiate a broad debate among social and political leaders on the shape of postauthoritarian economic and social policy.

Many centers undertook such activities. PIIE and CIDE, for example, monitored and analyzed the education sector and systematically developed policy recommendations. ILADES and PET focused on social policy more broadly, emphasizing its impact on the poor; GIA and GEA studied the agrarian sector; PROSPEL, FLACSO, and (after 1986) CLEPI worked on foreign policy; and the Academy of Christian Humanism, the Vicariate of Solidarity, and the Chilean Commission of Human Rights began discussing how a new democratic regime might address the delicate issue of human rights violations under the dictatorship. They began a lengthy process of discussion that cut across party lines and helped generate trust and consensus. The results of these deliberations began showing up in seminars, discussions, and publications. They figured prominently, for example, in the workshops organized under CED's "Political Concertation, National Project, and Democracy" program. (Several years later, these same academic centers would form the basis for the multiparty *equipos técnicos* that worked out the platform for Patricio Aylwin's presidential campaign, and in 1990 many of their staff members would take high-level positions in the new democratic government.)

Economic Policy: The Key Issue

Although intellectuals led virtually the entire opposition policy debate during this period, nowhere was their influence more important or more complex than on economic policy. Here traditional disagreements among Chile's political forces were sharpest and most emotional. Many of Chile's bitter political divisions during the 1960s were based on conflicts over private property, foreign investment, markets, and the economic role of the state.[57] Here, as well, the military regime had made its most radical changes, at the behest of the neoliberal Chicago Boys. And here the stance taken by the opposition would most crucially determine the breadth of its support, and its success, once democracy returned. Economic policy was one of the most political of social policy issues. Yet the economy could not be managed on purely political considerations. The structural reforms of the Chicago Boys had changed the economy drastically. It was more dynamic than in the past and more integrated into the global economic system, and it required more technical expertise. The heavy emphasis by the Pinochet regime on a sophisticated economic policy "created an awareness among nontechnical political leaders that they had to listen to technicians."[58] Politicians could no longer make glib economic promises. Economic policy had become more than ever the dominion of experts.[59] Thus economic management was not only one of the most political issues facing the opposition, but also one of the most technical.

This combination of political and technical demands gave opposition intellectuals a significant opportunity to influence policy. Virtually all technical economists allied with the opposition were based at private research centers. Few were in business or in politics. None, of course, were in government. Those centers, therefore, provided most of the opposition's economic technocracy. But because economic policy was such a contentious and often emotional issue, intellectuals had to walk a difficult line between political and technical concerns.

At the same time, conventional wisdom regarding economic policy was changing more generally among opposition leaders. The failure of Allende's economic policy had been dramatic and undeniable, and the successes of Chile's neoliberal approach were becoming increasingly apparent. The experience of exile in Eastern and Western Europe had exposed many left-wing leaders to both. With traditional approaches to economic policy under attack from many directions, a new doctrine was needed.

Not surprisingly, then, the impact of intellectuals on opposition economic policy was complicated. On the one hand, opposition intellectuals were compelled to criticize. The structural reforms of the Chicago Boys marked a sharp break from the past and were ideologically opposed to positions traditionally held by the left and much of the center. They initially imposed high social costs, particularly on the poor, while benefiting principally the wealthy. Moreover, because until the mid-1980s the opposition could publicly criticize the regime *only* on technical grounds, economic criticism became the principal form of political criticism. When opposition economists commented on the dictatorship's economic policy, they were thus playing not just a technical role but a political role as well. They were "substituting for politicians who could not act and struggling against a cruel, repressive dictatorship that was causing massive misery among the most vulnerable sectors of the population" (Foxley, 14 March 1991). Economic criticism had to fill in for other kinds of criticism that were impermissible.

On the other hand, when the economy emerged from the banking crisis in 1985 and began growing steadily, opposition intellectuals had to face the possibility that postauthoritarian economic policy might not be substantially different from the policies pioneered by the Chicago Boys. Many of the regime's structural reforms were working and enjoyed increasing public acceptance. The economy was growing, unemployment was dropping, and Chile was becoming an economic success story, in contrast to the stagnation or decline that afflicted much of the rest of Latin America. And as the prospect of assuming power became more real, the opposition realized that its success would depend heavily on economic performance, defined in terms not only of a more equitable distribution of income but also of macroeconomic stability, growth, and low inflation. The opposition could no longer simply criticize the regime's economic policy; it had to develop its own.

During this period, intellectuals were instrumental in helping the opposition shift from repudiating the regime's economic policies to devising an approach of its own that was both politically acceptable and technically sound. The process was lengthy, taking place in myriad meetings, seminars, and workshops, and extending until shortly before the presidential elections of 1989. It involved discarding many of the economic principles—such as protectionism, a strong role for the state in production, and price controls—that had long been central to the left and to much of the center, and accepting most of the structural changes instituted by the regime. And it involved combining traditional concerns for social justice and the poor with the new economic orthodoxy in a way that would unite the opposition rather than divide it. The process involved political actors at all stages. But it was led, for the most part, by intellectuals from the private research centers because of their special combination of political credibility and technical expertise.

The process began in the late 1970s with the study circle of economists organized by the Academy of Christian Humanism. That exercise regularly brought together fifty or more opposition economists and political actors for discussion during a period when communication was severely limited, and bitter divisions, particularly on economic policy, still characterized relations among opposition parties. Although the study circle did not produce a new approach, it "played an important communication role when that was very difficult," establishing a set of relationships among opposition economists that would endure over the next decade (Ffrench-Davis, 3 February 1992).

CIEPLAN

Among the early, and subsequently more important, protagonists was the Corporation for Latin American Economic Research (CIE-PLAN), known for its high academic standards, strong technical expertise, and persistent emphasis on policy. Its senior staff had completed doctorates at some of the best universities in the United States. They published academic books and articles regularly and maintained working relationships with reputable economists in such countries as the United States, Brazil, Colombia, and Argentina.

At one level, CIEPLAN constituted a bastion of technical expertise for the opposition. It was a serious academic institution with impeccable credentials and could not be accused of staking out a position for purely political advantage. It had studied the Chilean economy during more than a decade, reflecting on the failures of the past and the radical transformations of the present. If CIEPLAN took a position, the position was solid. It could, therefore, engage the Chicago Boys on their own scientific terms. And it could supply the technical expertise increasingly demanded by opposition leaders, and by the public more generally.

At another level, CIEPLAN had assumed a political role by relentlessly criticizing the regime's economic policy. It was, as Socialist economist Carlos Ominami points out, "a great critic of the military regime."[60] Its vigorous and strongly technical critique, coming at a time when other forms of criticism were impossible, had given it de facto political significance. CIEPLAN's willingness to assume that political role, particularly before 1983, generated substantial credibility among political leaders.

This credibility extended beyond the center and beyond politicians. Although much of its staff was identified with, and many were active in, the Christian Democratic party, CIEPLAN was clearly independent from the party apparatus. Foxley, CIEPLAN's president, had written at length of Chile's need to build a stable political consensus and had sharply criticized the rigid approach adopted by the Christian Democrats during the 1960s. CIEPLAN had developed, through the community dialogues program, its own contacts with social actors throughout the country. Its staff included several leftist scholars, and it regularly involved academics and political actors from the left in its activities. CIEPLAN was composed, as one of its leftist staff members recalls, of "people who have inside them the idea of change, . . . of taking the side of the poor, not of political parties."[61] It was not, therefore, a particularly partisan institution, nor did it set out to convert those on the left to its beliefs.

Thus CIEPLAN operated simultaneously at political and technical levels. Its technical strength made it a formidable political voice, and its political voice helped persuade politicians to heed its technical message. Indeed, it was CIEPLAN's unusual ability to balance its political and its technical functions successfully that eventually gave it so much influence. Foxley's observation on how political activism led, later on, to technical influence is insightful: "Our capacity for influence in the campaign, and after, in the government, was greatly increased not principally because our ideas were 'renewed' and supposedly attractive. Rather, what was important was that those traditional politicians saw us struggling with the dictatorship alongside them on their own turf. That generated for us a credibility and a degree of reciprocal trust and political respectability among [those] traditional sectors" (14 March 1991). CIEPLAN managed to make its political and technical roles mutually supportive.

With the outbreak of protests against the regime early in 1983, CIEPLAN began to shift from critic to proponent. As Oscar Muñoz recalls, "The economic model was in crisis, people had lost their fear and began taking to the streets. The scenario was one of regime termination. And that created in us a sense of urgency" (27 August 1991). CIEPLAN staff decided that the time had come to begin developing serious economic policy proposals. Within just five months, and after extensive discussions with economic and political actors, it produced the first of several efforts to lay out the bases for a new economic policy—an edited volume entitled *Economic Reconstruction for Democracy*.[62] Many books, working papers, seminars, and journalistic articles were to follow over the next five years, as CIEPLAN took on additional issues and honed its ideas in internal and external debate.

During this period CIEPLAN's contributions to the economic policy debate were based on traditional academic activities but extended well beyond them. It compared, for example, the macroeconomic management in Peru, Brazil, and Argentina during their transitions to democracy, extracting lessons for Chile. It reviewed labor legislation in Europe and the United States and sought its relevance for the potentially explosive labor problems Chile would face once democracy returned. It then engaged leaders from the country's major labor confederations in discussions over several years regarding appropriate approaches to labor relations under a democracy.[63] Under its community dialogues program, CIEPLAN staff members traveled throughout the country, meeting with local business, government, and civic groups to discuss policy options. That program not only enabled CIEPLAN to spread its ideas, it also exposed it regularly to the real concerns of local groups.[64] CIEPLAN published a monthly magazine on economic policy issues, written for a nonspecialist audience and circulated nationwide to a select group of social and political leaders. It organized a series of seminars for journalists covering economic policy issues. Foxley wrote three books outlining political and economic bases for a democratic Chile. Several staff members played key roles in preparing the economic section of the Christian Democrats' Proyecto Alternativo, a broad policy package developed under the leadership of Sergio Molina during the mid-1980s. At least two other staff members participated regularly in the economic commission established by the reorganized Socialist party in 1985 to develop its position on economic policy.

CIEPLAN staff members also began, around 1987, to take a more conciliatory stand with respect to the Pinochet regime's economic reforms. Their shift was prompted by a combination of intellectual and political factors. As Oscar Muñoz explains, the practical reality of positive economic developments gradually caused CIEPLANistas (and many others who opposed Pinochet) to alter their positions on economic policy: "Perhaps we had been very convinced of certain approaches and had developed at great length the arguments to defend [them]. When we saw that in fact things functioned well under a different approach, we began to pay more attention to those other arguments, to look at them more dispassionately, and to balance better the different types of arguments and find ultimately that there was no one truth." But acknowledging those changes, after so many years of criticizing the regime's economic policy, was not easy. Muñoz recalls realizing with some discomfort during this period that, were he responsible for industrial policy, he probably would not make many of the changes that he had, in the past, written were necessary. "Initially I didn't dare tell anyone. . . . But at some point, a little timidly, I told someone I particularly trusted at CIEPLAN how I felt. To my surprise, he was thinking the same thing. . . . And we began to exchange information about what others in CIEPLAN thought. . . . I imagine that most of us experienced this personal process. And shortly thereafter, we found that we were all transmitting a discourse that was much more about continuity than about change" (27 August 1991).

Foxley, on the other hand, emphasizes how broader political considerations also affected CIEPLAN's stance. First, he notes, after 1983 political protest became possible once again, permitting economists to shift some of the burden of criticism to other social actors. Second, the economy had in fact improved, with most of the costs of the reforms having already been borne and the benefits beginning to be felt. "You'd have to be awfully hard-headed and stubborn not to accept the facts as they were," he observed. Third, the new political conditions called for a deliberate gesture. "We were convinced rationally that this country had to learn to get along with itself, and we had studied game theory, and the theory of cooperation. . . . Thus [we sought deliberately] to initiate a game of cooperation in which we recognized more positive points than we had previously, more even than we really thought were positive. We prepared a document that we published at CIEPLAN entitled 'Democratic Social-Economic Consensus Is Possible,' which was an affirmation of . . . what was possible. And we defined it in terms so that the other side could say, 'Those guys have recognized our positive points. Now we are obliged to seek a greater understanding with them'" (14 March 1991). The shift, then, was prompted not only by recognition that some of the policies had worked but also by a desire to emphasize an ethic of political harmony more appropriate to the democratic regime that was approaching.

To be sure, no one at CIEPLAN ever approved fully of the economic reforms wrought by the Pinochet regime, finding them cruel in their impact on the poor, unnecessarily drastic, and riddled with unjustifiable windfalls for the rich. And CIEPLAN's conciliatory document did not appear until September 1988, at about the time of the plebiscite.[65] But many of the group's earlier criticisms were becoming passé. The exorbitant costs incurred by the government's efforts to bring down inflation, liberalize the financial sector, and control the debt crisis had already been paid.[66] CIEPLAN, like many others in the opposition, recognized that conditions had changed; progress had been achieved, and the old approaches would no longer do.

What was distinctive about CIEPLAN, however, was its capacity to reconcile the new economic orthodoxy with the realities of opposition politics. CIEPLAN managed to show, in the words of one of its senior staff members, Ricardo Ffrench-Davis, "that you could have a market economy that was more just, more equitable, that gave a space to people. . . . [It] helped counter the belief that all market economies—had to be very concentrated, very inequitable, very denationalized, et cetera" (3 February 1992). It constituted a guarantee that opposition economic management would be both serious and sophisticated. Yet it also guaranteed greater equity. In the context of Chilean opposition politics, only CIEPLAN had the combination of technical skill and broad political credibility necessary to reconcile free markets with social justice.

The Socialists

On the left, intellectuals were perhaps even more influential in revising approaches to economic policy than in the center. Leftist parties and politicians were weaker, and leftist economic doctrine under greater challenge, creating more opportunity for intellectuals to exert influence.

Here, more than in the center, as Socialist economist Carlos Ominami noted, "It was very difficult to establish a clear distinction between political and intellectual leadership." He continues: "Ideas rose with great strength from discussions among intellectuals and were carried quite rapidly to the world of political leadership because they were more or less the same people" (14 January 1992). Moreover, leftist intellectuals, including economists, had been exiled in great numbers, giving them firsthand experience with the economies of Europe and North America. Many pursued graduate study while abroad, coming into contact with new and more modern approaches to economic thinking.

The left had its own dynamic, however, and was only tangentially influenced by CIEPLAN. Impetus for new economic thinking came first from other sources, as Ominami explains: "The case of the left has a lot to do with the greater opening of intellectuals through their international experiences—the fact that many of us were obliged to live in exile, during which we developed a more universal, and less provincial, viewpoint. The fact of the defeat during the 1970–1973 period was a very important stimulus to rethink many things. When you have gone through a defeat, you are obligated to seek explanations about why things happened that way and, certainly, to have an approach that seeks to avoid repeating the same errors."

The trauma of failure and subsequent exile appears to have altered leftist thinking on economics as well as politics. The economic failure experienced under the Allende government, combined with direct exposure to the capitalist democracies of Western Europe and the socialism of Eastern Europe, generated a vigorous debate on economic policy. Political intellectuals such as Jorge Arrate, who had done graduate work in economics at Harvard University, became key actors in debates that ranged across several continents during the late 1970s and early 1980s. It is noteworthy that five of the most technically qualified economists on the left—Carlos Ominami, Ricardo Lagos, Jorge Arrate, Jaime Estévez, and Sergio Bitar—were also political actors, and that four of them spent nearly a decade living in exile. Leftist leaders began to change their views on economic policy while still in exile, and well before the domestic debate on economic policy picked up in the mid-1980s.

Inside Chile, the principal base for leftist economists before 1985 was PET, founded by Allende's former budget director, Humberto Vega, shortly after the coup and operated under the Academy of Christian Humanism. PET was basically a research center but had as well a strong outreach program that included furnishing direct advice to "economic organizations of the poor." In addition to its core research on labor economics and poverty, it had developed a capacity for general economic commentary. Beginning in 1983, it provided training on economic issues for more than a hundred labor leaders. Although it was a reservoir of economic analysis for the left and devised a set of policy recommendations for labor relations, it does not appear to have been a leader in reshaping the left's approach to economic policy.

Another institution, VECTOR, played a more central role. A small research center established in 1978 principally to give the socialists a platform for discussion with the Christian Democrats, VECTOR's strong suit was dialogue, and its chief emphasis economic policy. Ricardo Lagos, a Duke University–trained economist and former professor who was emerging as one of the left's leading political voices, for several years headed its board of directors, enhancing the organization's role as a center for policy discussion. Its monthly workshop on economic affairs regularly brought leading socialist, and some Christian Democratic, economists and politicians together for debate. It also published a monthly report on the economy.

Perhaps the most important vehicle for developing a new leftist stance on economic policy was the economic commission of the new Socialist party. The commission had been established in the mid-1980s, once the Socialist party had re-emerged, under moderate leadership, as a cohesive organization. Its director was Carlos Ominami, a former member of the radical Revolutionary Left Movement (MIR) who, while in exile, had earned a *doctorat de troisième cycle* and a *doctorat d'état* in economics from the University of Paris. The commission met regularly over the next several years and became the center of leftist debate over economic policy.

Dominated by foreign-trained intellectuals, the commission drew heavily on academic material for its policy recommendations. One of its members, Manuel Marfán, recalls being struck by how many academics who otherwise went their separate ways converged in the group: "It was very curious because, in these meetings of the commission . . . the members were all . . . a doctorate from the University of Paris, a doctorate from Berkeley, a doctorate from Harvard, me with a doctorate from Yale, someone else from Sussex. . . . Despite the fact that many of us were less militant, more technocratic, . . . less political, suddenly we were sitting down to talk with others whom we may not have seen for years, . . . we were coming together" (7 January 1992). Ominami, who later became minister of economic affairs under the new democracy, stresses how direct the relationship between academic and political roles was: "I had participated as an intellectual in the debates on economic policy, but as the political parties were reconstituted, I was the first person put in charge of the economic commission of the Socialist party. Then what I did . . . was to try and put things together around the basic ideas that came from my purely intellectual work" (14 January 1992).

The result was an approach to economic policy that was based firmly on modern economic theory and differed dramatically from traditional positions taken by the Chilean left. The new approach emphasized macroeconomic stability and economic growth, accepted the validity of free markets and private property, rejected a strong role for the state in production, and sought full incorporation into the world economic system. It was not, however, an acceptance of the economic model advocated by the Chicago Boys. Rather, as Ricardo Lagos notes, it was more "a profound debate over what kind of economic policy would lead to a more just and egalitarian society" (13 March 1991).[67] And it was chiefly the product of a group of intellectuals, most of them foreign trained, who then successfully convinced politicians of its merit. As Ominami explains: "I think we've advanced substantially in convincing a sector of the left that opening up [the economy] is progressive, that properly functioning market mechanisms are progressive—more just than protectionism . . . as we practiced it. But that has been an effort. These aren't ideas that one can, from one day to the next, decree are going to be the new ideas of a political party. They are ideas you have to fight for, and I think we're still fighting" (14 January 1992).

CED's Economic Dialogues

Yet another key actor in shaping a postauthoritarian economic policy consensus was the Center for Development Studies (CED), easily the largest and most influential of the new outreach activities initiated by intellectuals. Under the politically sensitive direction of Edgardo Boeninger, its economics workshop began in 1985 to convene some of the country's leading economists and policymakers from left, right, and center. They included Fernando Léniz (former minister of finance under Pinochet); Sergio Bitar (former minister of mines under Allende); Carlos Ominami (an economist initially associated with the Revolutionary Left Movement and later minister of economic affairs under Aylwin); and Sergio Molina (minister of finance under Frei and later minister of planning under Aylwin). Workshop participants discussed economic position papers prepared by representatives of all economic hues.[68] They also addressed specific topics, such as private property (traditionally a divisive issue in Chilean politics), the distribution of wealth, and mechanisms for economic decision making. And as a spin-off of the economics workshop, CED organized seminars for business leaders from different sectors on their policy concerns. The approach throughout was to clarify differences and then seek to reduce them.

One surprising result, according to Boeninger, was that each group found itself closer to the others on economic policy than it had realized. Some found their own ideas changing as a result of the discussions. Their interaction in the project "accelerated the process of convergence, modifying people's thought through continued reflection and reference to the international literature."[69] CIEPLAN economist Patricio Meller offered a similarly positive assessment: "CED caused economists on the right to realize that they could talk with the economists on the left, that they weren't proposing wild policies; it also helped the left realize that there were people on the other side who were concerned with distributional problems, people they could talk to. That was important, in a world as polarized as Chile was, that people who were on opposite sides got together."[70] The remarkable amount of consensus that emerged from the exercise—the first systematic exchange of views on economic policy by the left, right, and center in many years—provided a clear signal that a return to democracy in Chile need not mean a return to the conflict of the 1960s and 1970s.

The CED program also helped a new right-of-center economic position coalesce and take on a higher public profile. As a result of the workshops, highly respected Catholic University economist Felipe Larraín produced, in 1987, an edited volume on economic policy and democracy that supported most elements of the Pinochet economic model but criticized its limited emphasis on social welfare and argued that a return to full political liberties was essential for the model to succeed.[71] That book was widely discussed in the press, evoking considerable criticism from the hard right and demonstrating the viability of a prodemocratic, right-of-center approach to economic policy.

CED's workshops, then, were fundamentally important in pulling together the new threads of economic thinking that were developing across the political spectrum. At a time when a return to democracy began to seem possible but grave doubts remained about whether a democratic Chile could agree on economic policy, CED helped politicians resolve those doubts. It was particularly important in facilitating contact between the opposition and the right, "combining the Socialists and the Christian Democrats with those who would later form the National Renovation party, and then with business leaders" (Ffrench-Davis, 3 February 1992). It established the conditions for a broad democratic consensus on economic policy. As Ominami observes, "There, things began to become evident that today have crystallized in Chilean society, that is, the existence of strong points of convergence among the positions of the right, center, and left on economic policy. Today, . . . one of the important points of Chile's situation is the existence of a high degree of consensus regarding basic elements of economic strategy. . . . An important antecedent was all that was done . . . within the framework of work principally carried out at CED" (14 January 1992).

From Producers of Knowledge to Articulators

Through these multiple and varied activities organized by the research centers, the rudiments of a shared vision of postauthoritarian policy began to emerge. A policy debate was initiated among intellectuals, spread to politicians, and would continue for several years. Political leaders from across the opposition were convened to focus on specific policy issues. They discussed problems, priorities, differences, and agreements. They discovered that they had significant common ground on many, if not most, issues. They began to believe that, despite their historical differences, they could work together to develop viable economic and social policy.

Indeed, intellectuals were the source of the policy agreements that later constituted the opposition's platform for the 1989 presidential election. In the words of Alejandro Foxley: "The Concertación's *ideology*, if that's the term, was elaborated in a long process by intellectuals at the research centers. In that sense, the Concertación was the ideological triumph—and the revindication—of the value of ideas in a political-historical process as decisive as the one Chile was living. . . . The Concertación was the first expression of postauthoritarian policy. And subsequently, the policy of the democratic regime has been very strongly marked by that new approach to problems that emerged principally from the intellectual world" (14 March 1991).

Thus Chilean intellectuals raised their political profile after the protests against Pinochet began to stall in 1984. Through seminars, interviews, and publications, as conveners and as informal advisers, they achieved a greater political presence. Increasingly, they spoke out on political issues. Increasingly, people listened. They became articulators between the world of ideas and political actors. One intellectual-politician, Sergio Bitar, recalls the uncommon political relevance that intellectuals seemed to have when he returned from exile in the mid-1980s: "I was struck . . . by the . . . people who had no political vocation, who were neither political leaders nor even party members, but who, through their intellectual activity, their strategy proposals—I am talking of [people from] FLACSO and others—began to have more marked political leadership" (16 January 1991).

Similarly, Socialist leader Ricardo Núñez notes the marked influence research centers had on the political world during this period: "It was more around sectors linked to formal [party] leadership, [but] based in academies or research centers—places for more systematic, professional reflection on political, social, and economic events—where the greater degree of influence on the process of developing the country's political struggle resided. Hence the strength of organizations like CIEPLAN, VECTOR, FLACSO, the Academy of Christian Humanism, et cetera. It was no coincidence therefore that, together with the genuine inability of parties to operate, there emerged a genuine operational ability, and an enormous capacity, to work and reflect in these centers linked directly or indirectly, formally or informally, to the political forces . . . of the opposition" (18 March 1991).

Modernizing Politics: 1987-1988

And throughout the renewal of Chilean politics—its more pragmatic character, its shift toward political activity accessible to all citizens, the use of technology, the use of the social sciences—none of these would have been possible had traditional politicians predominated. They were only possible because of this new wisdom, these new concepts that intellectuals introduced into politics.

— ENRIQUE CORREA, 8 March 1991

The strategy followed by the Campaign for the No was based on a diagnosis of Chilean society elaborated during years by the social science community. The triumph of that option in the plebiscite revealed that their interpretation was correct.

— EUGENIO TIRONI, *La Invisible Victoria*

The two years following the discovery of arms caches in the north and the unsuccessful attempt to assassinate Pinochet in late 1986 began as a period of great depression for the forces opposing the military regime and ended in great triumph. The opposition entered the period discouraged and in disarray. All its efforts—peaceful and nonpeaceful— to topple the regime had failed. Its unifying mechanism, the National Accord, had been suspended because of disagreement among its members. A state of siege had once again been imposed. The economy was growing steadily. The regime's hated plebiscite was approaching. It would have been hard to imagine that the opposition, two years hence, would be celebrating Pinochet's defeat.

The first year, 1987, was a time of great internal change but little visible progress. The opposition had finally dropped its efforts to topple the regime with social protests but still could not bring itself to accept Pinochet's plebiscite. Instead, it sought to persuade the regime to replace the plebiscite with open, competitive presidential and parliamentary elections. And its factions remained divided, arguing bitterly over transition strategy.

The military regime, meanwhile, moved ahead according to the timetable established by the 1980 Constitution. It took each step necessary to prepare for the plebiscite, passing laws providing for voter registration, the reconstitution of political parties, and electoral mechanisms and establishing a process for choosing its candidate. It resolutely rejected all calls from the opposition to alter the transition scenario. It declared repeatedly that the Constitution would be respected, and that the transition process it set forth would be implemented.

Several crucial processes were unfolding simultaneously. The opposition's approach to transition strategy was changing but was not yet fundamentally different. The regime's approach to transition was not changing at all but had spawned a dynamic that moved increasingly beyond Pinochet's control. And the constitutionally mandated plebiscite was approaching. The opposition had to decide how to confront the transition that was imminent.

The institutional tide had turned, however, causing the action to drift from research centers back toward the political arena. Politicians with academic backgrounds who had depended for years on private research centers for discourse and, in some cases, sustenance were now finding new opportunities in politics. Intellectuals with a political bent were being enlisted to help the opposition promote democratic transition. Academic analysis was giving way to political analysis. Increasingly, the focus was on the immediate challenges posed by direct political contestation. Intellectuals still drew heavily on their academic training, but they applied it more and more to activities not traditionally associated with the academy.

During this period, intellectuals achieved their maximum expansion into the political sphere. Some left the academy to become political actors. Others functioned on the far edge of their academic roles, devising transition strategy, marketing it to political leaders, and even making sure that strategy was properly implemented. Their impact on politics now became deliberate and direct. They showed the opposition how it could use Pinochet's rules to defeat him, modernized politics, and designed the successful plebiscite campaign. The efforts and investments of several decades came together to help defeat the dictatorship. Intellectuals, for a brief period, influenced political events directly and fundamentally. They played their greatest role in Chilean politics during 1987 and 1988.

Devising a New Approach to Transition

By the end of 1986, it was clear that the opposition's efforts to structure a transition to democracy were not working. For nearly four years the opposition had refused to accept the transition mechanisms established by the Constitution of 1980, relying on social mobilization to force the regime to turn over power immediately. Yet, despite help from Chile's worst depression since the Great Crash of 1929, the opposition had failed to generate enough discontent to topple the regime. The broad, sustained wave of citizen protest necessary to pressure Pinochet into altering the itinerary established by the Constitution of 1980 had not materialized. The social mobilization strategy, therefore, was increasingly discredited (the Communist party remained its lone supporter, clinging on until well into 1988). The opposition was coming to realize that regime change would only occur through a political process, and with the only political process in place that established by the regime, it began to take seriously the arrangements set forth in the Constitution of 1980.[1]

The opposition, however, was unwilling to agree to participate in the regime's plebiscite. It remembered bitterly the undemocratic arrangements that had accompanied the 1980 plebiscite to approve the new constitution and assumed that the upcoming vote would be no different. Most believed it was designed merely to legitimate the regime for eight more years. Participation, therefore, would not only be futile but might constitute a stamp of approval for Pinochet's continued rule. Social mobilization was on its way out as strategy, but the plebiscite was not in.

And indeed there were, at the end of 1986, many reasons for the opposition to be pessimistic. Some of the basic prerequisites for a fair plebiscite were not yet in place. Political parties still could not legally function. No provisions had been made for voter registration, voting procedures, or oversight of the election process. The opposition had not been guaranteed the freedom of expression—and particularly, access to television—that would be crucial to waging a successful plebiscite campaign. Even if those conditions were established, the opposition assumed that the process would still be sufficiently stacked against them to ensure Pinochet's victory. As Socialist leader Jaime Gazmuri recalls, "We never thought the military would be willing to lose an election" (7 March 1991).

Thus the opposition shifted to a strategy that focused on electoral processes rather than on street protests but stopped short of embracing the plebiscite: it called for free elections.[2] Christian Democratic leaders Edgardo Boeninger and Gabriel Valdés, and Popular Democratic Movement (MDP) leader Germán Correa, issued calls for free elections in January 1987. In March, the opposition formally kicked off a broad campaign to persuade the military regime to amend the Constitution, replacing the plebiscite with open presidential and congressional elections.

By June, several party-based committees promoting free elections were operating. In August, Patricio Aylwin was elected president of the Christian Democratic party, replacing Gabriel Valdés, and called for free elections in place of the plebiscite.

The shift was significant for the opposition, for it implied tacit acceptance of the Constitution of 1980 and did not demand that the regime turn over power to an interim government prior to holding elections. It also included a call for citizens to register to vote, thereby validating the voter registration process the regime established early in 1987. Moreover, the initial free elections committee of fourteen famous personalities drawn from across the opposition—the National Council for Free Elections (CEL)—claimed a broader mandate, vowing to oversee the process of voter registration and to establish an independent mechanism for monitoring any future electoral process, including the plebiscite.[3] As the director of the free elections committee, Sergio Molina, recalled, "We reckoned that a fundamental ingredient was to have an organization that could eventually confront whatever might happen in terms of the plebiscite or elections or some other structure, even if it were not the one that we liked" (13 March 1991). Much of the opposition shared that concern, and the campaign quickly acquired an important subtext: securing adequate guarantees that the plebiscite, if held, would be fair.

Some argue that the free elections campaign was always more gambit than genuine objective, allowing the opposition to withhold a commitment to the plebiscite until minimally acceptable conditions had been established. "The slogan was free elections," recalls one opposition leader, "but it never entered anyone's head that the slogan was viable" (Vodanovic, 15 March 1991). Another asserted that "the free elections movement was important in terms of helping press for generating a reasonably level playing field" (Boeninger, 29 January 1991). Thus the campaign for free elections sought not only to reform the process mandated by the constitution but also to reposition the opposition, should the plebiscite prove unstoppable.[4]

The strategy was, however, "little more than a step forward in the search for new formulas."[5] It continued to be rupturist in character, seeking to alter the mechanisms and timetable the regime had established for transition to civilian rule. The regime, feeling no need to alter its plans, routinely rejected all such proposals. And the opposition encountered great difficulty in making its strategy credible. Looking forward, perhaps, to the congressional elections scheduled to follow the plebiscite, opposition parties were reluctant to unify. Instead, they insisted on establishing separate free elections committees—the center had theirs, led by the president of the Christian Democratic party Gabriel Valdés, succeeded in August 1987 by Patricio Aylwin; and the moderate socialists had another, led by Ricardo Lagos. Opposition parties were also torn by disagreement over whether to unite around a common candidate and program of government for any eventual election. And an initiative by Ricardo Lagos to unite the opposition through a nonideological party based solely on reestablishing democratic rule—the Party for Democracy—was rejected by the Christian Democrats concerned with maintaining their own party's image.

The result was an unruly, ongoing squabble that often resembled the chaos Pinochet so direly predicted would ensue should the regime's gradual transition to a protected democracy not be carried out in full. The personal and ideological divisions that had for so long divided the opposition remained a paramount force. They permeated debates over the wisdom of selecting a single opposition candidate and a program of government, should free elections be attained. They also caused parties to pause, in the discussion over unity against Pinochet, to consider the implications of the congressional elections that would follow Pinochet's plebiscite no matter who won. The prospect, even if small, of genuine political power initially caused the opposition to revert to its old partisan ways.[6]

Disarray among opposition leaders was great enough to stimulate calls for unity from the ranks. In July, leaders of eleven party youth organizations demanded that party leaders "come together to dialogue." The Women for Life movement, which spanned all opposition sectors, called for a party summit to elaborate a common proposal to end the dictatorship. Newsmagazines began to criticize the "incapacity of the opposition to talk and reach agreements."[7] In December, one of the country's leading human rights groups sent a letter to opposition leaders threatening to initiate a hunger strike if they did not unite.[8] Indeed, commenting on events in late 1987, two veteran observers noted: "Instead of acting like leaders and uniting to push Pinochet from office, his opponents remain too trapped in their past differences and too worried about alienating voters to form an alliance with potential rivals in a post-dictatorial era. Chile risks recreating the polarization that led to the collapse of the Allende government."[9]

The regime, meanwhile, moved steadily ahead with preparations for the plebiscite. In October 1986 it promulgated the Electoral Registration System and Electoral Service Law, establishing the machinery necessary for voters to register and for elections to be held. Voter registration began on 25 February 1987, with President Pinochet the first to register. Two weeks later, the regime promulgated a political parties law that established conditions under which non-Marxist political parties could organize and function legally. On 19 April a Voting and Tabulation Law was approved, providing for oversight and scrutiny of the electoral process, including participation by representatives of all legally constituted political parties. Throughout this period, the regime consistently declared that the transition would be carried out through the plebiscite, and that there would be no modification of the system established by the Constitution of 1980.[10]

The regime's systematic steps to establish a clear, relatively democratic set of conditions for the plebiscite came as a surprise to much of the opposition. Previous elections under the military regime (the 1980 constitutional plebiscite and the 1978 "consultation") had been marked by dubious legality and absolute unfairness. The regime was known for its dramatic violations of human rights and of democratic norms. Most opposition leaders therefore assumed that, one way or another, the regime would skew conditions enough to guarantee its victory. Conventional wisdom dictated, as Gazmuri observed, that the military would not permit the opposition to win.

This time, however, several factors were operating together to generate different conditions.[11] The regime's claims to legitimacy were based on the Constitution it had created in 1980, which mandated the plebiscite as part of a broader transition process. The armed forces had consistently reaffirmed their commitment to that Constitution, often using it to justify their rejection of opposition demands. They would not alter that position; any violation of the Constitution risked delegitimating the regime itself.

The regime also wanted the opposition to participate willingly in the plebiscite. An opposition boycott, particularly one based on the absence of democratic guarantees, would have made governance over the ensuing eight years—until the open elections envisioned for 1997—much more difficult. And the regime was confident that it could win, based on past plebiscites, its institutional resources, a buoyant economy, and the opposition's continued divisions. Thus the regime was willing not only to abide by the Constitution but to make concessions to opposition demands it could legally have avoided. It unilaterally decided to delay the plebiscite until substantial numbers of voters had registered, to lift all states of emergency for the first time in fifteen years, to allow most exiles to return, and to give the opposition's campaign minimal access to television.[12] The whole point, for the regime, was to renew its mandate through a patently legitimate plebiscite.

The regime's international reputation was also at issue. The world would be watching the country's plebiscite, and thousands of foreign journalists and election observers would be on hand when the voting took place. After fifteen years of international isolation, the regime genuinely wanted to improve its image abroad. It was well aware, as a report on the plebiscite by the Latin American Studies Association notes, of how rigged elections had destabilized authoritarian regimes in the Philippines and elsewhere.[13] In several ways, then, a fraudulent plebiscite would compromise the regime's efforts over nearly a decade to achieve political legitimacy.

The Constitution of 1980 had also begun to acquire its own dynamic. Despite many nondemocratic elements, the rule of law it established began to play an autonomous role in Chile's transition to democracy, imposing conditions not intended by the military regime. The plebiscite itself appears to have been the result of a compromise, while the Constitution was being drafted in 1980, between the Council of State's proposal for a five-year transition ending in presidential and congressional elections in 1986, and a sixteen-year transition subsequently proposed by the junta. Pinochet reportedly resolved the debate by suggesting a ratifying plebiscite eight years into the transition period. If the vote was positive, the regime would continue an additional eight years, adding a largely appointed Congress with only limited powers shortly after the plebiscite. If not, the full transition would occur a year later, through open presidential and congressional elections. That concession, which Pinochet almost certainly would not have made absent the pressure of his civilian supporters, proved to be crucial.[14]

Moreover, the junta apparently never intended the plebiscite to be held under the electoral standards and guarantees set forth in the 1980 Constitution. Those provisions, according to one of the Constitution's transitory articles, were to come into force only after the plebiscite, when the first congressional elections would be held. The Constitutional Tribunal, however, saw it differently. Composed of conservative jurists who supported but were not directly controlled by the regime, the Tribunal ruled four to three in September 1985 that the plebiscite must be subjected to the provisions for elections set forth in the 1980 Constitution.[15]

That decision, taken three years before the plebiscite and opposed by Pinochet's minister of justice, Hugo Rosende, was to have major implications. It subjected the plebiscite to constitutional norms rather than to the whims of the junta. It meant that the Electoral Qualifying Tribunal provided for by the Constitution had to function for the plebiscite. It meant that political parties had to be legalized before the plebiscite took place, voters had to be registered, only registered voters could vote, the Electoral Service had to be established, and registered parties would be permitted to oversee the voting, making fraud more difficult. It significantly reduced the scope of arbitrary restrictions on the plebiscite process and replaced them with constitutional guarantees. The result was a plebiscite scenario almost certainly different from the one the military government originally had in mind.[16] The system established by Pinochet to legitimate his regime was beginning to elude his control.[17]

By the end of 1987, regime preparations and opposition deliberations finally began to come together. The military government had made it clear that the plebiscite would take place as scheduled, and with at least minimal democratic guarantees. The opposition had launched a major voter registration drive and had advanced a good deal in debate over formulas for unity. Two of its parties, the Humanists and the Christian Democrats, had taken the initial steps to obtain legal status under the new political parties law. And a few opposition leaders were beginning publicly to float the idea of participating in the plebiscite. The opposition's demand for free elections was slowly giving way to the reality of the regime's determination to carry out the transition scenario established by the Constitution of 1980.

In December, Ricardo Lagos and a group composed principally of moderate Socialists launched the Party for Democracy as an ideologically neutral vehicle designed solely to contest the regime in elections. In January, Christian Democratic president Patricio Aylwin announced that the party had decided to participate in the plebiscite and was willing to collaborate with all other groups who favored voting "No to Pinochet," including the orthodox left. Then in early February, a majority of opposition political parties subscribed to a document calling on citizens to vote no in the referendum "to defeat Pinochet and his regime." After trying unsuccessfully for nearly five years to alter the regime's scheme for a transition to democracy, the opposition finally gave in and accepted it. The free elections campaign had been transformed into the Campaign for the No. The opposition Concertación, which eventually swelled to include sixteen parties, had been born. Eight months later, it would defeat Pinochet in the plebiscite with more than 54 percent of the vote.

The Role of Intellectuals: Modernizing Politics

During this period, intellectuals achieved their greatest direct impact on politics. The symbiotic relationship they had developed with politicians because of regime repression gave them extraordinary access to the process of political decision making, and extraordinary credibility within it. Opposition politics was characterized, perhaps more than at any time in the country's history, by politicians with a foot in the academy and by intellectuals with a foot in politics. It was, in Hirschmanian terms, a time of maximum "trespassing."[18]

These overlaps and interdependencies created a complex pattern. Intellectuals began to influence politics at even more levels than in the past. Some, like Ricardo Lagos and Jorge Arrate, had left the academy to become political leaders. Others, like Alejandro Foxley, Edgardo Boeninger, and Carlos Ominami, were in the process of doing so. Yet others, like Angel Flisfisch, Carlos Huneeus, José Joaquín Brunner, and Manuel Antonio Garretón, remained firmly in the academy but were important political voices in the media or in internal party debates. A small group, including Juan Gabriel Valdés, Eugenio Tironi, Javier Martínez, and Carlos Vergara, deliberately directed their academic skills toward the task of modernizing the opposition's political campaign techniques.

Indeed, the hallmark of intellectual influence on politics during this period was the idea of modernizing politics. Operating from knowledge and skills obtained in the academy, and taking advantage of their extraordinary credibility, Chilean intellectuals systematically introduced modern campaign techniques to Chilean politicians. The intellectualization of politics that had occurred in the late 1970s led, in the words of Edgardo Boeninger, to "the modernization of politics" in the mid-1980s (29 January 1991).[19]

This concept—the introduction by Chilean intellectuals of modern politics—was voiced repeatedly in interviews. Typically, it meant substituting pragmatism and science for ideology and intuition. Alejandro Foxley, for example, notes the appearance of a "modern politics" that "is less ideological, more flexible, understands better the modern world and is thus more adaptable, more inclined towards agreements, places greater value on the economy and on macroeconomic equilibria, et cetera" (14 March 1991). Ricardo Lagos argues that intellectuals "introduced elements of reason" into politics. More concretely, this often meant bringing new political techniques from abroad. As Lagos continues: "It was intellectuals who first used survey techniques, it was intellectuals who first used image techniques, it was intellectuals who carried out content analyses, it was intellectuals who convinced politicians of the importance of focus groups. . . . Thus there were all these modern techniques that intellectuals used daily, and that politicians only later on realized were important" (14 March 1991). Intellectuals began convincing politicians to drop old ways of doing politics and adopt new ones.[20]

One of the first important contributions by intellectuals during 1987 was to help politicians see that sufficient conditions existed to defeat the regime in the plebiscite, and that people were generally receptive to that strategy.[21] Opposition leaders entered 1987 depressed at their failure to topple the regime through social mobilization, and deeply pessimistic about their chances for victory under the regime's transition mechanisms. Although they saw no real alternative to continued resistance, they had little hope of success. Thus serious debate over participating in the plebiscite was rare. Instead, the emphasis was on modifying the regime's plans by demanding free elections, and on whether the opposition should unite behind a single candidate and program of government in confronting the regime.

The regime, nonetheless, was getting ready for the plebiscite, and its preparations began to pose decisions for opposition members: Should they urge their constituencies to register to vote, so they would be ready for whatever electoral scenario emerged? Should they legalize their parties under the regime's new legislation, giving them the right to normal political activities? Should they make preparations, presuming their demand for free elections failed, to participate in the plebiscite? In each case, a positive decision brought benefits but also risked helping legitimize a fundamentally unfair transition scenario.

Opposition leaders were hampered in making these decisions by their limited access to the constituencies they purported to represent. Political parties were still banned, and normal party activities could not legally be carried out. Few elections of any kind had been held since 1973.[22] Political meetings and rallies could be organized only at considerable risk. The press was still highly restricted in what it could report. The mechanisms that normally relate political leaders to their followers had not functioned for fifteen years. Carlos Vergara, a sociologist based at SUR, describes conditions: "All the social and political fabric that connected parties with their social bases had been bombarded. . . . For many years it was difficult to carry out any political activity at all, let alone operate as before, because people weren't there, structures didn't exist, and there were immense problems with infrastructure and resources. Political leadership was increasingly distanced from the majority of citizens during a period when profound transformations were occurring in Chilean society."[23] Thus politicians for the most part brought only intuition and ideology to the strategy debates. They had little reliable information on what people really thought.

Within this context of pessimism and uncertainty, intellectuals provided, in the words of one politician, "justification and rationality" for opposition decisions (Gazmuri, 7 March 1991). They informed opposition debate with the experiences of other countries in shifting from dictatorship to democracy. They pointed out, for example, that transition in Uruguay had been based on a plebiscite, that the democratic opposition in the Philippines had triumphed despite having fewer guarantees than Chile's opposition expected to have, and that transition in Spain had required the opposition to significantly moderate its demands. They analyzed the regime's preparations for the plebiscite and estimated their impact on opposition prospects. They discussed the nature of democratic governance, stressing its reliance on consensus and compromise. They also demonstrated, through sophisticated studies of political attitudes, that a majority of the electorate preferred a plebiscite to the free elections campaign.

The most prominent leader of the free elections campaign, Sergio Molina, describes the role played by intellectuals during this period: "The passage of the political laws caused a major internal debate in which intellectuals were influential in persuading the parties to enter into the framework imposed by the dictatorship despite being at a disadvantage, because it gave us visibility, voice, organization. That was very difficult for the parties to accept, and at first they strongly resisted. . . . There, intellectuals had great influence on the parties" (13 March 1991).

Similarly, Brunner notes that "intellectuals played a very important role, . . . showing that this was the best path, that it was the only viable path, that it was a morally acceptable path, that it was a path that would lead to success, . . . providing historical antecedents that showed, for example, that certain kinds of transitions begin only when the opposition is willing to play the game, to dance with the dictatorship, . . . and bringing in intellectuals and Spanish politicians who said those kinds of things. . . . They played an important role in that precise moment and with respect to that fundamental judgment regarding whether to register or not, whether to accept the Constitution or not, whether to participate in the plebiscite or not" (28 February 1991).

As a result, the chain of decisions that opposition leaders made beginning in March 1987 and culminating in the February 1988 coalition (La Concertación) to participate in the plebiscite, was based on careful calculation rather than on bitter capitulation to the regime's inexorable timetable. The opposition therefore entered the plebiscite proactively, with a clear rationale, feasible objectives, and a credible strategy. Rather than being subdued by the prospect of confronting Pinochet in the plebiscite, it was energized. That condition, as Núñez notes, owed a great deal to the protracted intermingling of politicians and intellectuals: "Behind the call for voter registration, behind the call to vote no later on, there was reflection, not just political intuition, not just an alternative we chose because no other existed, but also behind that a reflection about the type of democracy we wanted to construct, with the idea that we were in a stage of Chile's social-political process and in a world in which consensus takes priority over dissension, in which agreements take priority over disagreements, in which social actors must seek ways to combine efforts and common objectives rather than provoke big ruptures. . . .

During ten years, approximately, there was this interesting, creative over-lap" (18 March 1991).

Pioneering New Techniques: CERC and FLACSO

The first clear manifestation of the new politics was the emergence, between 1986 and 1988, of polling and focus groups as tools for political competition. The appearance of these instruments was totally the initi-ative of intellectuals based at Santiago's private research centers. They did not respond to any demand by politicians for new techniques or in-formation. Researchers at the Center for the Study of Contemporary Re-ality (CERC) and the Latin American Faculty of the Social Sciences (FLACSO) began, with foreign funding, to carry out survey research for purely academic purposes in 1984.[24] By late 1988, they had changed the way politics was done in Chile.

The introduction of political opinion polls, however, had a strong historical and academic base. High-quality survey research had devel-oped in Chile with the establishment of "scientific sociology" during the 1960s. The academic programs at FLACSO, the University of Chile, and the Catholic University had all been founded with a strong emphasis on empirical sociology. Eduardo Hamuy had begun carrying out systematic studies of political attitudes at the University of Chile in 1958 and had been remarkably successful in predicting the results of presidential elec-tions in 1958, 1964, and 1970.[25]

Hamuy's surveys were not, however, taken up by political parties as a tool in devising strategy, and they became virtually impossible to carry out after the 1973 military takeover of power because of the regime's pro-hibitions and the dampening effect of widespread fear. During the first decade of the military regime, private organizations carried out only commercial marketing research. The military government also commis-sioned regular polls—of debatable quality—by the local Gallup orga-nization on its own popularity but seldom made the results public.

Conditions changed with the political freedom that accompanied the protests of 1983, and broader surveys of public opinion once again became possible. The first of these new studies was carried out in 1983 by Diagnos, a for-profit venture formed by five unemployed social sci-entists as a survival strategy. Diagnos described its efforts as "sociolog-ical journalism" aimed at finding out what had happened in the country after so many years of dictatorship. It surveyed specific groups, such as youth and women, on their attitudes toward issues that included health, culture, the economy, religion, and types of government, and almost al-ways under contract to such organizations as radio stations or newsmagazines.[26] Although founded by people with academic training, Diagnos did not address academic or theoretical issues in its work. It was, however, one of the first groups to demonstrate that, authoritarian conditions notwithstanding, reliable surveys could be carried out on issues that went beyond the narrow confines of traditional marketing research.

More clearly academic initiatives followed close behind. CERC, a research center operating under the Academy of Christian Humanism, was one of the pioneers. Discussions at a 1984 seminar on democratic transition prompted CERC, with help from University of Miami political scientist Enrique Baloyra, to organize a workshop on the prospects for carrying out public opinion studies in Chile. That workshop led to a small study on attitudes toward democratic transition, and another workshop, in 1985, to discuss the results.

The second workshop convened several foreign experts on democratic transition, among them Juan Linz of Yale University, who had carried out some of the most influential survey research during the Spanish transition to democracy. It led to another small survey, in late 1985, on the political attitudes of university students that was designed to prepare the way for more ambitious studies. When the results of that survey proved reliable, CERC proceeded with a broader study in 1986 of political attitudes among Santiago residents and, in 1987, the first nationwide survey of political attitudes since the coup.[27]

These early studies were, in the words of a key staff member, "all academic, absolutely all of them, and it was basically the [ongoing] political processes that prompted us to include political questions that would later become publicized, more for use by parties or for general public opinion or for the media." They sought, as CERC's director, Carlos Huneeus later wrote, "to study the subjective changes" that had accompanied the major objective transformations wrought by the military regime over more than a decade.[28]

To be sure, the potential political relevance of the surveys was of interest from the start. The politically authoritarian conditions prevailing in Chile gave the surveys special significance and attraction. Huneeus, writing about the findings of the university student survey in 1986, noted that "political actors in Chile can say that they know what Chileans think and want regarding politics, but as long as those opinions are not expressed through free, secret and informed suffrage, such affirmations lack a necessary foundation. It's not only useful for academic reasons, but also necessary for political reasons to know what Chileans think about politics."[29] But with the plebiscite still two years off and the opposition firmly against participating in it, the political uses of such surveys were not at all clear. The initial impulse was certainly academic rather than political.

Indeed, a major motivation underlying CERC's efforts was to take advantage of Hamuy's earlier work and develop reliable time series data that would make possible comparisons of Chilean political attitudes over nearly three decades. As Huneeus explained: "This comparison of data has great relevance for the social sciences. In no other country have survey data from a democratic period been compared with a survey carried out under authoritarianism." CERC's studies were, therefore, strongly influenced by Eduardo Hamuy, who offered his data and methodological expertise to CERC. They sought, among other things, to "revive a tradition of empirical sociology that Hamuy had initiated during the 1950s and that had been interrupted by the military coup."[30]

CERC's studies soon developed a strong reputation for quality and reliability. Their provocative findings drew significant media coverage. They were instrumental in directing attention—first of intellectuals and later of political leaders and the general public—toward independently verifiable measures of public opinion on political issues. Soon their success attracted major funding from the Italian government and the European Economic Community for a regular series of surveys, and in 1988 CERC became the principal source of polling information for the opposition Concertación.

At about the same time, another private social science research center, FLACSO, was also beginning to undertake political opinion studies. Like CERC, its initial concerns were academic. A small survey on government decentralization carried out by CED in 1984 had prompted several FLACSO researchers to wonder whether such surveys could address more explicitly political attitudes. Shortly thereafter, the Spanish government contracted FLACSO to carry out a survey on the image of Spain in Chile as part of its plans to observe the quincentenary of the voyage of Columbus to the Americas. Although the questionnaire had been prepared in Spain, FLACSO researchers added two questions on politics to see whether they would work. As Angel Flisfisch explains: "They worked. So the next question was, why not do a more political survey? But there still was no political intention. It was an academic thing, and it seemed kind of seductive to be doing surveys in an authoritarian context" (17 January 1991).

In late 1985, with additional funding from the Spanish government, FLACSO carried out its first survey designed explicitly to gauge political attitudes among Santiago residents. The success of that survey soon prompted a whole new line of activity and generated substantial foreign funding. Over the next several years, FLACSO became one of the leading sources of political attitude surveys in Chile, often in collaboration with CED and CEP, and securing substantial financing from foreign sources that included the U.S. National Endowment for Democracy, the Ford Foundation, and the Spanish government.[31]

The early surveys carried out by both FLACSO and CERC generated findings that challenged conventional opposition views about public opinion. First, the studies consistently showed that most people held moderate, rather than radical, political attitudes. Only a small segment supported political violence or favored forcibly removing the military regime from power. Although a majority favored political change, they did so only if change could be accomplished without social disorder. At a time when social mobilization was the dominant theme in opposition strategy, the surveys suggested that most people opposed social mobilization.[32]

Second, the studies indicated that at least a third of the population supported the military regime, and that another third was neutral or undecided. Instead of being hugely unpopular, the regime had significant (albeit minority) popular support, even among less advantaged sectors. Pinochet's appeal was not confined to a small group of wealthy economic interests. Thus the opposition faced a regime whose defeat could not be taken for granted, even in free and fair elections. It had to be contested with great care.

Third, the surveys found a "tremendous continuity in democratic values" among the population (M. Lagos, 9 January 1991). People still arrayed themselves along the left-right continuum, correctly identified the positions of political parties, and evidenced overwhelming support for the institutions and processes of democratic governance.[33] Despite nearly two decades of conflict and repression, Chile's much-admired democratic culture remained intact and could be counted on in efforts to return the country to democratic rule.

The intellectuals carrying out the studies were quick to derive the political implications of their findings. That most of the population, although opposed to Pinochet, was politically moderate, rejected violence, and strongly favored using democratic procedures to resolve political conflict argued against trying to force the regime out of its transition scenario through social mobilization and supported instead the soft-landing thesis based on contesting the regime in the plebiscite. Edgardo Boeninger, according to Flisfisch, was one of the first to "recognize that the surveys had a potential for political impact."[34] He and others at the private centers realized that the findings constituted a strong argument for fundamentally changing opposition transition strategy.

What had begun, therefore, as an essentially academic exercise quickly acquired political overtones. Intellectuals, realizing the strategic importance of their findings, undertook to market them to politicians. As Flisfisch recalls: "So we did it. But upon doing it we suddenly began to see that it had political effects, and that led us to begin to seduce leaders—the political elites—with the idea that here we've found something; let's think about it" (17 January 1991). Through informal conversations, journalistic articles, seminars, workshops, and conferences, in- tellectuals presented their academic findings to political leaders. "There was," in the words of Guillermo Sunkel, "a kind of strategy of seduction by these intellectuals working on politics—to seduce politicians into seeing that this instrument was really useful—that it could be effective in the struggle."[35] The chief motivation for the studies thus began shift- ing from academic to political.

At first, political leaders were doubtful and the process slow. The initiative had come entirely from intellectuals. None of the studies had been commissioned or financed by political parties. As one of the key CERC staff members recalls: "The process was extremely slow because people, particularly those on the left, said, 'No, that can't be. That's a survey, a result, a theory, an interpretation,' in sum, 'There's not enough evidence to say this is what the population really wants'" (M. Lagos, 9 January 1991).

Over the next two years, however, the seminars and conferences be- gan to have an effect. Knowledge initially generated by intellectuals for academic purposes was steadily exerting pressure on the strategic think- ing of opposition politicians. Most of the polls, after all, had been carried out by reputable academics and met international standards of quality. Subsequent surveys validated the initial findings. And many of the in- tellectuals carrying out the surveys already enjoyed strong formal or informal relationships with the political leadership. Politicians, there- fore, could not ignore the findings. They came to believe, as Sunkel later observed, both that the surveys accurately expressed public opinion and that such instruments were necessary for designing electoral campaigns. CERC and FLACSO managed to persuade political leaders that "polit- ical communication in a mass society requires knowledge based on this type of instrument and not only knowledge based on direct contact with 'the people.'"[36]

The CIS Consortium

Much of the influence exerted by intellectuals on politicians during this period took place through channels that were already in place— research centers, informal consultations, and the press. But new mechanisms established deliberately to influence opposition strategy also began to appear. One of the most important of these was the CIS consortium, formed in mid-1987 by three academic research centers (CED, SUR, and ILET) to bring modern political campaigning techniques and political consulting more generally to Chile's political opposition. In contrast to the academic objectives of FLACSO and CERC, CIS was from the outset deliberately political. It sought, in the words of one of its leaders, to go "beyond purely intellectual influence" to achieve political influence as well.[37]

But CIS was not a standard exercise in political consulting. It did not respond to a demand by politicians for advice. Political leaders played no role in its formation and did not request its services. Instead, CIS was the initiative of intellectuals who marketed their advice, free of charge, to politicians. It represented a fundamental escalation in efforts by intellectuals to transmit the implications of their research to political leaders.[38]

The idea began with the academic curiosity of ILET's director, Princeton-trained political scientist Juan Gabriel Valdés. "For a long time—perhaps since 1975—I had been interested in the idea of political consultants, but knew nothing about them and didn't know anyone in Chile who knew anything about them" (29 May 1991).[39] While on a three-month research fellowship at Notre Dame University in early 1987, Valdés began asking questions about political consultants. He sent letters to several U.S. political consulting firms. The one that answered—the Sawyer/Miller Group—subsequently invited him to New York and then offered to visit Chile for free, if he would make the arrangements, Valdés recalls. "I was acting exclusively as an academic. . . . When I was at Notre Dame—the State Department invited me to Washington to talk with various people as a Socialist leader. So I went to Washington and then to New York. And at precisely the same time, my father [Gabriel Valdés, then president of Chile's Christian Democratic Party] was invited by the State Department to come to Washington. When I went to see the Sawyer/Miller Group, they showed me the Philippines campaign, and what they were doing, I think, in Ecuador for a candidate there. Well, I was fascinated with the idea, and they proposed a formula. They said, 'Look, we would like to go to Chile, but we need an intermediary there. So we're not going to charge for the trip. We'll go to Chile, and we'll explain to you on the ground what we do. Then we'll tell [your people] we are interested in doing a survey in Chile and that we would like to see what other kinds of social research you have.' And that's when I first knew of the existence of focus groups. Until then, I knew nothing about them."[40]

At about the same time, Valdés explains, the idea of establishing a joint operation with other private research centers to transmit the new approaches to Chile's opposition was emerging: "But just as I returned to Chile from Notre Dame, I ran into Ernesto Tironi (who's a good friend of mine), and he said, 'Look, you should get together with my brother Eugenio, because he's been thinking about doing something similar, and I think he would be very interested in what you have to say.' So I got together with him (I knew him because we had been exiled together in Mexico), and I told him about it, and from that came the idea, with Eugenio, to associate SUR with ILET. SUR was basically Eugenio Tironi, Carlos Vergara, and Javier Martínez—with [Guillermo] Campero, Diego Portales and me, to organize a team of people that would concern itself with carrying out surveys and designing some kind of team to cooperate with politicians on the issue of the plebiscite. That was in 1987."

The three institutions complemented each other nicely, according to Valdés: "CED provided basically a strong link with the world of politics, because Gabriel Valdés was there, because Edgardo Boeninger had been there, because CED was close to the Christian Democrats (my father was still president). Then what ILET provided was, frankly, my link with the Sawyer/Miller Group, and the idea of jointly managing the operation. . . . And the third component was SUR, which had three stupendous social scientists, and what's more was dedicated to working with the poor and youth groups that we also wanted to cover."[41]

In Chile, staff from the Sawyer/Miller Group spent three days in discussions and seminars at ILET, with the participation of social scientists from other private research centers and a few opposition political leaders. The result was an agreement that they would send to Chile one person who would teach CIS to carry out focus groups, would carry out a national survey jointly with CIS, and, finally, would provide some orientation regarding political advertising.

There remained the question of how to finance these new activities. "They [Sawyer/Miller] proposed that I contact someone I didn't know— a man named George Soros, whose identity I learned just about the time I went to see him. And I went to see George Soros in New York, . . . together with someone from Sawyer/Miller and Mariano Fernández [then a CED staff member]. They gave us approximately $30,000, which we were then going to give to the Sawyer/Miller Group, because we were not going to receive anything for our own institutions. This was done in the name of CIS, that is, there was no political backing—and what's more we hadn't any."[42]

With funds in hand, CIS and Sawyer/Miller organized, in August 1987, the first focus group ever carried out for political purposes in Chile.

(A focus group is a set of in-depth interviews designed to assess opinions and attitudes.) The findings were presented the next month at the first meeting of the Technical Committee for Free Elections, which had just been established to advise opposition parties in their campaign to force the regime to hold free elections. In November, CIS and Sawyer/Miller conducted a national political opinion survey, and, in January 1988, representatives from Sawyer/Miller returned to present a full report, along with detailed recommendations for strategy, to opposition leaders.[43] CIS continued its activities throughout 1988.

The assistance CIS received from Sawyer/Miller did not extend beyond January 1988, and thereafter CIS began carrying out political consulting functions, as it interpreted them, on its own. Valdés explains the shift: "The role of the Sawyer/Miller Group cannot be overblown, because the truth is that they were there. But they themselves . . . told us at a certain point . . . , 'We don't have anything more to teach you.' They realized that the people they were talking with had Ph.Ds., were doctors in sociology, like Tironi, knew how to do surveys, like Vergara. . . . Once we learned the techniques, . . . we understood the domestic political situation better than they did. So a situation developed where they didn't come back—they left. We spent the money we'd received, and good-bye. The technical team came twice . . . and there was a third visit by directors [to present the conclusions and recommendations]. So all the publicity we later developed for the plebiscite campaign had nothing to do with Sawyer/Miller. For us they were important because they gave us a vision of the role we could play as advisors to the political world" (29 May 1991).

By early 1988, CIS had absorbed the lessons taught by Sawyer/Miller and was functioning on its own. It continued to carry out surveys and focus groups with funds raised from abroad, and it consolidated its role as an informal but effective source of strategy and modern campaign techniques to the democratic opposition. It provided the core ideas that led to the plebiscite victory and became the harbinger of a new approach to politics in Chile. It would continue to function right through the presidential elections of 1989.

The Technical Committee for Free Elections

At almost precisely the same time, the Technical Committee for Free Elections, to whom CIS's first focus group findings had been presented, originated in the political parties. Another important initiative crucially shaped by opposition intellectuals, the committee was established in September 1987 under the leadership of Christian Democratic political leader (and accomplished intellectual) Genaro Arriagada to advise the three groups comprising the Free Elections Movement. Formed a few months after CIS and incorporating several of the principal CIS members, the committee was nonetheless a separate undertaking. In March 1988 it would be transformed into the Technical Committee for the No, which masterminded the opposition's plebiscite campaign.[44]

The Technical Committee for Free Elections was established by the political leaders who made up the Free Elections Campaign to help devise and coordinate their strategies. Directed formally by politicians, it was dominated at the technical level by intellectuals. Arriagada invited some of the opposition's best-trained and most accomplished social scientists to serve on the committee, including Angel Flisfisch, Ignacio Walker, Carlos Huneeus, Juan Gabriel Valdés, Eugenio Tironi, Manuel Antonio Garretón, and Carlos Vergara. The opposition was, at that time, firmly committed to pushing for free elections and to reaching agreement on a set of issues it called the "trilogy" (a single presidential candidate, program of government, and electoral coalition) to contest the Pinochet regime. The committee's task was to "generate the broad ideas and lines of strategy" for the Free Elections Movement.[45]

In late September, the group repaired to Olmué, a small town north of Santiago, to develop its ideas. It quickly realized that it disagreed fundamentally with opposition strategy. Instead of a campaign to force the regime to hold free elections, it favored dropping the free elections campaign and participating in the plebiscite. Instead of struggling to reach agreement on a common candidate and program of government, it favored agreeing on only one thing: saying no to Pinochet. Instead of dwelling on past offenses committed by the regime, it favored emphasizing the benefits that would accompany a return to full democracy.[46]

As Carlos Vergara recalls, "These were our first disagreements with the political leadership. . . . We said we must participate in the plebiscite" (28 January 1991). Thus the committee decided almost immediately to recommend abolishing the objective it had been formed to pursue— the campaign for free elections—and replacing it with a campaign to vote no in the plebiscite.

The group based its conclusions principally on academic analysis, and particularly on the findings of political attitude surveys and focus groups that academics had begun to carry out. Survey research had been indicating since 1985 that people were tired of street demonstrations and placed a relatively high value on public order. Results from focus group interviews carried out the previous month by the CIS consortium added a new element: profound and widespread fear among the population. People feared unemployment, disorder, repression, politics, and the future. That pervasive fear generated feelings of vulnerability, anguish, and personal weakness. As Eugenio Tironi, a key figure in carrying out the

focus groups, interpreted the findings, "With fear, people don't act according to their will. Thus rational appeals to conscience are not enough,
and may even be counter-productive."[47]
Fear was accompanied by frustration, humiliation and skepticism,
generating widespread apathy and withdrawal among the population.
People were skeptical of all political initiatives and profoundly pessimistic about the future. Characterizing the focus group results, Tironi
wrote, "The basic longing of Chileans is to live in a society where, in
place of fear, they find a sense of unity and transcendence" (22).
In the view of the Technical Committee, these findings posed real
problems for the opposition. An apathetic and skeptical population did
not augur well for a complex strategy aimed at forcing the regime into
holding free elections. The average citizen had little stomach for conflict,
and little confidence that the opposition's free elections campaign would
improve conditions.
Thus a different political approach was necessary. The opposition
had to adjust its strategy to the mood of the people. "We had to provide
a channel for this—to reconcile the political objective, which was to return to democracy, with the way in which the population was incorporated into national life. It was a very traumatic form [of incorporation]
with much fear, and it would not tolerate another initiative based on the
concept of overthrowing the regime" (Vergara, 28 January 1991). Instead
of exhorting people to fight for a new transition scenario, the opposition
had to offer them hope and dignity.[48]
The plebiscite, the group concluded, could play that role. "The plebiscite . . . is the kind of event that [can make] Chileans leave behind their
current subjective state, and act on the basis of their longings," Tironi
wrote. But "the attitude, in confronting the plebiscite, cannot be marked
by complaint, denunciation and skepticism. If it is, then it will deepen
[feelings of] impotence and fear—the psychosocial bases of apathy. Thus
it is urgent to break with the attitude of many opposition militants, who
have become professional denouncers. To do away with apathy, those
militants will have to transform themselves into prophets of hope, into
communicators of the new attitude: The plebiscite is an opportunity to
affirm the dignity of Chileans and to show the power of the people."
These interpretations of the initial focus group findings turned out to
be remarkably durable. They staked out a strategic position that was later
accepted by opposition leaders and maintained throughout the plebiscite
campaign.[49]
The Technical Committee also decided that the opposition's longstanding belief that it must reach agreement on a presidential candidate,
a program of government, and a formal coalition was wrongheaded and

had to be abandoned. Instead, it recommended that opposition parties seek only an informal agreement to work together to defeat Pinochet in the plebiscite and defer all other issues until later. Reaching agreement on anything else, the committee reasoned, would generate conflict and merely aggravate the voters' aversion to political disorder. "We argued," recalls Arriagada, "that a coalition around the No was the only possible base for unity, because this wasn't the time to be discussing programs and, even less, a presidential candidate. This was the hour of the No" (8 March 1991).

The group also decided that the significant decentralization Chile had experienced since the coup required politicians to change their approach to political campaigning. The transfer of many responsibilities to municipal governments, and the shift of most economic initiative to the private sector, had created a new political dynamic that was less responsive to traditional reliance on declarations by national leaders from the country's capital. Instead, a new approach keyed to local initiatives rather than national directives was necessary. As Arriagada recalls, "Traditional politicians were very convinced that the struggle revolved around their opinions on pages C2 and C3 of *El Mercurio* [the country's leading newspaper], but—this group of social scientists said that the fight was where they weren't. . . . So we recommended placing the accent at the local level, by creating community committees, et cetera" (8 March 1991).

Indeed, the contrast between the positions of political leaders and intellectuals on many strategy issues was striking. As Arriagada describes it: "In politics, intellectuals normally tend to complicate things, . . . emphasizing abstruse programs and difficult formulas. Here . . . curiously, intellectuals contributed brutally to simplifying politics and moving it toward much more concrete issues. That is, while politicians believed that the country wanted heroic things, intellectuals were arguing that what the country wanted was a little happiness, peace, modest programs, security, and the recovery of minimal dignity. The politicians believed we could keep struggling for free elections, a common program of governance, a common candidate—all very complex—while the intellectuals were saying, 'No, the only thing you should ask them to do is to vote no.' And that is a very interesting fact."

Thus the committee members returned to Santiago determined to convince political leaders to drop the free elections idea entirely and participate in Pinochet's plebiscite. "The Christian Democrats were arguing over whether to legalize themselves as a party or not [under the new political parties law]—suggesting participation in the plebiscite was a kind of treason. . . . The Socialists were thinking of forming a Party for Democracy. The great debate was over whether to enter into the [regime's] institutional framework or not. . . . We said, 'Let's do it. Everything has failed, we've got a plebiscite, it's an opportunity to overcome the fear.' . . . We were six or seven technicians—intellectuals from CIE-PLAN, from SUR. We told ourselves that on New Year's Eve we must celebrate with the political class by announcing a decision to participate in the plebiscite" (28 January 1991).

Moreover, the committee had already begun to sketch out the details of a plebiscite campaign. As Vergara recalls: "Not only did we say we had to participate in the plebiscite, we said we have to do it in a certain way. We had a prototype campaign ready when the agreement was signed on February 2. The central pillars of the campaign were based on that design" (28 January 1991).

Communicating the New Approaches to Politicians

Beginning in August 1987, then, two overlapping groups dominated by intellectuals—CIS and the Technical Committee for Free Elections—undertook a systematic campaign to teach opposition politicians about modern campaign techniques and to make the case for participating in the plebiscite. Through informal conversations and a series of formal meetings, committee members presented the findings from the focus groups and surveys and their implications for political strategy to political leaders.

Some part of those efforts, such as myriad conversations with politicians in settings ranging from party dinners to dinner parties, were informal and based on personal relationships, following traditional ways of discussing politics in Chile. But another set of efforts, organized by CIS, was more formal and represented a new approach to transferring technology from the academy to politics. The CIS initiative revolved around a Political Analysis Committee that regularly invited leaders from the principal opposition parties to gather at CED, usually over lunch, and discuss the knowledge being generated by social scientists. These sessions were not, as Sunkel points out, "instances of decision."[50] Rather, they were opportunities for social scientists to get their message across. They represented a new and deliberate attempt by intellectuals to convert their findings into political strategy.

CIS member Carlos Vergara explains the logic behind the meetings:

Insofar as you propose to contribute to orienting the campaign, you must necessarily modify—or better yet, invent—a link between your output of knowledge and the political leadership. Because in fact the people who direct political campaigns are the politicians, not the technocrats. So the problem is how to convey to the political leadership what one thinks ought to be done. In general, old guard politicians are not people to whom you can give 150 tables, have them read them, and draw the conclusions. What we did was consider ourselves a kind of "public service utility," not in the service of any particular political party, but in the service of the democratic cause in general. And what we did was convene a group of political leaders . . . and we explained to them what we were about and what we wanted to do. We met with them twice a month . . . where, in tandem with other work, we provided analysis and general recommendations on strategy. . . . This was very well received, and we kept doing it even after the plebiscite, because it generated an instance of very horizontal discussion . . . between technocracy . . . and political leadership. And secondly, it was an absolutely pluralist instance.[51]

The meetings of the Political Analysis Committee were held at CED, because CED had developed substantial credibility among political leaders and because CED's founder, former Christian Democratic party president Gabriel Valdés, strongly supported the CIS initiative. The committee invited leaders from all opposition political parties, including the Nationalists, Christian Democrats, Almeyda Socialists, Humanists, Radicals, Social Democrats, and moderate Socialists. As Eugenio Tironi recalls: "Starting in August or September 1987 until the plebiscite, we had a weekly lunch at CED with the opposition political establishment— perhaps fifteen or twenty leaders. . . . We would prepare briefs on what kinds of speeches to give, how to appeal to the undecided voter, et cetera."[52]

The meetings were serious technical sessions on political strategy and campaigning, led by academics from CIS and the Technical Committee. They were based on short papers, seldom more than four or five pages, summarizing recent analysis and written in a style calculated to appeal to political and social leaders. An early paper, for example, posed six fundamental questions for the opposition, answering each and justifying each answer, all in just over two double-spaced pages.[53] They represented a deliberate departure by intellectuals from standard intellectual output. "We were clear from the beginning that this was a kind of militancy in a larger cause, but over a limited time. We didn't define it as intellectual work. We defined it as our contribution, as intellectuals, to a particular political process" (Vergara, 28 January 1991).

These efforts reached top party leaders. As Gabriel Valdés recalls: "I remember seeing all the party chiefs . . . sitting back there, and Martínez giving them classes in politics. Classes! There were people who had been senators, deputies, sitting here in classes, all taking notes. It was very remarkable" (1 March 1991).[54] Similarly, Tironi recalls making his case to

Patricio Aylwin, then president of the Christian Democratic party: "I remember a meeting with Patricio Aylwin in December—just the two of us for a whole morning—showing him the data from the surveys and reading the memorandum I had written to explain why I thought we had to throw ourselves into the No [the plebiscite]" (19 December 1990).

Vergara provides a sense of how political leaders responded to the CIS meetings: "We convened a first lunch, and what happened, to our surprise, was that everyone showed up. Then after the lunch the only thing they wanted was that we repeat it. In other words, the demand was generated immediately, and we went on carrying out surveys, preparing reports and sharing them with these kinds of people. . . . There was a terrible tension with many other leaders to attend, and we could not, for reasons of space, increase the invitations. But it was a group that generated much influence and in that sense, we were the ones who took the initiative to generate that type of relationship, and it was defined in those terms" (28 January 1991).

The meetings emphasized the implications for political strategy of the survey and focus group studies being carried out by CIS, CERC, and FLACSO, and the lessons learned from the Sawyer/Miller Group. They stressed the population's pervasive sense of fear, its lack of interest in the free elections campaign, and its strong rejection of political disorder. They also analyzed Pinochet's support, concluding that he could be defeated in a fair plebiscite and with the right campaign. They began laying out the kinds of appeals that would have to be included in a successful plebiscite campaign.

In part because they were a completely new element, the focus groups appear to have had a particularly important impact. As Foxley recalls, "That was totally new. . . . It was a decisive, decisive element. It was fascinating. To understand what people were really feeling . . . that was what a focus group gave you in contrast to a survey. It provided a much richer texture. . . . From there came the theme of weakness, for example, as a central theme that later permeated the entire campaign. That was fantastic" (14 March 1991).

The sophisticated efforts by CIS and the Technical Committee to transform findings from surveys and focus groups into political strategy were unprecedented in Chile. Vergara's recollection illustrates the typically high level of analysis employed: "The problem was . . . how to express politically what was already present subconsciously in the people. It was almost a problem of political engineering—how to link the plebiscite with democracy—because the opposition had been linking the plebiscite with dictatorship. . . . 'We must win the plebiscite to get free elections'" (28 January 1991).

Doing that effectively required making political sense out of the confused and often contradictory impressions the surveys were picking up. Vergara explained that "what the intellectuals did, I think, was to make a clean copy of what probably many already had in draft and didn't know very well how to express. And much of the population was also in this draft state. At the middle levels of leadership, there was [the idea] that accepting the legitimacy of Pinochet's institutional arrangements was an act of moral treason and, what's more, would lead to defeat because of the precedent of the 1980 plebiscite, where the opposition lost and many said that Pinochet stole the votes and there was fraud."

Their conclusion was that the plebiscite could be won if the opposition adapted its strategy to the mood of the voters. Vergara said: "But there was an opening. And that feat of original conversion was accomplished by a group of intellectuals who said, 'We've got to link the plebiscite with democracy and not continue to insist on linking the plebiscite with dictatorship.' We were crazy, because the plebiscite would be held regardless, we had no chance of preventing it, the entire opposition would be caught without having registered to vote, Pinochet would win, and we would end up having a dictatorship until 1997."

A few sessions in early 1988 included staff from the Sawyer/Miller Group, who presented conclusions from the survey and focus groups they had carried out with CIS. Juan Gabriel Valdés recalls that "there were two meetings with people from Sawyer/Miller, that were really spectacular. . . . We made a joint presentation, I would start, then Tironi would talk, then the people from Sawyer/Miller . . . said: 'This country has cancer. This cancer is fear, and if you don't succeed in overcoming that fear, the plebiscite is lost. Therefore, your whole objective must be overcoming the fear in the people, because you are drawing a conclusion that is false—that if you register people in the voter rolls they will go and vote no. The people may register, but later the shift to going and voting No is something that requires a special courage, and if you don't work on that shift you're going to find out that people are not going to vote or will vote yes, or will abstain" (29 May 1991).

These presentations were a novelty, in the sense that they were the work of political consultants rather than academics and embodied a different approach to communicating survey findings. Juan Gabriel Valdés goes on: "One of the academics from Sawyer/Miller . . . gave a talk that had a tremendous impact on the politicians present. . . . He said: 'Chile is like a theater stage on which there's a man who has been there for many years with a steel bar, and every time someone from the public has raised his head, he has struck and killed him. And soon people are terrorized . . . , and then the man says he is going to bring out a box and people are going to express their opinion on a piece of paper. If the first man who goes up on the stage grabs the steel bar and starts hitting the big man with it, people are not going to dare to go up on stage, because they know very well that the big man is going to start hitting them again with the steel bar, and the game will be up. So the first guy who goes up on stage has to greet the man with the steel bar and tell him how happy he is with the decision. That way the rest will dare to go up on stage.'"

Quite apart from its substance, the style of the Sawyer/Miller presentation established new horizons for the CIS group. As Valdés continues: "That logic of nonconfrontation was very important because it gave basic examples, . . . the political world began to understand it, and, more importantly, something that was fascinating to us began to happen: we realized how we were seducing the political world." CIS began to understand the role political consultants play, and to adopt it.

Politicians did not always agree with the recommendations of CIS and the Technical Committee, however. The findings from the surveys and focus groups were surprising to many and often contradicted strongly held positions regarding the mood of the country and appropriate transition strategy. As Vergara recalls: "In December, 1987 there was a big Seminar for Free Elections, with delegates from the Free Elections Movement from all over Chile, at the Spanish Circle [a Santiago meeting center]. We, as the Technical Committee, were speakers. We . . . generated a tremendous discussion. I would say that over half the people there, from across the opposition, were against participating in the plebiscite" (28 January 1991). Recalling a similar meeting held at CED around the same time, Fernández describes the reaction of political leaders as "a scandal, because at that time it meant entering into Pinochet's Constitution—all those things we'd been repudiating all our lives."[55] The dominant mood among political leaders in late 1987 still favored pressuring the regime to change its transition arrangements and resisted participation in the plebiscite.

A few months later, on February 2, 1988, they changed their approach. Thirteen opposition parties formed the "Concertación para el No" to contest Pinochet in the plebiscite. They agreed to work together in a common plebiscite campaign. And they asked the same technical committee that had worked so hard, under Arriagada's leadership, for a new approach to develop the No campaign. The opposition had fundamentally altered its transition strategy. It had finally accepted the regime's arrangements.

Impact on Opposition Strategy

How important were intellectuals in the opposition's decision to change its transition strategy? Extraordinarily important. To be sure, the decision was influenced in complex ways by a variety of factors and was ultimately made by politicians, not intellectuals. Time was passing. The plebiscite was going to be held whether the opposition participated or not. Had it not acted in a timely fashion, urging its supporters to register, legalizing its parties, and devising a unified campaign, the opposition would probably have forfeited any chance of winning. The regime's timetable, therefore, forced the opposition to make choices.

But intellectuals crucially informed those choices. Edgardo Boeninger, easily the most important figure in the opposition's deliberations, comments on the complicated causal pattern that led to a change in approach: "It wasn't so simple as saying there were two groups, the politicians who believed white and the intellectuals who believed black . . . and finally the intellectuals convinced the politicians it should be black. No. Everything evolved. . . . The roots of the opposition position regarding the viable political strategy came from people two steps removed from the action, and the change in strategy probably would not have been possible had there not been, two steps behind the daily action, a center of reflection that politicians looked to for help. There was an intercommunication in which reasoning, analysis, daily experience, successes, and failures were changing perceptions and generating logically a consensus." He continues: "The real decisions were taken ultimately by politicians. For example, the decision of the DC [Christian Democrats] was taken in a national junta in which the political directorate, even though infiltrated, as in my case, by intellectuals, was a group elected by a national junta of political delegates who decided on a certain path. It's not as if you can say that this or that contribution came from intellectuals. That would be pretentious" (29 January 1991).[56]

Boeninger's emphasis on complexity, however, contrasts with the comment of sociologist Javier Martínez, who participated extensively in the discussions: "This time intellectuals played under their own colors. . . . The decision was practically imposed by opposition sociologists and political scientists on the politicians." From his perspective, intellectuals were crucial in recognizing the viable strategy and in making their case to politicians; they made a major difference. "What I remember from the first meetings we had with politicians was their great resistance to the idea of entering Pinochet's plebiscite. Their argument was, 'That's something Pinochet wants to impose on us and we must avoid it. If we participate Pinochet will defeat us and we'll be left with no alternative for opposing him afterwards.' Most of them had no idea whether people would vote for the No. It was completely confusing terrain for them. Nor did they have any idea who the opposition messages reached, and who they didn't. They didn't know who their audience was. . . . And then perhaps the most decisive element was an avalanche of public opinion studies that appeared around September 1987—from FLACSO, SUR, CERC, et cetera" (6 March 1991).[57]

Another participant, Eugenio Tironi, takes a position somewhere between Boeninger's and Martínez's but stresses the role of intellectuals: "I agree with Boeninger. But I also think that Boeninger fails to emphasize the role of people like him . . . who provide the link . . . between the intellectual world and the political world. . . . The decision to change strategies was taken by politicians but instigated, stimulated and motivated precisely by people like Boeninger. And a Boeninger took his arguments, his strategy, principally from the intellectual world" (20 March 1991).

Several other key participants in the deliberations credit intellectuals with a major role, even while noting that politicians made the final decisions. The leader of the first free elections committee, Sergio Molina, emphasizes the contributions of intellectuals in bringing reason and realism to the debates over strategy: "It's in the specific things where they had influence. . . . For example, entering into the Constitution [and] legalizing the political parties, specifically in those two expressions, the influence of intellectuals was very important. It forced people to reason and explain and justify and carry out studies and talk with leaders and introduce . . . a rationality. I would say there was more realism among the intellectuals, much more realism than in political discussion at the party level or the party leadership level" (13 March 1991).

Social Democratic leader Mario Papi stresses the role that surveys played in informing political leaders who otherwise had little reliable information on the mood of the people: "The fact is that, for lack of other kinds of information—because we were kind of acting in the shadows—it was difficult for us to measure what the population was feeling. For a political leader, even visiting a shantytown was risky, serious. So at that time, when politics was groping, these surveys . . . became powerful elements of argument. . . . They were . . . little lanterns in the night, let's say, that helped provide a foundation to political debate that was otherwise based on sniffing the air. . . . In that sense, they were a very, very important element" (7 March 1991).

Indeed, the introduction by intellectuals of modern political campaigning techniques—particularly surveys and focus groups—had a major impact on political strategy. They accurately mapped out the mood of the country, enabling opposition politicians to supplement beliefs and intuition with reliable, empirical information. They provided evidence that a strategy based on protests and struggle was unpopular and would not work. Because of the polls, as Socialist leader Ricardo Lagos recalls, "One began to realize that the strategy of confrontation and rupture was not the most appropriate" (13 March 1991). Similarly, Gabriel Valdés remembers: "They carried out the studies on what people thought and reached the conclusion that here the big problem was fear. This was very decisive, for never again did we think in terms of protests" (1 March 1991).

They also helped the opposition see that, with a different strategy, it might win the plebiscite. "The opinion surveys," in the words of Alejandro Foxley, "had the virtue of socializing the idea that it was possible to defeat Pinochet. And that was a dynamizing element for people who were deciding unconsciously whether to join the democratic struggle against Pinochet or not. The worst enemy of a struggle against a dictatorship is the lack of information—knowing or not knowing if the number of those who oppose the dictator is large or small. The surveys clarified that" (14 March 1991).

The surveys and focus groups, in Brunner's view, helped to moderate opposition strategy. "The work carried out through surveys by centers and some group of those we call intellectuals was, I think, the final factor that convinced the political class that a change of strategy was necessary, and that . . . they could win. The great factor that was behind the moderation of the transition in all its initial stages was the surveys. Intellectuals moderated the political class, to a great degree, through the surveys" (28 February 1991).

Intellectuals also played an important role in helping the opposition think through the form their collaboration should take, once the decision to participate in the plebiscite had been made. As Eugenio Tironi recalls, "Now a fundamental step here was the generation of this concept of 'La Concertación.' Historically, coalitions in Chile have been based on the concept of unity, that is, sharing principles, ideologies, and programs. . . . [We argued] for collaborating simply around a minimum objective: the triumph of the No. That would be our only commitment. . . . That would be better because it would attract a broader spectrum of voters—this common action around the No. Thus unity was dysfunctional to our objective" (19 December 1990).

Here the debate was often fierce—on whether the opposition coalition should be broad or narrow, and on whether they should agree on the trilogy before the plebiscite. Based on their analysis, intellectuals argued effectively for a broad coalition around just one issue: defeating Pinochet. Tironi continues: "This was the great debate—with the Chris-

tian Democrats, in some sense, as the sector that said that we had to agree
on a program, then on a candidate, and then we'll go united to the No.
We said, from our position, that the question was exactly the inverse.
Let's agree exclusively on the No and leave the rest open, because that
way we can include more people. The more dissimilar we are, the more
voters we will get for this common objective. I think that, even though
I may be guilty of false modesty, or of no modesty . . . that our analytical
sessions that ran between August and December 1987 were very influential—on Genaro [Arriagada], on the Technical Committee, on [Ga-
briel] Valdés, on [Patricio] Aylwin himself, on Ricardo Lagos."

And of course, the intellectuals took the initiative to bestow their
new ideas upon politicians. Through an elaborate process of seduction
that included bringing U.S. political consultants to Chile, convening
politicians for luncheon meetings, preparing specialized documents, and
generally infiltrating the political process, they engaged often incredu-
lous political leaders in debate over transition strategy. They were never
invited by political parties to carry out these activities. They supplied
information for which, initially, there was no demand.

Intellectuals, then, played a major role in causing Chile's democratic
opposition to change its strategy between late 1986 and early 1988. They
provided new ideas, information, techniques, and advice. And they persuaded politicians to listen to them. Clearly, the opposition's decision
to shift from demanding free elections to participating in the plebiscite
was made by politicians. But just as clearly, intellectuals played a crucial
role in proposing, informing, justifying, and promoting that decision.

Designing the Plebiscite Campaign

The opposition's decision on 2 February 1988 to form a coalition and
contest Pinochet in the plebiscite came relatively late in the regime's transition scenario and left little time to develop a campaign. To be sure,
many opposition parties had decided by mid-1987 to call for massive
voter registration, and a few had taken the initial steps to legalize themselves under the regime's new political parties law. But agreement on
campaign strategy, and the establishment of a campaign structure, had
just begun. Although the government had not yet set a date for the plebiscite, it was required by the Constitution to hold it by the end of the
year and needed to provide only sixty days' advance notice. Thus theo-
retically the Concertación could have faced a plebiscite just a few months
after it came into being. It had to shift quickly from spurning the plebiscite to competing effectively in it.

To do that, the thirteen (and later sixteen) parties of the Concertación established a Command for the No headed by a directorate that represented its major groupings. The directorate transformed the Technical Committee for Free Elections, which had helped engineer the decision to take part in the plebiscite, into the Technical Committee for the No with the same membership (some of Chile's most accomplished social scientists) and the same director (Genaro Arriagada).[58]

Because the opposition had agreed to run a single, joint campaign, the Command for the No was responsible for all decisions regarding campaign strategy. Significantly, however, it delegated most of that responsibility to the Technical Committee. Formally, of course, the directorate made the final strategy decisions. But in fact it accepted virtually all the recommendations made by Arriagada's Technical Committee. Indeed, on those occasions when politicians questioned the committee's recommendations, the leaders of the Command for the No often decided against the politicians.[59] Thus the Technical Committee for the No—a group led by an intellectual-politician and dominated by some of the country's leading social scientists—became the architect of the No campaign. Its strategy became the Concertación's strategy; its tactics became the Concertación's tactics. The campaign was designed by a group consisting principally of intellectuals.

Participants in the No campaign regularly mention the extraordinary influence exercised by intellectuals through the Technical Committee. In the words of Socialist leader Enrique Correa, it "comprised the best of Chilean social scientists, and their suggestions were the base for the decisions taken by political leaders" (8 March 1991).[60] Similarly, Social Democratic leader Hernán Vodanovic states that "there was a delegation of the capacity . . . to resolve all political operations from party leadership to this committee. . . . Thus the importance of Arriagada [and] of what the committee was doing exceeded the importance of the parties" (15 March 1991). For his part, Arriagada maintains that "the executive secretary's office basically gave the intellectuals a fundamental role— very, very fundamental. Thus the management of the campaign was highly technical" (8 March 1991).

Political leaders ceded such extraordinary influence to intellectuals for a variety of reasons. They had, after all, been sidelined for nearly fifteen years and still possessed only limited organizational capacity. Their experience with political campaigning was old and based on sharply different conditions. Their repeated attempts, since 1983, to unseat Pinochet had failed miserably. Several had come from the ranks of intellectuals and maintained strong ties with the academy.[61] They were, therefore, uncertain how best to contest the regime in the plebiscite, and willing to listen to some modern, technical advice.

For their part, intellectuals had, over a decade, developed substantial credibility among politicians. It was their initiative that brought modern political campaigning techniques to Chile. They persuaded politicians that the new approaches had merit. And they alone knew how to apply them. Politicians, in fact, had almost no capacity to select and apply the new campaign techniques. Thus between 1986 and 1988, intellectuals held a monopoly on the new politics. They had created a demand only they could supply.

Intellectuals achieved significant influence on the campaign as well because of the scrupulous efforts by Arriagada and others to respect the role and authority of politicians. The intellectuals who dominated the Technical Committee for the No were careful to avoid threatening the positions held by political leaders. As Arriagada recalls: "I always maintained that the Technical Committee had to distinguish between authority and influence. If we wanted to appear every day in the newspapers, the politicians would get frightened. We didn't have to appear in the papers. The Technical Committee had its own influence, and so we had to respect the domains [of others]. The Technical Committee had to be very influential, but public prominence would awaken jealousy among politicians and, consequently . . . diminish its influence" (8 March 1991).[62] Intellectuals sought to educate politicians rather than to supplant them—to help rather than to compete.

Thus the plebiscite campaign marked the emergence of a new political technocracy in Chile. It pioneered a modern, scientific approach to politics. The bulk of campaign strategy came not from politicians but from technocrats associated with the Technical Committee for the No. The directorate of the Command for the No became, in Vergara's view, a "highly efficient channel of communication" between the broader political leadership and the "intellectual technicians" of the Technical Committee. "These leaders had the wisdom to rely heavily on this team of people to direct the entire process of the 1988 campaign. And that technical team, if you think about it carefully, was in its majority intellectual. Angel Flisfisch is an intellectual; Eugenio Tironi—intellectual; Ignacio Walker—intellectual; Genaro Arriagada—in between; Manuel Antonio Garretón, et cetera" (28 January 1991).[63]

The result was what Arriagada has called the "technicalization of the campaign."[64] Political strategy was based less on ideology and intuition, and more on pragmatism and scientific analysis. The process began to depend heavily on a corps of specialized social scientists and media professionals who were not themselves politicians. "Politicians," as Correa observes, "no longer made their decisions based only on their dreams or their obsessions, but also . . . on surveys and scientific inquiry into what people wanted, or felt, or had. That was very modern" (8 March 1991). A political consulting function began to take root in Chile.

One manifestation of this new approach was the deliberate decision to give the campaign an upbeat, positive theme rather than to denounce the military regime for its outrages. That decision was based solidly on focus group results showing fear and passivity to be so widespread that even many who strongly opposed Pinochet might not vote in the plebiscite. "The strategy of the No consisted basically in formulating messages and organizing events that, instead of reinforcing conflictual and disintegrative tendencies dominant for years in Chilean society, responded to repressed desires for reconciliation and social cohesion."[65]

That approach ran counter to conventional wisdom and to the reflexes of many politicians. As Vodanovic recalls: "The traditional left, along with other traditional groups, wanted a campaign of denunciation. And many, particularly SUR, said no, what people want is joy, hope, security, pluralism, reconciliation" (15 March 1991).[66] Although a majority already appeared to favor the No, it was not clear how many would be willing to vote. "People need a future," Tironi wrote after carrying out the first focus groups with Sawyer/Miller staffers in 1987, "but fear the possibility that it will awaken the traumas of the past."[67]

Thus the campaign resisted the impulse of many politicians to focus on conflict and recriminations, deciding instead to accentuate the positive. The campaign's fundamental objective was "to overcome an attitude of resignation that was born out of fear and skepticism, so that people would act in accord with their opinions."[68] It incorporated a few of the themes suggested by politicians, but with a low profile and in terms calculated to avoid the fear of conflict so common among voters.[69] The campaign sought principally to shift voters into a new, optimistic frame of mind by stressing the exhilaration and happiness that would accompany a No victory. The campaign slogan became "Joy Is Coming" (*La Alegría Ya Viene*).

Another manifestation of the new approach was the campaign's strategy to persuade those who opposed the regime to register to vote. A CIS survey indicated in April 1988 that only 59 percent of those favoring the No had registered, compared with 79 percent of those who favored the Yes. Had the vote taken place in April, the Yes would probably have won. Further, the survey showed that the difference stemmed principally from under-registration by urban youth. CIS promptly carried out several focus groups that revealed profound resignation among urban youth, causing them to take refuge in a kind of "magic thought" in which they were willing to oppose the regime through armed struggle but not through the ballot box. The committee concluded it must make a special effort to convince this group to register, with appeals that stressed their historic opportunity to overthrow Pinochet in the plebiscite, and the "heroic" aspect of doing so. That effort was successful, and registration rates among urban youth soon caught up with those in the rest of the country.[70]

The surveys and focus groups also enabled the opposition to identify distinct segments of the electorate, targeting those that were least certain how they would vote, and developing appropriate messages for each.[71] Thereby, the No Command was able to monitor the status of its support and concentrate resources where they were most needed. That ability proved particularly important in winning over the undecided voters, who comprised a third of the electorate right up until just before the plebiscite took place. CIS determined that the group was predominantly female, with relatively low levels of formal education, but that two subgroups—men and well-educated women—were most likely to decide in favor of the No and thus deserved priority in the campaign. It also revealed that the principal barrier to winning these subgroups was their image of the opposition as divided, incompetent, and partisan. Those findings caused the opposition to target those two subgroups and to alter its campaign at the symbolic level, promoting an image of unity, organization, and moderation. Subsequent studies showed those efforts to be largely successful.[72]

Yet another manifestation of the new politics was the opposition's television campaign (*la franja*). The campaign was devised by a Creativity Committee of volunteers composed principally of academic social scientists and media professionals based at Santiago's advertising firms. Although the regime permitted only limited access to television for campaign purposes (fifteen minutes each night beginning at 11 P.M. during the month before the plebiscite), most observers credit the No Command's TV spots with a crucial role in the victory. And indeed, in surveys done after the plebiscite the No's TV campaign was rated as significantly more credible, entertaining, and positive than that of the Yes.[73]

The spots were simple, creative, and enormously effective. They favored strong, clear images over verbal information. They avoided radical and aggressive messages, even in the face of sharp attacks by the TV spots of the Yes campaign. Instead, they emphasized the dignity, order, and happiness in store if the No won. Initially, they featured people and scenes from everyday Chilean life, leaving politicians out entirely. When political leaders were introduced, about halfway through the television campaign, their presentations were staged so as to counteract the negative feelings focus groups had shown them to arouse among voters.[74] The tone of the TV campaign thus reflected more the culture of television than it did Chile's traditional culture of politics. Many spots had no explicit political message at all, relying instead on scenes and understated symbols to address concerns identified by the CIS surveys.

Not surprisingly, that approach generated protests from some political leaders. Ricardo Lagos, for example, is reported to have charged that the TV campaign might win an award at the Cannes Film Festival yet lose the plebiscite. Many politicians argued for a more aggressive, explicitly political approach. Those concerns led to negotiations within the directorate of the No Command and to occasional modifications. But the fundamental thrust remained unchanged.[75] The show still belonged, as Vergara asserts, to the intellectuals: "The month of television publicity was very decisive and managed by intellectuals that included Eugenio Tironi, Juan Gabriel Valdés, and Javier Martínez. And that was done in spite of, to put it in slightly extreme terms, the political parties. There was a struggle among the parties to meddle in it, and, very wisely, the top party leaders insisted on placing their confidence in this group of intellectuals" (28 January 1991).

The new political campaign techniques paid off. They led to a plebiscite victory, with 54.7 percent of the vote, on 5 October 1988. The victory thwarted the regime's plans to maintain power for eight more years and forced the open presidential and congressional elections in December 1989 that chose Patricio Aylwin to lead a new, democratic regime. It also prompted the military regime to agree, early in 1989, to a series of constitutional amendments that partially reduced the authoritarian character of the democratic system set out in the 1980 Constitution. The transition to democracy would now occur more rapidly and fully than the military regime had ever intended. Intellectuals had simultaneously designed a successful plebiscite campaign and fundamentally changed the way politics was done in Chile.

Reflecting on the role of intellectuals—and politicians—in that experience, Arriagada notes their departures from conventional stereotypes. Instead of emphasizing themes that were too complex or abstract for the average voter as intellectuals might be expected to do, they did exactly the opposite, reducing strategy to its simplest terms, and bringing politicians closer to the concrete problems of the people. "It was the intellectuals who struggled most against ideology and voluntarism." Instead of seeking, in the campaign, to convince voters through rational arguments, they focused on the nonrational—on the feelings of fear, apathy and isolation that were so widespread among the voters. "Curiously, the roles had become inverted. It was politicians, and not intellectuals, who showed a greater interest in rational debate, while intellectuals placed the accent on essentially motivational factors."[76]

Intellectuals transcended academic roles during this period and began acting like politicians. But they did not act the way politicians had traditionally acted. Instead, they brought new content to political roles, complementing ideology with psychology, and intuition with polls. They provided the impetus and the vehicle for bringing modern methods of political campaigning to the country. Politics in Chile would never be the same.

6

Conclusion

I too think the intellectuals should constantly disturb, should bear witness to the misery of the world, should be provocative by being independent, should rebel against all hidden and open pressure and manipulations, should be the chief doubter of systems, of power and its incantations, should be a witness to their mendacity. For this very reason, an intellectual cannot fit into any role that might be assigned to him, nor can he ever be made to fit into any of the histories written by the victors.
— VACLAV HAVEL, *Disturbing the Peace*

It is not our business to rule, and not our business to engage in politics. . . . Our first and most important function, the reason the people keep us and need us, is to preserve the purity of all sources of knowledge.
— HERMAN HESSE, *The Glass Bead Game*

Intellectuals Matter

Clearly, intellectuals can play remarkably important roles in democratic transition. Throughout nearly seventeen years of authoritarian rule in Chile, intellectuals—principally social scientists working from a network of private research centers—carried out activities that contributed significantly to that country's transition to democracy. Initially they provided a sanctuary for dissident thought. Then they led a forceful critique of opposition thinking that eventually produced a democratic left and a more tolerant and flexible center. They criticized the regime when politicians were prevented from doing so. They provided political leaders with information and analysis that were crucial to developing a more realistic approach to democratic transition. After open political activity again became possible, they helped opposition factions overcome their bitter divisions, creating conditions necessary for the coalition that was later to defeat Pinochet in the plebiscite. They took the lead in advocating fundamental changes in transition strategy. They participated directly in the transition process, importing a new campaign technology and successfully marketing it to political leaders. And then they used their analyses and credibility to design the successful 1988 plebiscite campaign. Intellectuals played a more important role in Chile's transition to democracy than they have in any transition in recent Latin American history.

To be sure, democracy was scheduled to return to Chile regardless— in a highly restricted form and at a slow pace—based on the provisions of the 1980 Constitution. Even had Pinochet won the 1988 plebiscite, he would have been required to share minimal power over the next eight years with a new legislature dominated by his appointees. In 1997, general elections were slated for the presidency and for a majority of the legislature. That would eventually have given the country a regime that was formally democratic, although riddled with authoritarian features.

But the issue in Chile after 1980 was not so much whether democracy would return, but how soon and in what form. Would Pinochet be compelled to relinquish power in 1989, or would he continue to rule until 1997? Could any of the Constitution's authoritarian features be eliminated? Could the opposition, if it did manage to gain power, govern successfully and democratically? The distinctive role of Chilean intellectuals was to ensure that democracy returned sooner rather than later, and to alter opposition thought and behavior in ways that deepened its commitment to pluralist democracy. Intellectuals fundamentally influenced the kind of transition that Chile had.

In the process, they performed functions that other actors either could not have performed or could only have performed more slowly and less capably. The church, for example, regularly strained the limits of its ability to oppose the dictatorship, generating tension within its ranks and attacks from without. Politicians and political parties were illegal until 1988. Even the limited political activity possible after 1983 carried with it substantial personal risk. Other elements of civil society, such as the labor movement, had been disbanded and scattered. It is hard to imagine any of those elements taking on greater roles, at least before 1988. A political vacuum had been created in Chile. Things needed to be done. Intellectuals rose to the occasion.

These findings address an issue—the role of intellectuals in transitions to democracy—that is seldom mentioned in the academic literature. Most analyses emphasize initiatives taken from within authoritarian regimes to institute transitions to democratic rule, and the role of elites more generally in leading the shift from authoritarian to democratic values. But the elites mentioned are, for the most part, military, political, or economic. Intellectual elites virtually never appear.

Yet our review of Chile's experience suggests that intellectuals have positive roles to play in democratic transitions. They need not remain on the sidelines, unsuited by training and orientation to the world of political action. Their products need not be confined to abstract analyses and complicated formulas. They can make solid, constructive contributions that draw on their strengths as intellectuals, yet satisfy the demands of political life. In short, the stereotypes of intellectuals as being irrelevant to social change in developing countries need not apply.

Factors Facilitating the Intellectuals' Political Role

In this book I have examined those roles and the factors that made them possible. I have argued that intellectuals influenced Chile's transition to democracy at many different levels over some fifteen years, often assuming roles not traditionally associated with the academy. No single factor accounts for this extraordinary behavior. The impact intellectuals achieved in Chile's case was made possible by an uncommon combination of training, commitment, initiative, and circumstance. It was that combination—not always present elsewhere, and often beyond the control of intellectuals themselves—that produced an extraordinary result. Thus Chile probably constitutes an extreme case that shows just how much intellectuals can accomplish when conditions are right. It establishes a benchmark against which to measure the performance of intellectuals in authoritarian regimes elsewhere.

Indeed, one of the lessons that emerges most clearly from our findings is that intellectuals do not play such roles automatically. Intellectuals are not, after all, natural political actors. Their domain is the world of ideas and criticism, not the practical concerns of political decision making. Historically, their relationship with power holders has been marked, as Coser suggests, by "mistrust and mutual incomprehension."[1] Their impact on politics has more commonly been delayed and oblique than immediate and direct. Thus when intellectuals have had major, direct impact on politics, it has been the result of some extraordinary combination of circumstances.

In Chile's transition to democracy, at least three broad factors led to the emergence of intellectuals as key actors: the country's political culture, the authoritarian context, and the investments made over nearly three decades in the country's academic social sciences.

Chile's political culture made it easier for intellectuals to play important roles. Politics in Chile had traditionally been more intellectual than elsewhere in Latin America. Politicians regularly looked to intellectuals for ideas, and intellectuals customarily addressed the major political issues of the day. Each, on occasion, looked to the other for approval. That relationship had intensified before the coup, with intellectuals helping sharpen ideological debate among political factions and thus feeling partially responsible for the breakdown that resulted. Consequently, when the need for intellectuals to expand more deliberately into politics appeared after the coup, their historical affinity with politics facilitated the process.

Similarly, the high ideological content of Chilean politics made it easier for intellectuals to play a role. The breakdown of democracy in 1973 was based fundamentally on a conflict of ideas—a battle between party leaders advocating utopian and mutually exclusive solutions to social problems. Polarization, radicalism, and ideological rigidity among Chile's political elites were major causes of democratic collapse and remained major obstacles to reestablishing democratic rule. Thus the task at hand, after the coup, was already substantially intellectual in character. As Foxley has pointed out: "Getting the political class and its intellectuals to look critically at themselves in their past roles constitutes perhaps a fundamental step in constructing a truly democratic and enduring political system."[2] That was a job intellectuals were already equipped to take on. Had the obstacles to democratic transition been less cerebral in character and more exclusively racial, ethnic, or economic, intellectuals might have found it much harder to be effective. Cultural factors conditioned the ability of intellectuals to play important roles in Chile's democratic transition.

A second important factor was the authoritarian context. Quite unexpectedly, the conditions imposed by democratic breakdown and authoritarian rule in Chile made it easier for intellectuals to take on significant roles in the transition. The trauma and repression that accompanied the military regime helped open opposition elites to new ideas and self-criticism. They weakened commitment to conventional politics and prepared the ground for subsequent changes in attitude and behavior. The country's political class—and to some extent its intelligentsia as well—had failed spectacularly and now was being brutally repressed. "Had 1973 been less traumatic," one observer noted, "conciliatory behavior later on would not have been so great" (Ffrench-Davis, 3 February 1992). Change-oriented intellectuals encountered an audience that was chastened and impressionable.

Moreover, the military regime's efforts to eliminate politics from the country created a political vacuum that intellectuals could expand into. Making politics illegal while tolerating academic activity gave opposition intellectuals a comparative advantage. In what may have been Latin America's most vigorous political culture, their locales—private research centers—became the only places where politics could legitimately be discussed. They simultaneously faced greater demand that they assume political roles and less competition in doing so. Efforts by a free-market regime to restrict political activity, ironically, gave intellectuals a temporary monopoly on opposition politics.

The authoritarian context, then, was an important factor. It set the stage, chose many of the actors, and partially determined the roles they could play. Perhaps most importantly, it weakened the established political order and created an opportunity for intellectuals to help a new order emerge. (Elsewhere, of course, the authoritarian context might operate quite differently, limiting the range of possibilities open to intellectuals, or even shutting them out completely.)

A third important factor was the substantial investments made over nearly thirty years to establish a modern social science in Chile. Social scientists were crucial in Chile's transition to democracy; other intellectuals were not. Virtually all the intellectuals who played important roles were sociologists, economists, or political scientists. Virtually none were artists, writers, natural scientists, or philosophers. Almost all had recently pursued graduate study abroad. Chile's transition was shaped not by a cross-section of the country's intelligentsia but by a sophisticated group of foreign-trained social scientists.

To be sure, transitions to democracy are themselves social phenomena and thus draw more naturally on the expertise of social scientists than on that of other intellectuals. Artists and natural scientists presumably bring fewer relevant skills to the task of democratic transition. Indeed, Chile's experience suggests that social scientists possess a combination of concerns and skills that match up especially well with the varied challenges posed by shifting from authoritarian to democratic rule. All other things being equal, social scientists might be expected to have a greater impact.

But Chile's case is significant precisely because all other things were not equal. The social sciences, in fact, were treated differently. The major investments that began around 1960 had established what was perhaps the region's strongest community of social scientists. Well-equipped programs had been set up at the country's major universities. Hundreds of scholars had been sent abroad for training. Government positions had been created. The social sciences had been valued in highly visible ways. Those efforts not only established a modern social science, they also undoubtedly attracted some of the country's most talented young scholars to the field.

After the 1973 coup, foreign donors provided funds over nearly two decades to keep many of those well-trained social scientists working in the country, despite the repression of the military regime. The network of private research centers that sprang up during the dictatorship was essentially a social science network. Dissident sociologists, economists, and political scientists—and not other intellectual groups—received foreign funding to establish an autonomous, parallel academy. Thus the investments that had been made in social science talent during the 1960s were safeguarded and even augmented during the 1970s and 1980s. No other group of dissident intellectuals in Chile was so favored over so long a period. (The only other group of intellectuals to experience comparable support both before and after the coup were the Chicago Boys, whose willingness to work within the military dictatorship enabled them to revolutionize the country's approach to economic policy.)

Moreover, Chilean social science became remarkably cosmopolitan. The social scientists who eventually played major roles in the transition had in common significant international experience through exile, graduate study abroad, or both.[3] Many hundreds of young scholars were given fellowships to pursue graduate training abroad before and after the coup. That experience exposed them to new ideas, new perspectives, and direct contact with other forms of social organization. They studied politics and economics at some of the best universities in Europe and North America, becoming acquainted with contemporary thinking on democracy, democratic transition, and economic growth. They developed strong personal and professional relationships with foreign colleagues. Many experienced firsthand the democratic socialism of Western Europe, and the "real" socialism of Eastern Europe. Most, as well, eventually returned home rather than remaining abroad, drawn in part by the professional prospects offered by Chile's strong network of private research centers.

Over nearly thirty years, then, the academic social sciences in Chile were significantly empowered in comparison with other disciplines and with politicians. They received substantial investment before the coup and were singled out by foreign donors for investment afterwards. Those efforts created and maintained an autonomous cadre of modern, highly committed professionals who were able to play an important role in their country's affairs. No longer were they the "passive intellectuals" mentioned by Moulian, who adapted and distributed the discourse of politicians. They had become independent, creative, and critical. They presided over the institutions that provided shelter, analysis, dialogue, and criticism to opposition politicians. They intellectualized politics. It should come as no great surprise, therefore, that it was principally social scientists, rather than intellectuals more generally, who played key roles in Chile's transition to democracy. Politics did not just take refuge in the academy after the coup, it took refuge in the social sciences.

The country's political culture, its authoritarian context, and the exceptional strength of its academic social sciences were thus important in shifting the balance of power temporarily from politicians to intellectuals, giving them the "acknowledged authority vis-à-vis an organized sector of society" necessary to have an impact on the regime.[4] The commitment, vision, and initiative of a few leading social scientists were also key. Had that combination been different, the pattern and magnitude of intellectual influence would probably have been different as well.

The Political Utility of Academic Perspectives

These findings suggest that intellectuals do not have to abandon traditional academic perspectives in order to play a positive role in democratic transitions, and perhaps in politics more generally. Here, the behavior of intellectuals during the first decade after the coup is noteworthy. Their activities were, for the most part, thoroughly academic: they gathered data, analyzed it, wrote it up, and discussed the results in seminars. They employed the theories, methods, and standards of the academy. Very few, during this period, left academic roles to take up politics.

Their work was nonetheless politically influential. They offered a sanctuary to critical, independent thinking when such thinking was banned elsewhere. They took the lead in helping opposition politicians examine the "causes of the defeat" and come to terms with their own role in the collapse of the democratic regime. They initiated a learning process that eventually reshaped opposition political thought. Their research often constituted solid criticism of regime policies.

Even after the protests of 1983, when politics became more feasible and a few intellectuals began moving out of the academy to assume more formal political roles, those who stayed made some of the most important political contributions. They helped establish relationships of trust and understanding among opposition factions. They helped politicians understand the nature of the authoritarian regime, and the major changes it was bringing to the country. They began to educate political actors regarding how democratic transitions had occurred elsewhere. Their research on political attitudes eventually caused politicians to change the way they did business.

Those were important political consequences of academic activity. They depended heavily on the fact that intellectuals were doing what they knew how to do well. Their firm base in the concerns and standards of the academy enhanced their credibility and the quality of their work. Even when intellectuals took on the role of political critics, as did CIEPLAN so successfully beginning around 1978, they presented themselves as academics and not as politicians. It was their position as intellectuals—their scientific status and role—that permitted them to carry out the political function of criticizing the regime. Had they abandoned their academic vocation, they would have lost their political effectiveness.

They did, however, develop a new relationship with politics. These were not ivory-tower intellectuals. They "infiltrated"—to use Boeninger's term—politics at all levels. In a few cases, they actually became political actors. More commonly, they remained "two steps behind the daily action" in roles that were less formal and less direct (Boeninger, 29 January 1991). Some, like Boeninger himself, played intellectual and political roles simultaneously, making it difficult to distinguish one role from another. There emerged an "organic linkage between intellectuals and politics" characterized not just by "intellectuals who know, telling politicians who do, what they know," but rather an amalgamation of the two groups (Puccio, 17 January 1991). Intellectuals engaged politicians, offering employment to some, inviting others to workshops, altering their discourse and seeking ways to make academic work politically relevant. They became intermediaries between the academy and politics—high-minded trespassers determined to make a contribution in unfamiliar terrain.

Chile's experience suggests that intellectuals may make their greatest contribution to democratic transition, and to politics, when they remain firmly rooted in their academic roles. Maintaining some independence from politics may be crucial to acting productively upon politics. Putting this another way, what makes intellectuals different from politicians—their academic perspective—may be what counts most in promoting democratization. If so, then it is the quality of the relationship between intellectuals and politicians that matters, and not a decision by intellectuals to renounce the academy for politics.

In Chile after the 1973 coup, the procedures and standards of science were applied to politics, rather than vice versa. The academy was not politicized; politics was intellectualized. That turnabout exposed politics to new ideas and subjected it to different criteria. One theme that underlies the entire Chilean experience is the shift from a politics based heavily on emotion, ideology, populism, and charisma to a politics based more on reason, analysis, pluralism, and informed judgement—values that have strong roots in the modern academy. Intellectuals promoted that shift less by displacing politicians than by infiltrating, educating, and persuading them. What was crucial was not so much that intellectuals abandoned the academy, but that they developed constructive relationships with politicians.

The Diversity of Possible Roles

These findings also suggest that intellectuals face a remarkably broad array of options in developing new relationships with politicians. Some of those options are purely academic. Others mix academic and political functions in highly unorthodox ways. A few are predominantly political. The possibilities vary according to circumstance, initiative, and the willingness of intellectuals to adapt. Clearly, however, the relationship between politics and the academy is not always dichotomous. One need not choose, at least during periods of democratic transition, to be either an intellectual or a political actor. Trespassers often make the greatest contributions.

In Chile's transition, the roles played by intellectuals evolved over time from producing knowledge, to advising political actors, to articulating between politicians and society, to direct political action. They evolved as well from broadly reflective and critical functions (the role of autonomous thinker) to the provision of expertise in narrow subject areas (the role of technocrat). Some of those roles, such as helping the opposition rethink its politics, were fundamentally intellectual in nature and drew on traditional academic skills. Others, such as CIEPLAN's success in criticizing the regime during the late 1970s, depended on authoritarian circumstances that gave intellectuals a comparative advantage. Yet others, such as bringing opposition factions together and introducing modern political campaign techniques, were based on the vision of specific individuals.

Some intellectuals ranged across many roles during that period; others occupied only one or two. In most cases, their incursions into political territory were temporary—a kind of trespassing made necessary and facilitated by extraordinary circumstances. As Angel Flisfisch suggests, early 1987 may have marked an inflection point, after which the impact of intellectuals on politics began to subside as politicians again became able to act (17 January 1991). But for some the shift was permanent—a response to the growing demand for technocrats in politics, or a decision to become professional politicians.

The hallmark of the Chilean experience was the ability of intellectuals to adapt their behavior to suit changing circumstances. Leftist intellectuals, for example, initially concentrated more on political thought, in line with the left's greater need to redefine its relationship to democracy. Centrist intellectuals were often more important on technocratic issues, such as reshaping economic policy. When politicians could not criticize the regime, intellectuals stepped up and played that role. When the social mobilization strategy faltered, intellectuals convincingly elucidated its shortcomings and offered a pragmatic alternative. When the time came for a plebiscite campaign, intellectuals became political operatives.[5]

It is instructive, in that regard, to compare Chile's experience with the categories developed several decades ago by Coser. In considering the relationships between "men of power and men of ideas," Coser emphasized five fundamental modalities: holders of power, advisers to power, legitimators of power, critics of power, and those who extol the power structures of other countries to the detriment of their own. He elaborated on each relationship through a series of historical case studies.[6]

What is interesting is that none of Coser's relationships, by itself, adequately characterizes the role intellectuals played in Chile's transition to democracy. Instead, all of them figured prominently. Some intellectuals held power in formal political positions, first within opposition parties and later in the new democratic regime. Others functioned as highly influential political advisers. Socialist intellectuals played crucial roles in legitimating democratic socialism within the mainstream of Chile's left and in legitimating participation in the plebiscite. Intellectuals became accomplished critics, both of the military regime and of the opposition's transition strategies. Intellectuals relentlessly hailed the virtues of foreign democracies in contrast to the offenses committed by the military dictatorship. Each of Coser's typical relationships was important.

Chilean intellectuals played at least two other roles not mentioned by Coser. First, they functioned during the worst years of political repression as conservators of opposition politics. The private research centers constituted a kind of sanctuary for the opposition, providing a place where it could meet, come to terms with its failings, and rethink its politics. They were one of the few "spaces of liberty" available and became the exclusive locus of critical, independent thought for nearly a decade. That conservation function was important in a setting where politics was outlawed, and where politicians were defeated and demoralized. It happened because intellectuals adapted more successfully to authoritarian conditions than did politicians and reached out to them, temporarily making politics an intellectual endeavor.

Second, intellectuals operated at the psychological level, as conveners of bitterly divided political factions. Here their role was partly deliberate, and partly the unintentional by-product of hundreds of seminars and workshops. By regularly assembling diverse political actors on the neutral ground of academic analysis, intellectuals helped a traditionally divided opposition come together. They provided social occasions that addressed psychological, as well as ideological, divisions. They enabled an atomized political class to develop personal relationships. They helped restore the mutual trust and understanding that had long been missing from Chilean politics and was essential for the seventeen-party coalition that later defeated Pinochet in the plebiscite. That bridge-building function is unusual for intellectuals. It was particularly important given the bitterness and division that had characterized Chilean politics for more than two decades. It was taken up principally because intellectuals acquired the power—temporarily—to bring opposition factions together, and because a few extraordinary intellectuals sought deliberately to "reconstruct the political and social fabric."

During periods of fundamental social change, intellectuals may have special opportunities to influence the course of events. Normal capacities and relationships may be altered and new needs created, enabling intellectuals to assume all sorts of extraordinary functions. Their potential for impact, whether from traditional roles or as trespassers upon the roles of others, may expand greatly, even if only temporarily. And intellectuals may be well equipped to play a variety of unorthodox but positive roles in the process of democratic transition.

The Change Potential of Autonomous Networks of Scholars

Finally, these findings underscore the positive role that networks of modern, talented scholars can play in the events of their countries, and the importance of establishing such networks even when their precise impact cannot be determined in advance. Chile's transition to democracy was influenced not just by individual intellectuals but by a community of intellectuals. The social scientists who transformed the country's political culture and modernized its political technocracy all knew each other and worked together. They were assembled gradually—the product of a strong, autonomous professional community that provided training, institutions, standards, colleagues, debate, and international contacts. That community, in turn, had developed over three decades, with sustained support from domestic and foreign funders.

Chile's vigorous social science community, however, was created with few assumptions about its impact on democratic transition, or its broader ability to influence politics. The Chilean government began the effort during the late 1950s with the goal of institutionalizing scientific research in the country's major universities. It was joined in that endeavor by foreign donors seeking to establish a stock of high-level human resources that could address the country's social and economic policy needs. Both groups emphasized policy rather than politics.

After the coup, foreign donors supported the private social science research centers in an effort to maintain critical, independent thought in an otherwise repressive setting, and to keep on hand able technocrats for high-level government posts once democracy returned. To be sure, many foreign donors were motivated by their distaste for the repression that characterized the Pinochet regime. And some certainly hoped that support for dissident social scientists and their research centers would increase pressure on that regime. What was being funded, however, was almost exclusively academic research and policy analysis.

But once established, Chile's social science community acquired a potential that transcended its original objectives. It became a kind of multipurpose national resource, capable of taking on many different tasks, depending on circumstances, funding, and its own inclinations. When the opportunity arose to assist the process of democratization, the network of social scientists was able to respond. And it possessed the size, autonomy, and vision to operate in a sustained and significant fashion. Few would have predicted, during the 1960s and 1970s, that funds invested in Chile's social science community would have such a profound impact on that country's transition to democracy ten or twenty years later.

The change potential of autonomous networks of scholars deserves more attention, both from academics studying democratic transitions and from foreign donors seeking to promote them. Sustained investment in creating a stock of talented social scientists can qualitatively change a country's political culture and its political technocracy. Keeping a critical mass of talented intellectuals in place and active during periods of great uncertainty and danger can provide a major counterbalance to the forces of repression and authoritarianism. Well-trained, internationally connected intellectuals can play fundamental roles in providing a democratic opposition with insights and techniques that are crucial in facilitating democratic transition. Intellectuals, as Chile's experience demonstrates, offer a capacity for creation and leadership that can be a formidable resource in moving from dictatorship to democracy.

Notes

Chapter 1. Introduction

1. See, for example, Dankwart A. Rustow, "Transitions to Democracy: Toward a Dynamic Model," *Comparative Politics* 2 (1970): 337–63; Samuel P. Huntington, "Will More Countries Become Democratic?," *Political Science Quarterly* 99 (1984): 193–218; Guillermo O'Donnell, Philippe C. Schmitter, and Laurence Whitehead, eds., *Transitions from Authoritarian Rule: Prospects for Democracy* (Baltimore: Johns Hopkins University Press, 1986); Larry Diamond, Juan J. Linz, and Seymour Martin Lipset, eds., *Democracy in Developing Countries*, vol. 4 (Boulder, Colo.: Reinner, 1989); Terry Lynn Karl and Philippe C. Schmitter, "Modes of Transition in Latin America, Southern and Eastern Europe," *International Social Science Journal* 128 (1991): 269–84; Adam Przeworski, *Democracy and the Market: Political and Economic Reforms in Eastern Europe and Latin America* (Cambridge: Cambridge University Press, 1991); and John Higley and Richard Gunther, eds., *Elites and Democratic Consolidation in Latin America and Southern Europe* (Cambridge: Cambridge University Press, 1992). Worth review in this context is an article written over thirty years ago on the role of intellectuals in economic development. See John Friedmann, "Intellectuals in Developing Societies," *Kyklos* 13 (1960): 513–44.

2. Guillermo O'Donnell and Philippe C. Schmitter, *Transitions from Authoritarian Rule: Tentative Conclusions about Uncertain Democracies* (Baltimore: Johns Hopkins University Press, 1986), 49; O'Donnell and Schmitter also provide an excellent summary on the role of the elites, 37–39. See also Michael Burton, Richard Gunther, and John Higley, "Introduction: Elite Transformations and Democractic Regimes," in Higley and Gunther, *Elites and Democratic Consolidation*. This emphasis derives substantially from Robert Dahl, *Polyarchy: Participation and Opposition* (New Haven: Yale University Press, 1971). Diamond and Linz note that "in Latin America, intellectuals play an important role in their societies and are quite open to the world of ideas." They do not develop this line of analysis, however. See Diamond, Linz, and Lipset, *Democracy in Developing Countries*, 11. On political elites, see, for example, Francisco Delich, "La Construcción Social de la Legitimidad Política en Procesos de Transición a la Democracia (I)," *Crítica y Utopia* (1983): 9.

3. Timothy Garton Ash, *The Uses of Adversity: Essays on the Fate of Central Europe* (New York: Vintage, 1990), 199.

4. Lawrence Goodwin, *Breaking the Barrier: The Rise of Solidarity in Poland* (New York: Oxford University Press, 1991), xxiv; see also 369–74. Roman Laba, *The Roots of Solidarity: A Political Sociology of Poland's Working-Class Democratization* (Princeton: Princeton University Press, 1991), 178. On failures of intellectuals, see, for example, Miklós Haraszti, *The Velvet Prison: Artists under State Socialism* (New York: Basic, 1987); and George Konrád and Ivan Szelényi, *The Intellectuals on the Road to Class Power* (New York: Harcourt Brace Jovanovich, 1979).

5. See, for example, O'Donnell, Schmitter, and Whitehead, *Transitions from Authoritarian Rule*; Diamond, Linz, and Lipset, *Democracy in Developing Countries*; Robert A. Pastor, ed., *Democracy in the Americas: Stopping the Pendulum* (New York: Holmes and Meier, 1989); James M. Malloy and Mitchell A. Seligson, eds., *Authoritarians and Democrats: Regime Transition in Latin America* (Pittsburgh: University of Pittsburgh Press, 1987); and Higley and Gunther, *Elites and Democratic Consolidation*.

6. See Luciano Martins, "The Liberalization of Authoritarian Rule in Brazil," in O'Donnell, Schmitter, and Whitehead, *Transitions from Authoritarian Rule*; and Thomas Bruneau, "Brazil's Political Transition," in Higley and Gunther, *Elites and Democratic Consolidation*. La Mounier does suggest a relationship, before 1945, between elite socialization and the country's law schools and mentions in passing the more recent impact of a "sizeable and cosmopolitan academic community." He does not develop these ideas, however. See Bolivar La Mounier, "Brazil: Inequality against Democracy," in Diamond, Linz, and Lipset, *Democracy in Developing Countries*, 142.

7. See Julio Cotler, "Military Interventions and 'Transfer of Power to Civilians' in Peru," in O'Donnell, Schmitter, and Whitehead, *Transitions from Authoritarian Rule*; Luis A. Abugattás, "Populism and After: The Peruvian Experience," in Malloy and Seligson, *Authoritarians and Democrats*; Cynthia McClintock, "Peru: Precarious Regimes, Authoritarian and Democratic," in Diamond, Linz, and Lipset, *Democracy in Developing Countries*; and Henry Dietz, "Elites in an Unconsolidated Bureaucracy: Peru during the 1980s," in Higley and Gunther, *Elites and Democratic Consolidation*.

8. Jonathan Hartlyn, "Colombia: The Politics of Violence and Accommodation," in Diamond, Linz, and Lipset, *Democracy in Developing Countries*, 65.

9. See Marcelo Cavarozzi, "Patterns of Elite Negotiation and Confrontation in Argentina and Chile," in Higley and Gunther, *Elites and Democratic Consolidation*; Carlos Waisman, "Argentina: Autarkic Industrialization and Illegitimacy," in Diamond, Linz, and Lipset, *Democracy in Developing Countries*; and Adolfo Canitrot, Marcelo Cavarozzi, Robert Frenkel, and Oscar Landi, "Intellectuales y Política en Argentina," *Debat* 4 (1985): 4–8.

10. Several references to the impact (or lack of same) that Latin American intellectuals have had on politics include: Sol Serrano, "América Latina y el Mundo Moderno en algunos Ensayistas Latinoamericanos," *Opciones* 4 (1984): 56–100, summarizes the efforts, in the late nineteenth and early twentieth centuries, by such intellectuals as Rodó, Martí, Vasconcelos, Zea, Paz, and Mariá-

tegui to interpret Latin American identity in the light of European and North American "modernity." Tomás Moulian, *Democracia y Socialismo en Chile* (Santiago: FLACSO, 1983), 9–19, sketches how a "fascination with Marxism" and a "religious vision of politics" led leftist intellectuals in Chile to undervalue democracy and subject themselves to the dictates of political parties during the late 1960s and early 1970s. Robert Barros, "The Left and Democracy: Recent Debates in Latin America," *Telos* 68 (1986): 49–70, summarizes recent literature on the "re-evaluation" of democracy by the left in Latin America. Roderick A. Camp, *Intellectuals and the State in Twentieth-Century Mexico* (Austin: University of Texas Press, 1985), analyzes the role intellectuals have played in Mexican politics but says little about their relationship to democratization. José Joaquín Brunner, "La Intelligentsia: Escenarios Institucionales y Universos Ideológicos," *Proposiciones* 18 (1990): 180–91, analyzes the "cultural transformations" experienced by the intelligentsia in Chile under the Pinochet dictatorship, noting how new intelligentsias of the left, right, and center emerged out of the authoritarian experience. Canitrot et al., "Intelectuales y Política," discusses the relatively limited political influence enjoyed by Argentine intellectuals.

11. See, for example, Pamela Constable and Arturo Valenzuela, *A Nation of Enemies: Chile under Pinochet* (New York: Norton, 1991); Paul W. Drake and Iván Jaksić, eds., *The Struggle for Democracy in Chile, 1982–1990* (Lincoln: University of Nebraska Press, 1991); Joseph S. Tulchin and Augusto Varas, eds., *From Dictatorship to Democracy: Rebuilding Political Consensus in Chile* (Boulder, Colo.: Rienner, 1991); and Ascanio Cavallo, *Los Hombres de la Transición* (Santiago: Andres Bello, 1992).

12. See, for example, Lewis A. Coser, *Men of Ideas: A Sociologist's View* (New York: Free Press, 1965); Edward Shils, *International Encyclopedia of the Social Sciences* 7 (New York: Macmillan and Free Press, 1968); Antonio Gramsci, *Prison Notes* (New York: Simon and Schuster, 1971); Hans Gerth and C. Wright Mills, eds., *From Max Weber: Essays in Sociology* (New York: Oxford University Press, 1965); Alvin W. Gouldner, *The Future of Intellectuals and the Rise of the New Class* (New York: Oxford University Press, 1979); and Seymour M. Lipset, *Political Man* (Garden City, N.Y.: Doubleday, 1960).

13. For "those who create," Lipset, *Political Man,* 333; "experts," James A. Smith, *The Idea Brokers: Think Tanks and the Rise of the New Policy Elite* (New York: Free Press, 1991), xiii; Robert Michels, "Intellectual Socialists," in *Encyclopedia of the Social Sciences* 8 (1932), 118; Robert K. Merton, *Social Theory and Social Structure* (New York: Free Press, 1968), 263; as related to culture, Max Weber, *Economy and Society* (Berkeley and Los Angeles: University of California Press, 1978); as related to power, Gouldner, *The Future of Intellectuals.*

14. Sergio Bitar, interview, 16 January 1991. Subsequent quotations from this interview are cited by date in the text or notes.

15. José Joaquín Brunner, interview, 28 February 1991. Subsequent quotations from this interview are cited by date in the text or notes.

16. This distinction is elaborated by Patricio Silva, "Intellecuals, Technocrats, and Social Change in Chile: Past, Present, and Future Perspectives," in Allen

Angell and Benny Pollack, eds., *The Legacy of Dictatorship: Political, Economic, and Social Change in Pinochet's Chile* (Liverpool: Institute of Latin American Studies, University of Liverpool, 1993). He contrasts humanist intellectuals (social scientists who produce societally significant ideas and symbols, and who tend to criticize the status quo) with technocrats (highly trained economists and engineers who believe that social problems are better resolved by scientific and technical methods than through politics and politicization). See also Veronica Montecinos, "Economics and Power: Chilean Economists in Government, 1958–1985," Ph.D. diss., University of Pennsylvania, 1988.

Chapter 2. The Historical Context

1. Paul E. Sigmund, *The Overthrow of Allende and the Politics of Chile, 1964–1976* (Pittsburgh: University of Pittsburgh Press, 1977), 21–22; Mark Falcoff, *Modern Chile, 1970–1989: A Critical History* (New Brunswick, N.J.: Transaction, 1991), 4.

2. U.S. economic assistance (donations and credits) increased from $112 million during the eight years of the Eisenhower administration to $750 million during the Kennedy and Johnson administrations, while Eximbank credits rose from $95 million to $340 million. See Heraldo Muñoz and Carlos Portales, *Una Amistad Esquiva: Las Relaciones de Estados Unidos y Chile* (Santiago: Pehuén, 1987), 48–74. Those figures do not include some $3 million in covert aid for Eduardo Frei's 1964 election campaign, "more money per capita than had previously been spent in any U.S. election," according to Abraham F. Lowenthal, *Partners in Conflict: The United States and Latin America in the 1990s* (Baltimore: Johns Hopkins University Press, 1990), 32.

3. On literacy, C. L. Taylor and M. C. Hudson, eds., *World Handbook of Political and Social Indicators*, 2d ed. (New Haven, Conn., 1972), 205. See also U.S. Government Printing Office, *Area Handbook for Chile* (Washington, D.C.: U.S. Government Printing Office, 1969), 125–50. On schools, Joseph P. Farrell, *The National Unified School in Allende's Chile: The Role of Education in the Destruction of a Revolution* (Vancouver: University of British Columbia Press, 1986), 31.

4. Ernesto Schiefelbein and Joseph P. Farrell, *Eight Years of Their Lives: Through Schooling to the Labour Market in Chile* (Ottawa: International Development Research Center, 1982), 26.

5. On the higher education system, Daniel C. Levy, *Higher Education and the State in Latin America: Private Challenges to Public Dominance* (Chicago: University of Chicago Press, 1986), 78. An excellent source of information is Programa Interdisciplinaria de Investigación Educacional (PIIE), *Las transformaciones educacionales bajo el régimen militar* (Santiago: PIIE, 1984). Regarding foreign influence, for example, when Valparaíso's private Federico Santa María Technical University was founded in 1931, it was modeled on the German technical school, and its faculty was to be composed entirely of foreigners for the first ten years; see Levy, *Higher Education*, 73. On promoting scientific research, José Joaquín Brunner, *Informe Sobre la Educación Superior en Chile* (Santiago: FLACSO, 1986), 26.

6. One spectacular example of foreign assistance was a ten-year, $10 million

commitment by the Ford Foundation in the early 1960s to strengthen the University of Chile through a program of exchanges with California's university system; see Edmundo Fuenzalida, "Institutionalization of Research in Chile's Universities: 1953–1967," in Roger M. Garrett, ed., *Education and Development* (New York: St. Martin's, 1984), 95–III.

7. Brunner, *Informe Sobre la Educación Superior*, 31–40. Examples of new forms of organization include the Center for the Study of National Reality (CEREN) at the Catholic University and the Center for Social and Economic Studies (CESO) at the University of Chile.

8. U.S. Government Printing Office, *Area Handbook for Chile*, 48.

9. Fuenzalida, "Institutionalization of Research," 63.

10. Fuenzalida (ibid.) thoroughly documents and analyzes the institutionalization of scientific research in Chile. Support was provided by the Chilean government, the Rockefeller and Ford foundations, the U.S. Alliance for Progress, and several European governments to develop research capacity in such fields as medicine, seismology, astronomy, physics, biology, engineering, agronomy, and veterinary medicine.

11. Francis X. Sutton, "Foundations and Higher Education at Home and Abroad," *Center for the Study of Philanthropy Working Papers* (New York: Graduate School and University Center, City University of New York, 1986), reviews the extraordinary efforts by private U.S. foundations to promote higher education in the United States and abroad.

12. Most of this information is drawn from Fuenzalida, "Institutionalization of Research."

13. Edmundo Fuenzalida, "The Reception of 'Scientific Sociology' in Chile," *Latin American Research Review* 18, 2 (1983): 95–97.

14. Hamuy studied at Columbia University and worked as a researcher at the City College of New York and at the University of Wisconsin; initial funding for the new venture came entirely from the university or the central government; see ibid., 98–99. Other excellent sources include José Joaquín Brunner, *El Caso de la Sociología en Chile* (Santiago: FLACSO, 1988), and Hernán Godoy Urzúa, "El Desarrollo de la Sociología en Chile," *Estudios Sociales* 12 (1977): 33–56.

15. José Joaquín Brunner and Alicia Barrios, *Inquisición, Mercado y Filantropía: Ciencias Sociales y Autoritarismo en Argentina, Brasil, Chile y Uruguay* (Santiago: FLACSO, 1987), 77; see also Brunner, *La Sociología en Chile*, 220–32.

16. See Brunner, *La Sociología en Chile*, 226–32; and Fuenzalida, "'Scientific Sociology' in Chile," 98–99.

17. A detailed account of Vekemans's interaction with the church hierarchy and of the evolution of DESAL appears in David Mutchler, *The Church as a Political Factor in Latin America: With Particular Reference to Colombia and Chile* (New York: Praeger, 1971), part 3; see also Fuenzalida, "'Scientific Sociology' in Chile," 102–5; and Brunner, *La Sociología en Chile*, 232–36.

18. Brunner and Barrios, *Inquisición, Mercado y Filantropía*, 77–78; see also Norbert Lechner, "Las Condiciones Políticas de la Ciencia Política en Chile," *Documento de Trabajo No. 453* (Santiago: FLACSO, 1990). On the rise in social science majors, Brunner and Barrios, *Inquisición, Mercado y Filantropía*, 21.

19. Ronald G. Hellman, "The Impact of the Ford Foundation on the Economic Sciences in Chile" (mimeo) provides useful detail on the program.

20. Juan Gabriel Valdés, *La Escuela de Chicago: Operación Chile* (Buenos Aires: Editorial Zeta, 1989), provides extraordinary detail and analysis on the relationship between the University of Chicago's Department of Economics and Chile's Catholic University.

21. On Ford, Hellman, "Impact of the Ford Foundation," and internal Ford Foundation files. On USAID, Valdés, *La Escuela de Chicago*, 194. On Rockefeller, Fuenzalida, "Institutionalization of Research," 74–75.

22. Hellman, "Impact of the Ford Foundation" table 1, for economists; for foreign degrees, 13.

23. Brunner and Barrios, *Inquisición, Mercado y Filantropía*, 80.

24. Brunner, "La Intelligentsia," 181.

25. Silva, "Intellectuals, Technocrats, and Social Change," 201. Silva has noted elsewhere, as an example of the antitechnocrat bias that was so common in Chile, that one of the charges leveled by radical elements against Salvador Allende's minister of agriculture, Jacques Chonchol, was that he was a "technocrat." See Patricio Silva, "Technocrats and Politics in Chile: From the Chicago Boys to the CIEPLAN Monks," *Journal of Latin American Studies* 23, 2 (1991): 389.

26. Brunner, "La Intelligentsia," 181; Brunner and Barrios, *Inquisición, Mercado y Filantropía*, 82. The reference is to Berlin's distinction, drawn in turn from the Greek poet Archiloqus, between "the fox [who] knows many things" and "the hedgehog [who] knows one big thing." See Isaiah Berlin, *Russian Thinkers* (New York: Viking, 1978), 22–81.

27. José Antonio Viera-Gallo, "Crisis y Reafirmación del Ideario Democrático: Trayectoria de Una Generación," in CIEPLAN, *Democracia en Chile: Doce Conferencias* (Santiago: CIEPLAN, 1986), 46. Mario Papi, interview, 7 March 1991. Subsequent quotations from this interview are cited by date in the text or notes.

28. Norbert Lechner, *Los Patios Interiores de la Democracia: Subjectividad y Política* (Santiago: FLACSO, 1988), 23.

29. Moulian, *Democracia y Socialismo en Chile*, 11, 13–14.

30. Alejando Foxley, "Reflexiones sobre los cambios en la democracia," in CIEPLAN, *Democracia en Chile*, 260, 265.

31. Brunner, "La Intelligentsia," 181–82.

32. Silva, "Intellectuals, Technocrats, and Social Change," 200. Moulian, *Democracia y Socialismo en Chile*, 94–99.

33. Lechner, "Las Condiciones Políticas," 6. Alicia Barrios and José Joaquín Brunner, *La Sociología en Chile: Instituciones y Practicantes* (Santiago: FLACSO, 1988), 50, argue that the highly ideologized nature of the discipline of sociology in the country was a result, in part, of "the absence of a cultural tradition that would guarantee the distinction between scientific practice and political practice."

34. Brunner, "La Intelligentsia," 181. He excepts a "thin segment of the intellectual right" from this position.

35. Vierra-Gallo, "Crisis y Reafirmación," 47.

36. For the standard argument, Adam Przeworski, *Capitalism and Social Democracy*, 2d ed. (Cambridge: Cambridge University Press, 1987), chapter 1; see chapter 9 for the general concept of the instrumental approach. Its application in Chile was first elaborated in Moulian, *Democracia y Socialismo en Chile*, and developed also in Ignacio Walker, *Socialismo y Democracia: Chile y Europa en Perspectiva Comparada* (Santiago: CIEPLAN-Hachette, 1990), chapter 4.

37. Brunner and Barrios, *Inquisición, Mercado y Filantropía*, 81.

38. Edgardo Boeninger, interview, 29 January 1991; subsequent quotations from this interview are cited by date in the text or notes. Foxley, "Reflexiones," 260. See Canitrot et al., "Intelectuales y Política," 4–8, for a discussion of the marginal role traditionally played by Argentine intellectuals in their country's politics.

39. Iván Jaksić, *Academic Rebels in Chile: The Role of Philosophy in Higher Education and Politics* (Albany: SUNY Press, 1989), 1, traces the influence of Chilean philosophers on higher education since that country's independence, arguing that "this close linkage between philosophy and politics constitutes the fundamental basis for understanding the history of the discipline in Chile and in many instances some of the most significant educational and political events of the nation."

40. See Timothy R. Scully, *Rethinking the Center: Party Politics in Nineteenth and Twentieth Century Chile* (Stanford: Stanford University Press, 1992), and Michael Fleet, *The Rise and Fall of Chilean Christian Democracy* (Princeton: Princeton University Press, 1985).

41. Eugenio Tironi, interview, 20 March 1991. Subsequent quotations from this interview are cited by date in the text or notes.

42. Javier Martínez, interview, 6 March 1991. Subsequent quotations from this interview are cited by date in the text or notes.

43. Alejando Foxley, *Para una Democracia Estable* (Santiago: CIEPLAN, 1985), 102.

44. Brunner and Barrios, *Inquisición, Mercado y Filantropía*, 80.

45. See Arturo Valenzuela, "Chile: Origins, Consolidation, and Breakdown of a Democratic Regime," in Diamond, Linz, and Lipset, *Democracy in Developing Countries*, 160–61.

46. Gonzalo Vial, "Algunas condiciones para una democracia estable en Chile," in CIEPLAN, *Democracia en Chile*, 93. On demands on the system and voter figures, see Tomás Moulian, "Estabilidad democrática en Chile: Una mirada histórica," in ibid., 135. Scully, *Rethinking the Center*, provides a comprehensive analysis of changes in Chile's political center.

47. See Genaro Arriagada, "De la república de 1925 a la constitución de 1980: El sistema político chileno," in CIEPLAN, *Democracia en Chile*, 146–47.

48. Valenzuela, "Chile," analyzes these problems; Sigmund, *Overthrow of Allende*, also discusses the contribution of structural factors to Chile's democratic breakdown. See chapters 1, 13.

49. Arriagada, "De la república de 1925," 147.

50. See Vial, "Algunas condiciones," 106–8.

51. Valenzuela, "Chile," 182–83; see also Scully, *Rethinking the Center.*

52. Moulian, "Estabilidad democrática en Chile," 141. Mario Góngora, *Ensayo Histórico Sobre la Noción del Estado en Chile en los Siglos XIX y XX,* 3d ed. (Santiago: Editorial Universitaria, 1986), 246–71.

53. See Arturo Valenzuela, "The Breakdown of Democratic Regimes: Chile," in Juan J. Linz and Alfred Stepan, eds., *The Breakdown of Democratic Regimes: Latin America* (Baltimore: Johns Hopkins University Press, 1978), 10–11.

54. Falcoff, *Modern Chile,* 13–24, reviews a variety of studies and concludes that political radicalism was not widespread among the Chilean electorate during this period. See also Carlos Huneeus, *Los Chilenos y la Política: Cambio y Continuidad en el Autoritarismo* (Santiago: CERC/ICHEH, 1987), 167–70; James Prothro and Patricio Chaparro, "Public Opinion and the Movement of the Chilean Government to the Left, 1952–1972," *Journal of Politics* 36 (1974): 2–43.

55. Valenzuela, "The Breakdown of Democratic Regimes," 10. Foxley, *Para una Democracia Estable,* 70. Manuel Antonio Garretón, "La oposición política partidaria en el regimen militar chileno. Un proceso de aprendizaje para la transición," in Marcelo Cavarozzi and Manuel Antonio Garretón, eds., *Muerte y Resurrección: Los Partidos Políticos en el Autoritarismo y las Transiciones del Cono Sur* (Santiago: FLACSO, 1989), 403; see also Garretón, *The Chilean Political Process* (Boston: Unwin Hyman, 1989), 9–10. Juan Gabriel Valdés, "Cultura y política: una mirada desde la clase política," in CIEPLAN, *Democracia en Chile,* 186–87.

56. Alejandro Foxley, Michael S. McPherson, and Guillermo O'Donnell, eds., *Development, Democracy, and the Art of Trespassing: Essays in Honor of Albert O. Hirschman* (Notre Dame, Ind.: University of Notre Dame Press, 1986), 194.

57. Moulian, *Democracia y Socialismo en Chile,* 165. Walker, *Socialismo y Democracia,* 117.

58. Moulian, *Democracia y Socialismo en Chile,* 86–87; see also Walker, *Socialismo y Democracia,* 129–47; and J. Samuel Valenzuela and Arturo Valenzuela, eds., *Military Rule in Chile: Dictatorship and Oppositions* (Baltimore: Johns Hopkins University Press, 1986), 210.

59. Walker, *Socialismo y Democracia,* 138.

60. Moulian, *Democracia y Socialismo en Chile,* 87–91; the Leninization of the Socialist party is also documented in Julio Faúndez, *Marxism and Democracy in Chile* (New Haven: Yale University Press, 1988), 159–222; and in Paul W. Drake, *Socialism and Populism in Chile* (Urbana: University of Illinois Press, 1978).

61. Cited in Walker, *Socialismo y Democracia,* 141.

62. Arriagada, "De la república de 1925," 149.

63. Analyses of the Christian Democratic position include Moulian, *Democracia y Socialismo en Chile,* especially 136–47; Valenzuela, "The Breakdown of Democratic Regimes," 33–39; Garretón, *The Chilean Political Process,* part 1; Scully, *Rethinking the Center*; Javier Martínez and Eugenio Tironi, *Las Clases Sociales en Chile: Cambio y estratificación, 1970–1980* (Santiago: Ediciones Sur, 1985); and Foxley, *Para una Democracia Estable,* 71–77.

64. See Foxley, McPherson, and O'Donnell, eds., *Development, Democracy,* 196; and Valdés, "Cultura y política," 178–80.

65. Walker, *Socialismo y Democracia*, 142–43.

66. Quoted by Vial, "Algunas condiciones," 105.

67. See Valenzuela, "The Breakdown of Democratic Regimes," 37–38; and Moulian, *Democracia y Socialismo en Chile*, 143–47.

68. Valenzuela, "The Breakdown of Democratic Regimes," 106.

Chapter 3. Reinstitutionalization and Self-criticism: 1973–1982

1. Baraona is quoted in Silva, "Technocrats and Politics in Chile," 393. This approach is documented and analyzed in Pilar Vergara, *Auge y Caída del Neoliberalismo en Chile* (Santiago: FLACSO, 1985), 71–156. Oscar Godoy, "Algunas Claves de la Transición Política en Chile," *Estudios Públicos* 38 (1990): 144.

2. Carlos Huneeus, "La Política de la Apertura y sus Implicancias para la Inauguración de la Democracia en Chile," *Revista de Ciencias Políticas* 7 (1985): 48–50. The one exception to the overall personalistic character of the Pinochet regime was the influence on economic policy wielded by the Chicago Boys.

3. In a phrase that sounded ironically like the Socialists' call for a "new man," the junta declared its intention to "change the mentality of the Chileans." Cited by Arriagada in Valenzuela and Valenzuela, *Military Rule in Chile*, 120. The foundational character of the regime is treated most completely in Vergara, *Auge y Caída*.

4. Genaro Arriagada, interview, 8 March 1991. Subsequent quotations from this interview are cited by date in the text or notes.

5. See Brian H. Smith, *The Church and Politics in Chile* (Princeton: Princeton University Press, 1982).

6. See Vergara, *Auge y Caída*, and Garretón, "The Political Evolution of the Chilean Military Regime and Problems in the Transition to Democracy," in O'Donnell, Schmitter, and Whitehead, *Transitions from Authoritarian Rule*, 98–111.

7. Among the most useful analyses are Foxley, *Latin American Experiments in Neoconservative Economics* (Berkeley and Los Angeles: University of California Press, 1983); Vergara, *Auge y Caída*; Arturo Fontaine Aldunate, *Los economista y el presidente Pinochet* (Santiago: Zig Zag, 1988); and Valdés, *La Escuela de Chicago*. On product figures, Foxley, *Latin American Experiments*, 43.

8. See Vergara, *Auge y Caída*, 215–29; Foxley, *Latin American Experiments*, 103–9; and Brian Loveman, *Chile: The Legacy of Hispanic Capitalism*, 2d ed. (New York: Oxford University Press, 1988), 331–39.

9. Ascanio Cavallo, Manuel Salazar, and Oscar Sepúlveda, *La Historia Oculta del Regimen Militar: Chile, 1973–1988*, 3d ed. (Santiago: Editorial Antártita, 1990), 273.

10. Loveman, *Chile*, 339.

11. See Jeffrey Puryear, "Higher Education, Development Assistance, and Repressive Regimes," *Studies in Comparative and International Development* 17, no. 2 (1982); reprinted by the Ford Foundation, New York, 1983.

12. See Manuel Antonio Garretón, "Las Ciencias Sociales en Chile," *Documento de Trabajo* (Santiago: FLACSO, 1982); Puryear, "Higher Education"; Brunner and Barrios, *Inquisición, Mercado y Filantropía*, 132–34.

13. See Puryear, "Higher Education."

14. CIDE and ILADES were both Jesuit institutions. CPU was identified closely with the Christian Democrats. Because FLACSO was, before the coup, a regional institution based on an intergovernmental treaty, it was generally considered an international organization rather than a private national institution. See Brunner and Barrios, *Inquisición, Mercado y Filantropía,* 133; and María Teresa Lladser, "Los Centros Independientes de Investigación en Ciencias Sociales en Chile: 1973–1985" (1985, mimeo), 6.

15. Mario Zañartu, interview, 19 December 1991; subsequent quotations from this interview are cited by date in the text or notes. The other principals in ICHEH's founding were Jesuit economist Zañartu, Christian Democrat analyst Genaro Arriagada, and Catholic University economist Ramón Downey.

16. Each of the books carried on the inside front cover the Latin inscription *"Ad instar manuscripti,"* which identified them as class notes rather than completed works, so as to avoid ecclesiastical censorship. Arriagada suggests, however, that the inscriptions were also prompted by Claudio Orrego's theory, based in part on his black sense of humor, that a little Latin might discourage soldiers bent on confiscating copies. Contributors included Eduardo Frei, Patricio Aylwin, Manuel Sanhueza, Enzo Faletto, Tomás Moulian, Raúl Atria, Ignacio Balbontín, Francisco Orrego, and Genaro Arriagada.

17. Hugo Frühling, interview, 15 March 1991.

18. María Teresa Lladser, "The Emergence of Social Science Research Centers in Chile under Military Rule," *UC/Berkeley Center for Studies in Higher Education Occasional Papers No. 59* (Berkeley: Center for Studies in Higher Education, 1988), 11, 20.

19. Brunner and Barrios, *Inquisición, Mercado y Filantropía,* examine the emergence of these centers in four countries: Chile, Brazil, Argentina, and Uruguay. Daniel Levy, *Private Research Centers in Latin America* (forthcoming), surveys the appearance of these centers across Latin America more generally.

20. Brunner and Barrios, *Inquisición, Mercado y Filantropía,* 138.

21. María Teresa Lladser, "Breve Historia de la Academia de Humanismo Cristiano, 1975–1988" (1988, mimeo), 1.

22. Duncan Livingston, interview, 14 January 1992. Subsequent quotations from this interview are cited by date in the text or notes.

23. A notable exception was the academy's study circle on women, which was forced out by Cardinal Silva's successor, Mons. Juan Francisco Fresno Larraín, in 1983 because of its stand on such issues as abortion and sexuality.

24. Participants included Patricio Aylwin, Edgardo Boeninger, Germán Correa, Manuel Antonio Garretón, Eduardo Palma, Claudio Orrego, and Tomás Moulian (Livingston, 14 January 1992). The MAPU party was generally considered the most intellectual segment of the Chilean left. Its leadership later played a crucial role in bringing an explicitly democratic element into the renovated Socialist party that emerged during the early 1980s.

25. María Teresa Lladser, "La investigación en ciencias sociales en Chile: su desarrollo en los centros privados, 1973–1988," in Taller de Cooperación al De-

sarrollo, ed., *Una Puerta Que Se Abre: Los Organismos no-Gobernamentales en la Cooperación el Desarrollo* (Santiago: Taller de Cooperación al Desarrollo, 1989), 224. Affiliated programs included the Center for Study of Chilean Reality (CERC); the Agro-Regional Studies Group (GEA); the Agrarian Research Group (GIA); the Program on Labor Economics (PET); the Interdisciplinary Program of Educational Research (PIIE); the Latin American Foreign Policy Monitoring Program (PROSPEL); the Human Rights Research Program (PDH); the Circle on the Condition of Women; FLACSO; and the Institute of Latin American Transnational Studies (ILET).

26. The academy's board was heavily dominated by the church and the Christian Democratic party. Reflecting the bitter divisions that had plagued Chilean politics for several decades, some board members initially resisted the incorporation of FLACSO on the grounds that some of its staff were atheists, and most were leftists. Here, the vision and ecumenicism of Cardinal Silva appears to have been crucial in persuading dissident members to drop their objections.

27. Lladser, "La investigación en ciencias sociales," 225.

28. These groups included, for example, the Corporation for Latin American Economic Research (CIEPLAN), PET, PIIE, CIDE, FLACSO, the Chilean Commission of Human Rights, the Vicariate of Solidarity, portions of the medical school faculties at the Catholic University and University of Chile, the Group of 24, and professors from the University of Chile's Department of Economics.

29. Lladser, "Breve Historia," 4.

30. Initial support was provided by the Ford Foundation, the United Nations Development Program (UNDP), and the International Labor Organization's Regional Employment Program for Latin America and the Caribbean (PREALC).

31. Lladser, "La investigación en ciencias sociales," 233.

32. Brunner and Barrios, *Inquisición, Mercado y Filantropía*, 136–37.

33. Brunner and Barrios, *Inquisición, Mercado y Filantropía*, 201–4, describe the research concerns of the new centers in four countries, including Chile. See also Lladser, "La investigación en ciencias sociales," 232–36.

34. Lechner, "Las Condiciones Políticas," 3. Lechner, 12–14, identifies four lines of research (descriptive, historical, theoretical-normative, and policy-oriented) that characterized work on democracy during this period.

35. See Lladser, "La investigación en ciencias sociales," 234–35.

36. Brian Loveman, "Private Development Organizations and International Cooperation: Chile 1973–1990" (1991, mimeo).

37. The single best review of postcoup foreign aid to Chile is Alan Angell, "International Support for the Chilean Opposition, 1973–1989: Political Parties and the Role of Exiles," in Laurence Whitehead, *International Aspects of the Transition to Democracy* (forthcoming). See also Taller de Cooperación al Desarrollo, *Una Puerta Que Se Abre*; and Puryear, "Higher Education."

38. When possible, the military government sought to dissuade foreign assistance organizations from funding these independent centers. Many observers argue that regime pressure explains the failure of the World Bank to channel research funds to private centers during the military regime, even while supporting research at the Catholic University.

39. Michael Pinto-Duschinsky, "Foreign Political Aid: The German Political Foundations and Their U.S. Counterparts," *International Affairs* 67 (1991): 56.

40. Brunner, "La intelligentsia," 186.

41. Enrique Barros, interview, 29 February 1991. At the same time, the emphasis by foreign donors on social relevance and immediate impact also left local scholars little funding for serious theoretical studies, conserving, as Lechner has suggested, the "perverse division between theoretical production (in the North) and empirical application (in the South)." See Lechner, "Las Condiciones Políticas," 18.

42. Lechner, "Las Condiciones Políticas," 9.

43. Brunner recalls receiving a letter in the early 1980s from a bishop comparing the work of FLACSO to the efforts of early Christians to defend the ideas and values they held sacred (28 February 1991).

44. Garretón explores this idea in "La oposición política partidaria," 398; and in "The Political Opposition and the Party System under the Military Regime," in Drake and Jaksić, *The Struggle for Democracy in Chile*, 214.

45. For the causes-of-defeat studies, see Garretón, "La oposición politica partidaria," 406; and Brunner and Barrios, *Inquisición, Mercado y Filantropía*, 139–40. "Radical self-criticism" is from Walker, *Socialismo y Democracia*, 173. For "extraordinarily sincere dialogue," Lladser, "La investigación en ciencias sociales," 232–33. For rethinking on the left, Brunner, "La Intelligentsia," 188. On the "learning process," Garretón, "La oposición política partidaria," 401.

46. Garretón, "La oposición política partidaria," 408.

47. Ricardo Núñez, interview, 18 March 1991. Subsequent quotations from this interview are cited by date in the text or notes.

48. Oscar Muñoz, interview, 27 August 1991. Subsequent quotations from this interview are cited by date in the text or notes.

49. Ricardo Lagos, interview, 13 March 1991. Subsequent quotations from this interview are cited by date in the text or notes.

50. Nonetheless, it was some time before critical research could be distributed freely. CIEPLAN's widely read compilation of critiques on economic policy, *Trayectoria de una crítica*, was held up by government authorities for over a year before finally being distributed in 1983.

51. Illustrating the intellectual nature of political discourse during this period, Núñez added: "We Socialists started speaking in Gramscian terms about organic intellectuals."

52. Walker, *Socialismo y Democracia*, 12.

53. Heraldo Muñoz, interview, 19 August 1991. Subsequent quotations from this interview are cited by date in the text or notes.

54. Brunner, "La Intelligentsia," 188.

55. The principle sources for this section are Moulian, *Democracia y Socialismo en Chile*; Walker, *Socialismo y Democracia*, 173–219; and Garretón, "La oposición política partidaria," 444–51: on the two main issues, Garretón, 406; for not "sufficiently Leninist," Walker, 178.

56. Walker, *Socialismo y Democracia*, 174.

57. Eric Hirschberg, "Changing Interpretations of Democracy and Socialism: The Transformation of Socialist Thought in Spain and Chile" (1991, mimeo), 15.

58. Quoted by Walker, *Socialismo y Democracia,* 180–81.

59. Enrique Correa, interview, 8 March 1991. Subsequent quotations from this interview are cited by date in the text or notes.

60. Lagos holds a doctorate in economics from Duke University, Núñez a doctorate in geography from the University of Prague; Arrate pursued doctoral studies in economics at Harvard University.

61. Publications that illustrate the renewal process include: Flisfisch, *Hacía un realismo político distinto*; Arrate et al., *Siete ensayos sobre democracia y socialismo*; Moulian, *Democracia y socialismo en Chile*; Tironi, *La torre de Babel: ensayos de crítica y renovación política*; Arrate, *La fuerza democrática de la idea socialista*; and Lagos, *Hacía la Democracia.* An early set of essays exploring new socialist perspectives on politics and based on a July 1981 seminar organized by SUR was published as the second issue of a journal called *Margen,* principally because *Margen* already had government permission to publish and thus could be placed in bookstores, while a book, it was assumed, would not gain approval.

62. See Walker, *Socialismo y Democracia,* 207.

63. Norbert Lechner examines this shift among Latin American intellectuals more generally in *Los Patios Interiores,* chapter 1.

64. Manuel Antonio Garretón, interview, 8 March 1991. Subsequent quotations from this interview are cited by date in the text or notes.

65. Timothy Scully, "Reappraising the Role of the Center: The Case of the Chilean Party System," *Kellogg Institute Working Paper Series* No. 143 (South Bend, Ind.: University of Notre Dame, 1990), 33, refers to Frei's apparent change of position. In a personal interview (21 March 1991) party leader Mariano Fernández talks of a meeting that took place in 1976 or 1977 and was attended by Raúl Troncoso, Claudio Orrego, and possibly Andrés Zaldívar (but not Fernández), in which Frei argued that the party must work in tandem with other political groups to defeat the dictatorship.

66. Jaime Castillo, "Una Patria Para Todos" (1977, mimeo). Mariano Fernández, interview, 21 March 1991. "If you watch what Castillo writes," Fernández adds, "It's what the Christian Democrats do. Always." Subsequent quotations from this interview are cited by date in the text or notes.

67. An earlier initiative, the Chilean Institute of Humanistic Studies, also sprang basically from party leaders with an intellectual bent. It predated the shift in party thinking toward flexibility and coalition building, however.

68. It is interesting to note, however, that Valdés mentions several intellectuals, including New York University's Kalman Silvert and the Sorbonne's Alain Touraine, as having influenced his decision to launch the new center. See Francisco Castillo, *La Fuerza del Diálogo* (Santiago: Centro de Estudios del Desarrollo, 1991), 18.

69. Ibid., 19. According to Fernández, Valdés had rejected a suggestion by former president Eduardo Frei that he return to Chile and assume the presidency of the Christian Democratic party, on the grounds that Frei was the party's nat-

ural leader. Two months after Frei's untimely death in early 1982, Valdés was elected president of the party (21 March 1991).

70. See Foxley, *Para una Democracia Estable,* 71–74; also Oscar Muñoz, "Antecedentes y causas de la crisis de la Democracia en Chile," Working Paper No. 93 (Santiago: Apuntes CIEPLAN, 1990).

71. Silva, "Technocrats and Politics in Chile," elaborates this idea in considerable detail.

72. For criticism, see Foxley, *Para una Democracia Estable* and "Reflexiones." For the blueprint for governance, Alejandro Foxley, *Chile y su Futuro: Un País Posible* (Santiago: CIEPLAN, 1987). Walker, *Socialismo y Democracia.*

73. Brunner, "La Intelligentsia," 189.

74. Osvaldo Puccio, interview, 17 January 1991. Subsequent quotations from this interview are cited by date in the text or notes.

75. Foxley, "Reflexiones," 260; Moulian, *Democracia y Socialismo en Chile,* 94–99.

Chapter 4. Convergence and Reenvisioning the Future: 1983–1986

1. These arrangements closely approximate the "limited democracy" or "*democradura*" case outlined by O'Donnell and Schmitter, *Transitions from Authoritarian Rule,* 9.

2. Patricia Verdugo and Carmen Hertz, *Operación Siglo XX* (Santiago: Las Ediciones del Ornitorrinco, 1990), provide an extensive journalistic treatment of these events.

3. Cavallo, Salazar, and Sepúlveda, La Historia Oculta del Regimen Militar, 273.

4. For example, Socialist leader and intellectual Jorge Arrate lived first in Rome, then in East Germany, and finally in the Netherlands, where he established the Institute for the New Chile and played a major role in the debates over leftist political thinking. Alan Angell and Susan Carstairs, "The Exile Question in Chilean Politics," *Third World Quarterly* 9 (1987), and Angell, "International Support for the Chilean Opposition," provide useful detail on Chilean exiles.

5. Jorge Arrate, cited by Walker, *Socialismo y Democracia,* 183. Walker documents vividly the impact of European exile on Socialist thinkers; see particularly 181–88.

6. Garretón, "La oposición política partidaria," 415–17; and "Political Opposition and the Party System," 216–27, analyzes the deficiencies of the debate over political strategy among the opposition.

7. See Joseph Ramos, *Neoconservative Economics in the Southern Cone of Latin America, 1973–1983* (Baltimore: Johns Hopkins University Press, 1984); and Silvia T. Borzutzky, "The Pinochet Regime: Crisis and Consolidation," in Malloy and Seligson, *Authoritarians and Democrats,* 75–79.

8. See Cavallo, Salazar, and Sepúlveda, *La Historia Oculta del Regimen Militar,* 396–98.

9. Particularly useful treatments of the protests include Genaro Arriagada, "Negociación política y movilización social: la crítica de las protestas," *Materiales para Dicusión del CED 162* (Santiago: CED, 1987), and Gonzalo de la Maza and

Mario Garcés, *La Explosión de las Mayorías: Protesta Nacional, 1983–1984* (Santiago: Educación y Comunicaciones, 1985).

10. O'Donnell and Schmitter, *Transitions from Authoritarian Rule*, 48–56; and Ignacio Walker, "La Dinámica Regimen-Oposición bajo la Dictadura Militar Chilena (1973–1988)," *Debat* 12 (1988): 33–47, apply this concept to the Chile case.

11. Huneeus, "La Política de la Apertura," provides perhaps the best analysis of these changes.

12. Garretón, "La oposición política partidaria," 413.

13. The incorporation into the Democratic Alliance was possible because of a split between the democratic left and the orthodox left, stemming from the decade-long renewal process Chile's Socialist parties underwent after the coup. That split was to become increasingly important over the next several years.

14. See Genaro Arriagada, *Pinochet: The Politics of Power* (London: Unwin Hyman, 1988), 70–74. Although the organized protests ended in July 1986, the opposition maintained its rupturist stance until early Februrary 1988, when it decided to participate in the regime's plebiscite.

15. Ignacio Walker, interview, 7 March 1991. Subsequent quotations from this interview are cited by date in the text or notes.

16. Huneeus, "La Política de la Apertura"; de la Maza and Garcés, *La Explosión de las Mayorías*; Javier Martínez, "Miedo al Estado, Miedo a la Sociedad," *Proposiciones* 12 (1986): 32–42; and Arriagada, "Negociación política y movilización social," all document and analyze this split.

17. Walker, "La Dinámica Regimen-Oposición," provides a useful analysis of the social mobilization strategy and its failings.

18. *APSI* 171 (1986): 4.

19. Instituto Chileno de Estudios Humanísticos (ICHEH), ed., *Una salida político constitucional para Chile* (Santiago: ICHEH, 1985), 145–54.

20. Andrés Sanfuentes, interview, 1 March 1991. This incident is described in Cavallo, *Los Hombres de la Transición*, 38–39.

21. Gabriel Valdés, interview, 1 March 1991. Subsequent quotations from this interview are cited by date in the text or notes. See Walker, "La Dinámica Regimen-Oposición," 35–39, for a description.

22. According to Cavallo, *Los Hombres de la Transición*, 41, Christian Democratic leaders were particularly impressed by the revelation of Pentagon official Nestor Sánchez, in a briefing at the U.S. Embassy, that the clandestine arms caches were packed for long-term storage and thus were intended for use not only against the military regime but also against the democratic regime that might eventually replace it.

23. Walker, "La Dinámica Regimen-Oposición," 37. Garretón, "La oposición política partidaria," 415–17.

24. Because of these inconsistencies, Garretón argues that the existing strategy was one of opposition rather than of transition (8 March 1991).

25. Walker, "La Dinámica Regimen-Oposición," 37.

26. Alfred Stepan, "On the Tasks of a Democratic Opposition," *Journal of Democracy* 1 (1990): 44–47.

27. Loveman, "Private Development Organizations," 53, notes the obstacles to a unified opposition movement.

28. Stepan, "Tasks of a Democratic Opposition," 47.

29. Arriagada, *Pinochet,* 68, points out, for example, that three of the four previous presidents of the Christian Democratic party were in exile when the protests broke out. Similarly, Huneeus, "La Política de la Apertura," 61, notes that a survey of the Christian Democratic party's national junta in 1985 revealed that 37% had been arrested, tortured, banished to a distant town, or exiled by the military regime; 20% had been dismissed from a job; and 16% had received anonymous threats.

30. Guillermo Campero and René Cortázar, "Lógicas de Acción Sindical en Chile," *Colección CIEPLAN* 18 (1985); and Allan Angell, "Unions and Workers in Chile during the 1980s," in Drake and Jaksić, *The Struggle for Democracy in Chile,* analyze the decline of Chile's labor movement under the dictatorship.

31. Ricardo Lagos, interview, 13 March 1991; subsequent quotations from this interview are cited by date in the text or notes. On the media, a decree law passed in 1984 after the protests began, for example, severely limited the ability of media to address political issues; see Cavallo, Salazar, and Sepúlveda, *La Historia Oculta del Regimen Militar,* 459. Also, although several opposition weekly newsmagazines appeared in the early 1980s, no opposition newspaper was permitted until March 1987, when *La Epoca* began publication.

32. Alejandro Foxley, interview, 14 March 1991. Subsequent quotations from this interview are cited by date in the text or notes.

33. CIEPLAN, "Report to the Ford Foundation," December 1986.

34. Castillo, *La Fuerza del Diálogo,* 51–52, 54.

35. Constable and Valenzuela, *A Nation of Enemies.*

36. Castillo, *La Fuerza del Diálogo,* 58.

37. The ten themes were: (1) social mobilization and political negotiation; (2) options for political coalition; (3) the role of the armed forces in a democratic Chile; (4) the role of the Communist party; (5) human rights, the administration of justice, public order, and political violence; (6) governability and political competition; (7) political parties and democracy; (8) the United States and Chilean democracy; (9) political regime options; and (10) transition scenarios and strategies. See ibid., 56–57.

38. Angel Flisfisch, interview, 17 January 1991. Subsequent quotations from this interview are cited by date in the text or notes.

39. Hernán Vodanovic, interview, 15 March 1991. Subsequent quotations from this interview are cited by date in the text or notes.

40. Sergio Molina, interview, 13 March 1991. Subsequent quotations from this interview are cited by date in the text or notes.

41. Centers carrying out such work included CIEPLAN, FLACSO, PET, CERC, GIA, GEA, PIIE, SUR, ILADES, ILET, and CIDE. Illustrative publications include Manuel Antonio Garretón, *El Proceso Político Chileno* (Santiago: FLACSO, 1983); Vergara, *Auge y Caída;* E. Tironi, ed., *Marginalidad, Movimientos, Sociales y Democracia,* No. 14 (August 1987); Martínez and Tironi, *Las*

Clases Sociales en Chile; José Joaquín Brunner, "Ideología, Legitimación y Disciplinamiento: nueve argumentos," in *Autoritarismo y Alternativas Populares en América Latina* (San José de Costa Rica: FLACSO, 1982), 71–103; Rodrigo Baño, *Lo Social y lo Político* (Santiago: FLACSO, 1985); Jorge Ruíz-Tagle, *El sindicalismo chileno después del Plan Laboral* (Santiago: PET, 1985); Guillermo Campero and J. A. Valenzuela, *El movimiento sindical en el régimen militar chileno* (Santiago: ILET, 1984).

42. See Martínez and Tironi, *Las Clases Sociales en Chile;* Alfredo Rodríguez and Eugenio Tironi, "El Otro Santiago: Resumen de la Encuesta Sur 1985," *Proposiciones* 13 (1987): 12–21; and Eugenio Tironi, "Pobladores e Integración Social," *Proposiciones* 14 (1987): 63–83. Also, volumes 14 and 15 of SUR's journal, *Proposiciones,* address these themes in considerable detail.

43. Tironi, "Pobladores e Integración Social," 78.

44. For example, Genaro Arriagada's 1987 critique of the opposition's social mobilization strategy, which influenced many Christian Democratic leaders, drew heavily on such studies. See Arriagada, "Negociación política y movilización social," especially 16–18.

45. Ricardo Solari, interview, 8 March 1991.

46. José Joaquín Brunner, interview, 29 August 1991. Subsequent quotations from this interview are cited by date in the text or notes.

47. Castillo, *La Fuerza del Diálogo,* 51–52, 57.

48. See Cavallo, Salazar, and Sepúlveda, *La Historia Oculta del Regimen Militar,* 488.

49. Arriagada, "Negociación política y movilización social," 2. Arriagada estimates that middle- and upper-middle-class participation began to decline by the fourth protest, which took place in August 1983.

50. The Radio Cooperativa poll showed that 63% of the poor had been in favor of the state of siege, compared with 18% of upper-class respondents. See ibid., 23.

51. *CAUCE,* no. 57 (1986), 11.

52. *APSI,* no. 107 (1986), 4–6.

53. *CAUCE,* no. 72 (1986), 26.

54. Juan Gabriel Valdés, interview, 29 May 1991. Subsequent quotations from this interview are cited by date in the text or notes.

55. See Núñez's "Open Letter to Leaders and Militants of the Chilean Left," *APSI,* no. 29 (December 1986).

56. Jaime Gazmuri, interview, 7 March 1991. Subsequent quotations from this interview are cited by date in the text or notes.

57. These conflicts persisted until the late 1980s. At a seminar organized in late 1986 by CEP, for example, two prominent Socialist economists, Gonzalo D. Martner and Eduardo García, sparked controversy by recommending that the government reassume control of significant sectors of the economy and sharply limit the activity of private capital. See *El Mercurio,* 28 December 1986, B1–B2.

58. Ricardo Ffrench-Davis, interview, 3 February 1992. Subsequent quotations from this interview are cited by date in the text or notes.

59. Patricio Silva, "Intellectuals, Technocrats, and Social Change," provides a detailed account of the growing role of technocracts in Chilean economic policy. See also Montecinos, "Economics and Power."

60. Carlos Ominami, interview, 14 January 1992. Subsequent quotations from this interview are cited by date in the text or notes.

61. Manuel Marfán, interview, 7 January 1992. Subsequent quotations from this interview are cited by date in the text or notes.

62. *Reconstrucción Económica para la Democracia* (Santiago: CIEPLAN, 1983).

63. The director of that program, René Cortázar, later became minister of labor in the new democratic regime.

64. Reflecting on the Community Dialogues experience, one staff member, Manuel Marfán, observed: "Having to explain your ideas to a group of labor leaders or businessmen or farmers is a hard test. Sometimes you realize that your ideas are foolish . . . sometimes people ask questions you've never asked, but turn out to be very important for them" (7 January 1992).

65. The document was circulated informally in September 1986 and appeared in *Revista CIEPLAN* 14 (November 1988): 36–44.

66. I am indebted to Joe Ramos for pointing out this aspect of the opposition's evolving approach to economic policy.

67. Another leftist economist, Humberto Vega, argues that the left opted for the World Bank model rather than the model of the Chicago Boys. "Anne Krueger," he notes, "is not the same as Milton Friedman." Humberto Vega, interview, 13 January 1992.

68. These were later published in a single volume. See Centro de Estudios del Desarrollo (CED), ed., *Orden Económico y Democracia* (Santiago: Centro de Estudios del Desarrollo [CED], 1985).

69. Castillo, *La Fuerza del Diálogo*, 55.

70. Patricio Meller, interview, 28 January 1991.

71. Felipe Larraín B., ed., *Desarrollo Económico en Democracia: Proposiciones para una Sociedad Libre y Solidaria*, 2d ed. (Santiago: Ediciones Universidad Católica de Chile, 1987).

Chapter 5. Modernizing Politics: 1987–1988

1. See Garretón, "La oposición politica partidaria," 426; and "Political Opposition and the Party System," 226–27, for a discussion of this shift.

2. Like many of the opposition's initiatives, this one was based in part on learning from the experiences of other countries. A Socialist leader recalls: "At first we were imitating a little the Brazilians, with a struggle for free elections" (E. Correa, 8 March 1991). Similarly, a Christian Democratic leader states: "The failure of Marcos and the triumph of this nonviolent approach taken by nuns, priests, . . . everyone . . . were very decisive. Various people . . . went there and brought back the idea of free elections as a way of organizing the struggle" (Gabriel Valdés, 1 March 1991).

3. CEL was significant in part because it included distinguished figures from the right, such as Catholic University political science professor Oscar Godoy, among its membership.

4. Strictly speaking, of course, voting no in the plebiscite would be a vote for free elections, because the Constitution provided for open presidential and congressional elections to be held should the plebiscite result in a majority voting no. Ricardo Lagos made this point in a public interview as early as September 1987. See *La Epoca*, 11 September 1987.

5. Garretón, "Political Opposition and the Party System," 226.

6. The divisive potential of free elections for the opposition at that point was such that several analysts argue that Pinochet would have easily won them. The major parties within the opposition, according to that analysis, would not have been able to resist running their own presidential candidates.

7. *APSI*, no. 210 (1987), 4; and *ANALISIS*, no. 185 (1987), 20.

8. Senen Conejeros, *Chile: de la Dictadura a la Democracia* (Santiago de Chile: Central Latinoamericana de Trabajadores, CLAT, 1990), 15.

9. Arturo Valenzuela and Pamela Constable, "Plebiscite in Chile: End of the Pinochet Era?" *Current History* 87 (1988): 32. A January 1988 appraisal by the Sawyer/Miller Group stated: "If we were asked today, on the basis of our research, should the opposition in its present state of readiness participate in the plebiscite, our answer would have to be no. You are not ready; you are not organized; you are not united; you do not have a single message; you do not have a single strategy. . . . On present evidence the democratic opposition in Chile is being outcampaigned by a 72-year-old general." Sawyer/Miller Group, "Chile: Year of the Plebiscite" (1988, mimeo), 2–3.

10. Electoral rolls had been destroyed in July 1974 and were not used for the 1980 constitutional plebiscite. Americas Watch, *Chile: Human Rights and the Plebiscite* (New York: Americas Watch Committee, 1988), discusses in considerable detail most of the "political" laws passed during this period. See also National Democratic Institute for International Affairs, *Chile's Transition to Democracy: The 1988 Presidential Plebiscite* (Washington, D.C.: National Democratic Institute, 1988). The Voting and Tabulation Law was subsequently amended to permit independent groups to designate observers, providing they submitted 20,000 signatures to the Electoral Service five days before the plebiscite was convoked.

11. Many of the points made here are suggested by the report of a Latin American Studies Association commission to observe the plebiscite. See Latin American Studies Association, "The Chilean Plebiscite: A First Step toward Redemocratization" (1989, mimeo).

12. There appear to have been virtually no direct negotiations between the opposition and the regime on these issues. According to Boeninger, "There was no negotiation with the military. There was pressure, and there was a scenario being developed, steps being taken, but there was no sitting down to agree explicitly on the rules of the game" (29 January 1991). This apparently contradicts Cavarozzi's assertion that Chile's transition featured elite settlements among the opposition and supporters of the regime regarding the openness and fairness of the plebiscite. See Cavarozzi, "Patterns of Elite Negotiation," 224. The motivations behind the regime's decisions remain unclear. Little reliable information

on debates within the military junta has so far surfaced. Existing journalistic accounts suggest disagreement within the junta on many of these issues and point to the heads of the air force (General Fernando Matthei) and the carabineros (General Rodolfo Stange) as proponents of additional democratic guarantees.

13. See Latin American Studies Association, "The Chilean Plebiscite," 3.

14. See Cavallo, Salazar, and Sepúlveda, *La Historia Oculta del Regimen Militar,* 310–32; and Ascanio Cavallo, *Los Hombres de la Transición,* 15–16, for an account.

15. See Cavallo, Salazar, and Sepúlveda, *La Historia Oculta del Regimen Militar,* 554–57.

16. The Constitutional Tribunal was to continue to demonstrate independence from the military junta. In August 1987 it found twenty-four inconstitutionalities in the junta's draft law on political parties, causing many of the restrictions proposed by the regime to be eliminated. See ibid.

17. The ironic character of these events prompted journalist Santibañez to entitle his account *The Plebiscite of Pinochet: Snared in His Own Trap.* See Abraham Santibañez, *El Plebiscito de Pinochet: (Cazado) en su Propria Trampa* (Santiago: Editorial Atena, 1988).

18. Albert Hirschman, *Essays in Trespassing: Economics to Politics and Beyond* (Cambridge: Cambridge University Press, 1981).

19. Boeninger makes similar remarks in Castillo, *La Fuerza del Diálogo,* 62–63.

20. Tironi elaborates on the modernization that occurred in Chilean politics in CIS (CED-ILET-SUR), *La Campaña del No Vista por sus Creadores* (Santiago: Ediciones Melquiades, 1989), 3–4.

21. Little has been written on the role played by opposition intellectuals during this period. An exception is Cavallo's profile of Patricio Aylwin, which mentions the influence of social scientists on his thinking. See Cavallo, *Los Hombres de la Transición,* 46–47.

22. For example, the election of Gabriel Valdés as president of the Christian Democratic party after Eduardo Frei's death in 1982 took place clandestinely. According to Cavallo, ibid., 192, only 124 votes were cast.

23. Carlos Vergara, interview, 28 January 1991. Subsequent quotations from this interview are cited by date in the text or notes.

24. Guillermo Sunkel, "Las Encuestas de Opinión Pública: Entre el Saber y el Poder," *Documento de Trabajo No. 439* (Santiago: FLACSO-Chile, 1989); and "Usos Políticos de las Encuestas de Opinión Pública," *Documento de Trabajo No. 18—Serie Educación y Cultura* (Santiago: FLACSO, 1992), traces in detail the emergence, between 1983 and 1988, of public opinion polling as a political instrument among Chile's opposition parties. Much of this section draws on his analysis.

25. According to Sunkel, Hamuy carried out forty-five political attitude surveys between 1957 and 1973. See Sunkel, "Las Encuestas de Opinión Pública," 20.

26. Diagnos was formed by four sociologists and a psychologist. See ibid.,

6–7. It carried out, for example, the surveys for Radio Cooperativa mentioned in the previous chapter.

27. Most of CERC's early work on political attitude surveys was funded by the Ford Foundation, which was exploring avenues for developing a program on governance in Chile.

28. Marta Lagos, interview, 9 January 1991; subsequent quotations from this interview are cited by date in the text or notes. Huneeus, *Los Chilenos y La Política*, 21.

29. Carlos Huneeus, "Lo Que Piensan los Universitarios," *HOY*, no. 456 (1986): 11.

30. Huneeus, quoted in Sunkel, "Las Encuestas de Opinión Pública," 20, 21.

31. See, for example, Angel Flisfisch, "Consenso democrático in el Chile autoritario," *Documento de Trabajo No. 330* (Santiago: FLACSO, 1987); and "Determinantes de la hostilidad al multipartidismo en el público masivo chileno," *Documento de Trabajo No. 334* (Santiago: FLACSO, 1987).

32. See, for example, Huneeus, *Los Chilenos y La Política*, 154–70; and Arturo Fontaine Talavera, "Sobre el pecado original de la transformación capitalista chilena," in Barry B. Levine, ed., *El Desafío Neoliberal: El Fin del Tercermundismo en América Latina* (Bogotá: Editorial Norma, 1992), 127.

33. See, for example, Huneeus, *Los Chilenos y La Política*, 54–66; Brunner, "Notas sobre la situación política chilena a la luz de los resultados preliminares de una encuesta," *Material de discusión*, no. 80 (Santiago: FLACSO-Chile, 1986); and Flisfisch, "Determinantes de la hostilidad al multipartidismo."

34. Cited in Sunkel, "Las Encuestas de Opinión Pública," 15.

35. Guillermo Sunkel, interview, 18 December 1990; subsequent quotations from this interview are cited by date in the text or notes. See also Sunkel, "Las Encuestas de Opinión Pública," 75. Sunkel argues convincingly that social scientists, having produced the political attitude studies, then took the initiative to generate a demand for them among politicians. See Sunkel, "Usos Políticos de las Encuestas," 35–44.

36. Sunkel, "Usos Políticos de las Encuestas," 36.

37. Guillermo Campero, cited in ibid., 20.

38. Little has been written about CIS, even though its existence and accomplishments were common knowledge in Chilean political and intellectual circles. The most complete compendium of information was published by CIS itself, as proceedings from a seminar it organized to analyze the No campaign right after the plebiscite victory. See CIS, *La Campaña del No*. Summary information also appears in Sunkel, "Las Encuestas de Opinión Pública," 23–29; and "Usos Políticos de las Encuestas," 20–21; and in Castillo, *La Fuerza del Diálogo*, 42–43. Much of the strategic thinking that CIS generated is reflected in Eugenio Tironi, *La Invisible Victoria: Campañas Electorales y Democracia en Chile* (Santiago: Ediciones SUR, 1990).

39. Like many Chilean intellectuals, Valdés had been active in politics alongside his academic career. He was part of the generation that left the Christian Democratic party in 1968 to found the Movement for Popular Unitary Action

(MAPU) party and then participated in the renewal of the Socialist party during the 1980s. He also helped establish the Party for Democracy in 1987.

40. Because Juan Gabriel Valdés's father, Gabriel Valdés, had just completed his term as president of the Christian Democratic party and was somewhat at loose ends, it is natural to ask whether he provided some of the original impetus for contacting political consultants. Two interviewees, Eugenio Tironi and Mariano Fernández, suggested that he did. And Gabriel Valdés mentioned in his interview that U.S. Senator Edward Kennedy had recommended the Sawyer/Miller Group to him. Juan Gabriel Valdés, however, stated that his father played no role ("zero") in coming up with the idea but was very supportive once activities got under way.

41. Valdés's father, Gabriel Valdés, had founded CED in 1982 and at that time was president of CED's board of directors.

42. The Open Society Fund, which Soros founded, made a grant of $35,000 to ILET in 1987.

43. Sawyer/Miller Group, "Chile." Findings from the first focus group are summarized and interpreted in Tironi, *La Invisible Victoria*, 19–25.

44. At this point, the free elections campaign comprised three separate committees: (1) the National Council for Free Elections (CEL), composed of fourteen distinguished personalities drawn from across the opposition; (2) the Operative Committee for Free Elections (COPEL) that represented the political center and was led by the Christian Democrats; and (3) the Committee of the Left for Free Elections, led by Ricardo Lagos.

45. Arriagada in CIS, *La Campaña del No*, unpaged prologue.

46. Reference to the decision to push for participating in the plebiscite can be found in Cavallo, *Los Hombres de la Transición*, 47.

47. Tironi, *La Invisible Victoria*, 19.

48. In interviews, "dignity" was one of the themes most recalled from the Olmué discussions, based on a document by that title prepared for the meeting by Eugenio Tironi, a revised version of which appears in *Mensaje*, no. 367 (1988), and in Tironi, *La Invisible Victoria*, 22–23.

49. Tironi, *La Invisible Victoria*, 24–25. This line of thought appears throughout CIS, *La Campaña del No*, and is summarized in Sawyer/Miller Group, "Chile."

50. Sunkel, "Usos Políticos de las Encuestas," 37.

51. Carlos Vergara, cited in ibid.

52. Eugenio Tironi, interview, 19 December 1990; subsequent quotations from this interview are cited by date in the text or notes. Among political leaders attending were Ricardo Lagos, Enrique Silva Cimma, Eduardo Loyola, Jorge Arrate, Gabriel Valdés, Germán Riesco, Mario Papi, Andrés Zaldívar, Germán Correa, René Abeliuk, Eduardo Frei, Eugenio Ortega, Raúl Troncoso, Jaime Gazmuri, Claudio Huepe, Luis Maira, Carlos González Márquez, Ricardo Navarrete, and José Tomás Saénz.

53. See CIS, "Preguntas y Dilemas de la Oposición" (1987, photocopy). Once the opposition decided, in February 1988, to participate in the plebiscite, the

Technical Committee for Free Elections was converted into the Technical Committee for the No, with essentially the same membership.

54. Valdés is referring to Javier Martínez, a sociologist from SUR who was a key participant in CIS.

55. Mariano Fernández, cited in Sunkel, "Usos Políticos de las Encuestas," 40.

56. A prominent Christian Democratic politician, Adolfo Zaldívar, also played a leading role in urging his party to accept the Constitution and participate in the plebiscite.

57. Martínez also notes that the first prominent opposition leaders to call publicly for participating in the plebiscite—Ricardo Lagos and Gabriel Valdés—were then out of office. "I don't know to what extent this is because they had always thought that way, or because it was their way of engaging those who at that time exercised power in their parties. . . . The fact is that high leaders who were at that moment semidisplaced were the first ones to take up the idea of the plebiscite" (6 March 1991).

58. The directorate of the No Command was composed initially of Enrique Silva Cimma (Radical party), Ricardo Lagos (Party for Democracy), Andrés Zaldívar (Christian Democratic party), and José Tomás Sáenz (Humanist party), with Genaro Arriagada (Christian Democratic party) as its executive secretary. Sáenz was later replaced by Tomás Hirsch. Luis Maira, representing a coalition of orthodox Socialist parties, was added when those parties joined the Concertación. In the later stages of the campaign, Patricio Aylwin (Christian Democratic party) became the directorate's spokesperson.

59. Arriagada addresses this issue obliquely in his prologue to CIS, *La Campaña del No.* Examples include the decision to base the campaign on a joyful future (*La Alegría Ya Viene*) rather than on the outrages of the past, and the decision to limit and control appearances by politicians on television.

60. Correa, along with Carlos Figueroa and orthodox Socialist Ricardo Solari, all served directly under the directorate as part of the executive secretary's office, under the supervision of Arriagada.

61. Two of the six members of the No Command's directorate—Ricardo Lagos and Luis Maira—had spent substantial portions of their careers in teaching and research.

62. Arriagada expresses similar views in CIS, *La Campaña del No,* unpaged prologue.

63. The best sources of information on the plebiscite campaign are CIS, *La Campaña del No*; Tironi, *La Invisible Victoria*; and Sunkel, "Usos Políticos de las Encuestas." See also Americas Watch, *Chile.*

64. Arriagada in CIS, *La Campaña del No,* unpaged prologue.

65. Eugenio Tironi in ibid., 13.

66. Staff members from SUR played key roles on the technical committee.

67. Tironi, *La Invisible Victoria,* 24.

68. Eugenio Tironi in CIS, *La Campaña del No,* 13.

69. This point is elaborated in Sunkel, "Usos Políticos de las Encuestas," 41–44.

70. On the survey findings, see ibid., 27–28. This analysis was first presented in an internal campaign document. See CIS, "Esperanza: Orientaciones ante el problema de la sub-inscripción de la juventud urbana" (1988, photocopy). It was later summarized by Eugenia Weinstein in CIS, *La Campaña del No,* 19–25.

71. See Vergara in CIS, *La Campaña del No,* 15–18; and Tironi, *La Invisible Victoria,* 32–34.

72. On the subgroups, CIS, "La Demanda de los Indecisos" (1988, photocopy). On the follow-up studies, see Martínez in CIS, *La Campaña del No,* 27–34.

73. See Tironi, *La Invisible Victoria,* 37–44; CIS, *La Campaña del No,* 87–132; and Roberto Méndez, Oscar Godoy, Enrique Barros, and Arturo Fontaine Talavera, "¿POR QUE GANO EL NO?" *Estudios Publicos* 33 (1989): 83–134.

74. Tironi, *La Invisible Victoria,* 42.

75. Sunkel, "Usos Políticos de las Encuestas," 43–44.

76. Arriagada in CIS, *La Campaña del No,* unpaged prologue.

Chapter 6. Conclusion

1. Coser, *Men of Ideas,* 136.

2. Foxley, *Para una Democracia Estable,* 131–32.

3. The Pinochet regime's use of exile on an unprecedented scale over more than a decade also caused opposition politicians to receive considerable foreign exposure and substantial assistance from foreign governments and political parties. Some of those political leaders, of course, were intellectuals as well as politicians. See Angell, "International Support for the Chilean Opposition"; and Angell and Carstairs, "The Exile Question."

4. Burton, Gunther, and Higley, "Introduction," 9.

5. The adaptability of Chilean intellectuals extends across the political spectrum. Right-of-center intellectuals imitated their adversaries after democracy returned in 1989, forming several new think tanks to confront the democratic government with intellectualized political alternatives.

6. Coser, *Men of Ideas,* 135–243.

Index

Abeliuk, René, 194n
Abugattás, Luis A., 174n
Academy of Christian Humanism, 36, 52, 117, 122; as convener of opposition, 66, 86; established, 44–46; and human rights, 110; study circle of economists, 112
Adenauer Foundation. *See* Konrad Adenauer Foundation
Allanamientos, 76
Allende government. *See* Popular Unity government
Allende, Salvador: bypassed negotiations, 26; and democracy, 30; and government's demand for social scientists, 17–18, 24–25; and higher education, 12; lack of support for, 32; margin of victory in 1958, 26
Allessandri, Jorge: and government's use of technocrats, 18; margin of victory in 1958, 26
Alliance for Progress, 11, 177n
Altamirano, Carlos, 62
Americas Watch, 191n
Análisis, 35, 191n
Angell, Allen, 176n, 183n, 186n, 188n, 196n
APSI, 79, 189n, 191n
Arellano, José Pablo, 41
Armed forces (Chilean), 35
Arms caches, 2
Arrate, Jorge, 59, 62, 63, 85; economic policy of, 117; impact of exile, 74, 186n; Political Analysis Committee, 194n; as politician, 131
Arriagada, Genaro, 182n; and Christian Democrats' weakness, 188n; and Constitution of 1925, 26, 180n; and impact of

foreign donors, 53–54; as intellectual, 7, 155; and postcoup intellectuals, 39; social mobilization strategy, 81, 105, 106, 186n, 187n, 189n; and Technical Committee for Free Elections, 141, 144, 194n; and Technical Committee for the No, 149, 153–56, 158, 195n; and "two Chiles," 34–35; and samizdat, 40; and universities, 38
Assembly of Civility, 81
Atria, Raúl, 182n
Authoritarian context, 163–64
Aylwin, Patricio, 1, 41, 110, 182n; as candidate, 158; and Command for the No, 195n; and Constitution of 1980, 79; and free elections movement, 126, 127; and Group of 24, 42; and plebiscite, 130; and Political Analysis Committee, 147, 153

Balbontín, Ignacio, 182n
Baloyra, Enrique, 135
Banking failure (1982), ix, 72, 75–76, 112
Baño, Rodrigo, 189n
Baraona, Pablo, 34
Barrios, Alicia: and intellectuals, 25; and private research centers, 182n, 183n; and sociologists, 19, 22, 177n
Barros, Enrique, 184n, 196n
Barros, Robert, 175n
Berlin, Isaiah, 178n
Bitar, Sergio, 63; and economic policy, 117, 119; and political intellectuals, 57, 121, 175n; and private research centers, 48; and socialist renewal, 64
Boeninger, Edgardo, 1; and Academy of Christian Humanism, 44, 45; and CED